An American Woman Living in Egypt

An American Woman Living in Egypt

Life during an Islamic takeover

Cheri Berens

MASR Academic Press

Copyright © 2018

ISBN 9780692121498
ISBN 9781733855402
ISBN 9781733855419

Cover photo of Cheri Berens by Essam

MASR Academic Press
MasrAcademicPress@live.com

DISCLAIMER

The First Amendment of the Constitution of the United States guarantees the right to free speech and expression. A person cannot be held liable, either criminally or civilly, for anything written or spoken about a person or a topic, so long as it is truthful or based on honest opinion and statements.

In America, no ideology is above honest analysis and investigation.

In the case of Islam, where it explicitly seeks political and social dominance over all people* honest analysis and investigation harms no one. On the contrary, analysis and investigation encourages the basic principles of freedom.

This book gives first hand experiences and investigates and analyzes what took place in Egypt. It also gives a summarized overview and analysis of the history of Islam via academic-based research. Never does this book promote harm to anyone. It does however, point out what can happen when people do promote harm, most specifically, in the name of a religion.

The author of this book believes no one should be treated differently solely for being a member of a religion, whether Islam or any other religion. The author of this book believes no person should be harassed, harmed or stereotyped for their religious beliefs.

In Muslim-majority countries, censorship and social and government enforcement is used to protect Islam from intellectual analysis. In America, freedom of intellectual analysis and opinion are lawful rights.

We, as Americans, are free to exercise our right to debate. These debates include the effects of an Islamic system and its advantages or disadvantages.

The Quran says men are superior to women (4:11; 4:176; 2:282; 5:6; 2:223). Are we not allowed to question and debate this? Does America not stand for equality among men and women?

The Quran condones slavery (2:178; 4:24; 8:69; 16:75; 23:5-6; 24:32; 33:50). Are we not allowed to question and debate this? Does America not stand against slavery?

The purpose of this book is simply to analyze and question. It does not condone or encourage any type of harm or stereotype on any one person or any group of people.

* Quran 2:191, 9:29, 21:44, 25:52, 48:29, but there are many examples in *hadith* as well.

To those who encouraged me to write this book.
To those who kept me motivated during its lengthy process.
To those who prayed for me and stood by me when things got rough.

CONTENTS

Introduction   **1**

1. Egypt 101   **5**

The Lowest of the Lowest   7
Orgasms   10
Marriage in Egypt   13
Divorce, wife beating—and blaming the woman   15
The remedy for the evilness of women—the veil and circumcising!   19
Once a prostitute, always a prostitute   24
The Dancing Dick   27
Removing culture   29
Islamic Law: a female swimmer must be punished as an adulteress   32
Kom Ombo Security Police   34
Social Enforcement: An Islam-ization Strategy   38

2. The Revolution: U.S. Involvement   **43**

Terrorism and the Security Police   47
President Mubarak   56
Egypt's Protest   63
Rage, chaos, and violence against Christians   74
Egypt's first "free and fair" presidential election?   78
Days of Wine and Roses? Or, days of no wine and no noses!   81

3. The Christian Origins of the Quran   **85**

The Near East before, during, and after Muhammad   86
Mecca   88
The Arab transition to power   91
Rock inscriptions and the story they tell   96
The transition to Islam   98
Hadith and Islamic Law   102
Islam: Fact or Fiction?   107
The Dome of the Rock   124
Words of God? or Man-Made Language?   134
The Yemeni Manuscripts: the oldest Qurans in existence   138
To Veil or Not to Veil—That is the Question   141
How Islam is implemented into the modern world   145

4. The Beginning of the End   **149**

Morsi's One Year in Power   150
An Islamic Constitution   153

Morsi Declares Himself Dictator — *157*
Morsi Eliminates the Supreme Court and Removes 3500 Judges — *159*
Rising Attacks on Journalists, Women and Christians — *166*
Morsi Replaces Governors with Terrorists — *177*

5. The End — 183

Western Media Collusion — *186*
Morsi is Arrested: The Bloodshed Begins — *191*
Intensified attacks on Christians — *201*
The State Department under Hillary Clinton and Gehad Haddad — *213*
Resistance? — *215*

Conclusion: What can we do? — 221

Appendix — 227

The years 633-833 — *227*
The Islamification of biblical history — *231*
Further evidence that the Quran was originally a Christian liturgical book — *233*
Important facts that took place during Mu'awiya — *235*
Iconoclasm: it was the Christians who destroyed icons, images and monuments — *236*

Sources — 239

About the Author — 257

INTRODUCTION

Chapter One recounts first-hand experiences and insights into a Muslim culture. These insights are meant to give you an introduction to the effects Islam has on society. Then, as you read the chapters that follow, give thought to events that have taken place in America, and by Chapter Five, you will be aware of the crisis lurking inside America.

In Egypt, the Muslim Brotherhood laid the foundation of their takeover by placing activists inside universities. In America, the same strategy was put in place. The Egyptian Muslim Brotherhood entered America in 1962 and began inserting Muslim student organizations in American universities. Today, there are more than 800 chapters of these Muslim Brotherhood organizations on American university campuses (UTT 2019).

In the 1970s, the Muslim Brotherhood in Egypt set up militant training camps and developed a strategy of recruiting in prisons. Upon release, recruits were funneled into the training camps and formed militias.

In the 1970s, the Pakistani branch of the Muslim Brotherhood entered America and set up 22 jihadi training camps. They began conversion programs in American prisons and began recruiting in prisons. Today, there are 35 known jihadi training camps in America (WND 2012).

In the 1980s, the Muslim Brotherhood in Egypt intensified the Islamist agenda inside universities and began a strategy of removing anything related to Egyptian heritage or nationalism. They preached that all Muslims, no matter what country they lived in, should be united under Islam with no distinction of nationality or cultural traditions to separate them from their Islamic identity.

In 1981 the Palestinian branch of the Muslim Brotherhood entered America and intensified the Islamist agenda on American university campuses. They promoted Islamic lifestyle on American campuses and encouraged Muslims to have separate Islamic communities and resist assimilation into American culture. The Muslim Brotherhood also placed *sharia* councils on American university campuses to encourage Muslim students to implement *sharia* into their daily life.

In Egypt, by the 1990s, Islamists had gained positions at every university. They became faculty members and administrators and were able to further the Islamist agenda.

In America, we have seen the co-opting of our youth via a liberal agenda placed in our universities. This liberal agenda plays an integral part in accelerating the Muslim Brotherhood's Islamist agenda into mainstream America.

Since the insertion of this agenda, we have seen:

- Demands for changes to school calendars to recognize Muslim holidays while simultaneously removing Christian holidays
- The insertion of Islam into our K-12 school curriculum while simultaneously removing American history
- Demands to integrate Muslim prayer rooms into schools while demanding the removal of crosses at Christian schools
- Demands to remove the pledge of allegiance due to its reference to God and allegiance to American values

In Egypt, the Muslim Brotherhood removed Egyptian history from textbooks and the national anthem was banned. In America, we've seen a similar effort to remove American history and there has been a campaign against nationalism.

Within weeks after Obama was elected president, the State Department held an Alliance of Youth Movements Summit. Chapters Two and Five detail how members of the Egyptian Muslim Brotherhood were recruited via this Summit and were funneled into CIA coup training camps. These camps taught militants how to mobilize large protests where they could conduct false flag events that would facilitate the removal of governments.

Representatives from Facebook, Google, NBC, ABC, CBS, CNN and MSNBC attended the Summit (Cartalucci "Google's Revolution Factory"; Howley "Hillary Clinton Sponsored Secret"; Youth Movements 2008).

Facebook and Google aided the Muslim Brotherhood in creating and promoting the Arab Spring protests and then mainstream media spread false news to cover up the Islamic takeover that was actually taking place.

In Egypt, the Muslim Brotherhood worked subversively with activist front groups in order to covertly work towards their goals. Members of Muslim Brotherhood in America work covertly with activist front groups such as Black Lives Matter, Women's March and others to achieve their goals.

As you will learn in Chapters Two and Four, the Muslim Brotherhood in Egypt demonized police in order to destabilize them and force them to stand down. Once they were destabilized, police were replaced with Islamist militias.

In 2008, Obama promised to create a "Civilian National Security Force" that would be "just as powerful, just as strong, just as well funded as the U.S. Military."

Throughout Obama's presidency we witnessed a massive effort to demonize police and there were several instances where police were told to stand down. Was Obama's "Civilian Security Force" ready in the waiting?

As detailed in Chapter Two, the Muslim Brotherhood and al-Qaeda worked together to remove governments. The Muslim Brotherhood and al-Qaeda work subversively in various countries creating militias. These militias are meant to overthrow governments.

As detailed in this book, starting in 2011, the Obama administration backed the Egyptian Muslim Brotherhood, al-Qaeda in Iraq, al-Qaeda in Libya, and the "rebel" opposition groups attempting to overthrow the Syrian government. The opposition groups in Syria were Muslim Brotherhood and al-Qaeda.

Islam is spreading rapidly throughout the world and with its spread, slavery is returning, rape is skyrocketing and pedophilia is being promoted as an acceptable practice. These were behaviors of Muhammad.

The life of Muhammad and Islamic history are taught in our K-12 curriculum and in our universities as "fact" without any avenue or options to question them. Graduate students and doctorate candidates are not allowed to introduce evidence that contradicts Muslim sources on Muhammad, the Quran and Islamic history. Research studies that introduce evidence contradicting Islamic history have been removed from our university libraries and research programs.

Chapter Three gives an overview of studies and books that need to be reinserted into our university programs and our libraries. All Americans need to learn the questionable aspects of Islam outlined in this book in order to halt further Islamification of America.

Chapters Four and Five detail the horrors of what happens to a country once Islam has infiltrated, but also demonstrates what happens when people become complacent and do nothing to stop it.

Read this book — and do not be complacent.

Chapter 1. Egypt 101

I approached the man holding the sign with my name on it and said to him, "That's me!" When he asked where he would be taking me, I answered, *il-haram*. He gave me a startled look, then one of confusion. Students enrolled in the Arabic Intensive Program at the American University in Cairo are usually family members of diplomats, wealthy individuals entering international banking, or some other "upscale" field or position in life. The village neighborhood of *il-haram*, my destination, has always been *ghehlaba* (poor, lower class).

The people of *il-haram* are at the bottom of the Egyptian class structure. They live at the base of the sphinx and pyramids, but most come directly from poor farming villages along the Nile or the villages of the Delta.

As we drove towards *il-haram* the driver continuously eyed me in the rearview mirror with a look of suspicion. His expression turned into astonishment when we pulled up to my destination, the entrance to an alley of mud-brick one and two-room houses without running water. The driver handed me a packet of information and a letter of greeting from the American University and left without a word. It seems this driver wasn't too enthused about my destination and judged me unfairly because of it.

During my enrollment in the Arabic Intensive Program, I lived with various families in *il-haram*. I settled into village life and got to know the neighborhood people. There are many horse and camel stables along the streets and alleys around the pyramids, so I began to take horseback riding lessons almost every evening after a long day of classes.

I would end each day on a high sand dune observing the transition to nightfall. Slowly the lights of Cairo would begin to light up one by one in the distance. Then suddenly, Cairo would light up all at once—a wave of lights in a magical blur. Soon after, the spotlights aimed at the pyramids would turn on. Often, the pyramids appeared to be glowing in a hazy mirage—enormous but blurred from light mixed with fine Saharan dust.

I will always look back on my earliest years in Egypt as some of the best years of my life.

Living amongst average Egyptians taught me the Egyptian culture. It was like taking a class: Egypt 101. Part of what I had to learn had to do with the country's well-defined class structure and how each class expected to be treated (or not treated, in some cases). Poverty had forced many Egyptians to remain in their village-like areas and alleyways of Cairo. You could turn a corner into an alley off a main, modern street and find yourself in Egypt in the mid-1800s.

By living in these village neighborhoods, I experienced all of their festivities and celebrations and came to understand the belief systems attached to those festivities. The lower class and poor are the majority in Egypt and they hold on to the very oldest traditions.

Unlike most foreigners who visit Egypt, I lived like an Egyptian and lived with Egyptians. I went to countless engagement parties, henna nights and weddings. I participated in the four days of feasting during the Corban Feast which included the ritual slaughtering of sheep. Many of my friends bought baby sheep months ahead with the sole purpose of having them full grown by the date of the feast. Often they would raise the lambs on their rooftops along with a few bunnies (to be eaten, not as pets).

I lived in these village homes while celebrating *eid il-fettira* (the feast at the end of Ramadan), *shem el-nisseem* (a holiday that is a remnant from an old Pharaonic tradition), and I've been to countless *subuah*, the 7th-day birthday party. Due to high death rates, Egyptians are afraid to celebrate the birth of a baby until it has lived seven days.

I attended all the other festivities and celebrations as well, both secular and religious. Egyptians love celebrations and have many. I did not "observe" the culture; I became a part of it. I lived it. It became my life. It was my life for many years.

I lived with different families over the years, but eventually I began to rent apartments of my own in various parts of Cairo. Each of the areas within greater Cairo are like separate villages. I'd get to know my neighbors and the people in the local community, the shop owners, and the people who sold things from the little kiosks that speckle every area of Cairo. I became friends with my neighbors and owners of shops. I hung out in their homes, at their shops, and was always invited to their events.

One of my favorite homes during my earliest years in Egypt was that of my first horseback riding teacher. My teacher, Hassan, would often invite me to his house to have a meal. Once he discovered that I knew all the classic Egyptian songs, he would sing them while we took long rides in the Sahara.

Eating at Hassan's house was always a treat. Not only was his wife a fantastic cook and taught me how to cook the traditional foods of Egypt (which came in handy when I later married an Egyptian), she was also my first insight into the life of the average Egyptian woman.

At first Hassan's wife, Aiya, served me. I was her husband's guest. Following tradition, she would not eat with us—she would serve us and then disappear. But after a few visits I talked Hassan out of this special treatment. I wanted to be part of the family and not treated special.

Aiya loved it when I helped her. She would grin at me when I showed interest in how she made traditional Egyptian food, and eventually, she showed me the tricks of her cooking skills. She then began to allow me to carry food in from the small area outside where she cooked, to the dirt floor of their main room where we all ate together on the floor.

Their small mud brick home had a dirt floor and no real furniture to speak of, just one hand-made mattress on the floor and one very simple dresser-type piece of furniture that held the wardrobe of the entire family of six. In other words, not much clothing.

They had no bathroom inside the home; they shared one with other people in the alley. That I did not seem fazed by their toilet, a hole in the ground, was a relief to them. Their neighbors had seen foreigners show disgust at the hole in the ground system. But the truth was, I had already become used to it. It is the norm for many in Egypt.

There was no running water inside Hassan's home. There was a pump outside in the alley that was used for cooking and washing dishes. After eating and clearing the floor, an ancient cassette player would be taken off the dresser and *beledy* music would be played. *Beledy* is traditional music with a very recognizable drum rhythm recognized by all as "Egyptian."

Beledy music and a well-used, tattered Monopoly game in Arabic was all Hassan and Aiya had for entertainment. But their favorite form of entertainment was dancing. After eating, we would dance. Usually the youngest child would go first, a three-year old boy who was one of the most impressive dancers I had ever seen, though as the years went by, I saw that all children, both male and female, begin dancing at the same time they learned to walk. Music and dance are deeply ingrained into the culture and play a central part of most festivities.

The Lowest of the Lowest

For several months I rented a very tiny one-room apartment with an incredible view of the pyramids. I was thrilled with this room with a view, but my relationship with the owner of the building, and the shop on the ground floor, was a difficult and tricky one.

Although he treated me with great respect because, as he often said, "You aren't like the other foreigners who come here for sex," he also made me uncomfortable because he managed to bring up sex in every conversation!

I came across this sexual stereotype about foreign women constantly. And to be honest, I came to find the stereotype somewhat true. Many foreign women come looking for a summer romance type of experience. And many offered casual sex. It was assumed that if these women offered casual sex to one man, they probably offered casual sex to many—and this is considered extremely bad by most all Egyptians.

The owner of the building respected me. I knew the culture well enough to know that being chaste was a must. I was in Egypt to learn the culture and to speak Arabic, but even if I was tempted at some point, I knew better. This chaste conduct served me well over the years. I had a good reputation wherever I went and with whomever I made friends. Years later, my husband went around to neighborhoods he knew I had lived and asked questions about me. He later reported to me that he could not find one dishonorable story about me, and in fact, heard raves about my being "like an Egyptian." He was very proud that I was well respected and loved (and that I hadn't had sex with anyone).

Every day the owner of my apartment building would tell me some story of a foreigner who had hit on him or did something bad (had sex). I was uncomfortable because I wasn't sure why he was always talking to me about sex. Was he bragging? Or was he hitting on me? I wasn't sure. So I avoided him as much as possible.

But I had another problem with the owner. He had an employee at his shop who helped at the counter and retrieved goods from the backroom. This employee had a son, and the son kept the shop clean and ran errands for the owner. One time I was sitting having coffee in the shop and also having a pastry. I had dropped the tissue I was using as a napkin and when I bent over to pick it up, the owner yelped "No!" He called his employee over and made him pick up my tissue.

Then, as if this was not enough, the owner pointed at some invisible speck of lint on the floor and told the employee to pick it up. The employee looked, but nothing was there. He was told again to pick it up. I bent over to get a close look and nothing was there. In fact, the employee's son had just finished sweeping the floor. I looked at the owner in puzzlement, but he just yelled at his employee to clean it up. The employee finally pretended to pick something up—making a big show of it—and walked away. Sadly, this type of thing happened most every day between the owner and his employee.

Even worse was the treatment of the employee's son, Ayman. Ayman was a bit slow, and because of this, people in my neighborhood treated him poorly. Kids made fun of him and shopkeepers shunned him when he came around.

When a person has a defect of any kind, whether mental or physical, that person is considered to be the lowest of the lowest, and depending on how different he is, he can become an outcast. But I found Ayman to be bright and very lovable and I made friends with him, first out of pity, because he had no one treating him well in my neighborhood, then, truly out of fondness.

Ayman began walking me to the corner where I caught the minivan bus that connected me to the main bus that would take me to downtown Cairo every day to get to the university. Ayman would also be waiting for me when I returned, which I loved because I'd be tired from a long day of classes and taking three buses to get home. The smile on his face when he saw me step off the bus made my long day new again.

The owner of my apartment building started a joke in the neighborhood about Ayman following me around like a dog. This joke was told in a most cruel and ugly way. Stray dogs often came into our neighborhood because there was a spot nearby where people dumped all types of waste and food scraps. Rats, cats, dogs and donkeys could always be found scavenging for food around the dumpsite. The owner of my building hated dogs more than any other creature, even preferring the rats to the dogs.

One day when the owner was gone for the afternoon I asked Ayman to accompany me to the post office to mail some letters. I knew he loved walking with me in this neighborhood where he was normally scorned and treated badly.

At first I thought he was leading me the long way for the fun of it, and that was fine with me. But then I realized he was walking me to his own neighborhood. People said hello to him and eyed me with a smile. He led me to a home where he was fussed over. It was his aunt's home and there were many children and a few female relatives there. They jumped to serve me tea.

Ayman's aunts asked me the same questions I am always asked when people first meet me:

Are you married? (my answer: divorced)

Do you have children? (my answer: yes)

How many boys? (my answer: none) Having no male children always received a reaction of great sadness, or sometimes people were "embarrassed" for me. Some men will divorce their wives if their wives produce no male children.

How old are you? (this meant, are you still young enough to marry and have male children in the future?)

After finishing tea and thanking Ayman's aunt profusely, we left for the post office.

We continued on down the alley but then Ayman darted into another home. Soon women came out and smiled at me and begged me to come in. It was another aunt and several cousins. We had another cup of tea and there was lots of joy expressed that Ayman had made a new friend.

We left, and it happened again, this time his mother's. I think maybe someone called ahead or sent a child as messenger because she was standing outside waiting with a huge grin on her face. I met all of Ayman's small brothers and sisters and I lingered longest at his home.

By the time we left, a large mob of neighborhood kids had gathered outside and they followed us through the streets as if we were the Pied Piper— all the way back to the border of my neighborhood. When we eventually returned to my building the difference in atmosphere was hard felt. The smile left Ayman's face immediately as he humbled himself in front of the owner.

The owner's poor treatment towards people he felt were less than him was endless, and over time I found it difficult to take. It was the main reason I ended up moving out of my wonderful little room with the pyramid view. But the final straw came in an awakening of sorts.

There was a taxi driver who I used often and who I had befriended. The owner would not allow my friend to meet up with me inside the ground floor shop. The owner made him wait outside like an outcast. People living in the building often met with friends in the shop and the owner normally welcomed it. He allowed others to meet up in his shop, but never my friend. Fed up one day, I asked the owner why he would not let my friend inside. He replied, "He's just a taxi driver."

At first this was a puzzle.

My taxi driver friend was very well educated and from an upper-class family. I had many dinners with his family and got to know them well. My friend's father was a historian and author of several books. There just weren't enough jobs for graduates and that's why my friend bought a taxi. It was an easy way to make an income while he found a job. My friend and his family were well respected in their community.

But my taxi driver friend was a Christian. And the owner of my apartment building had voiced his dislike for Egypt's Copts on many occasions. This was to be my very first inkling into a deeper underlying hatred some Muslims have for Christians.

Orgasms

As I moved around to different villages and suburbs, I continued to go horseback riding and tried new stables.

At one particular stable, the guides, and even the owner, who had many experiences with foreigners over the years, truly believed that foreign women always wanted sex. The men at this new stable not only believed that foreign women always wanted sex, they believed that foreign women rode horses to have orgasms!

Many stables have a multi-purpose meeting room where you wait for a guide. This room is also where you could go after the ride for a drink of water, soft drink, or to socialize a bit with other riders. Many ex-pats own horses in Egypt. Arabian horses are a fun ride, so there is a large community of foreigners who ride and socialize at stables.

It was there in this meeting room that my guide told me it was a well-known fact that foreign women rode horses to have an orgasm. Moreover, since Western women weren't circumcised, he believed they couldn't help but have an orgasm. He believed they couldn't control it from happening.

Images began to race through my mind as I contemplated this. Egyptian women who ride on the back of a motorcycle ride sidesaddle. I had thought it odd, but was now beginning to realize women did this to prevent people from thinking anything bad about them. It would be social death for a girl if people thought she was allowing her vagina to be stimulated.

I also thought of a time when I was visiting a friend. There were no chairs in the home, but there was a bed in the front room. This room was used as a bedroom at night, but doubled as a reception area by day. As in many middle-class Egyptian homes, this front room included the TV, the landline telephone, and a boom box. I was told to sit on the bed, which doubled as a couch during the day. The mother came over and draped a cloth over my lap.

This was not the only time this had happened, this covering of my crotch when I visited someone's home.

I was now beginning to put everything together.

Since I was wearing pants, my crotch needed to be covered. The average Egyptian woman wears a *galabeya*, a full-length, baggy dress. A *galabeya* conceals the crotch. I was wearing pants, the "V" of my crotch was visible. Crotches are scary things—and tempting.

After I got over the shock of this guide's statement of why he thought I rode horses, I asked for a different guide, without realizing all men at this stable held this belief about foreign women.

My new guide, Malek, loved to race in the desert. I loved racing, too, so we hit it off immediately. One evening we had plans to race to a cliff top to watch the pyramids light up at sunset.

While in the meeting room waiting for our horses, the owner of the stable made a deal for a young Saudi Arabian boy and me to ride with Malek. Malek liked riding with me alone so we could race through the desert unhindered, so he became noticeably irritated at this development.

Stable hands came in who were making the transition to starting the evening chores, but before they started their duties, they lit up some hash in the meeting room. Malek joined in when normally he didn't smoke until after he was done being a guide.

Malek was very stoned and had copped an attitude about being stuck with the young Arab. The young Arab was not a good rider and at one point could not get his horse to move.

Guides know the tricks to make the horses stop or go. The guide makes a certain noise that will stop the horse and makes another noise to make the horse move. But instead of helping this amateur rider, Malek suddenly raced off and left us!

Since I knew the area well, I took charge and the young Arab and I made it back safely. I did not mention anything about Malek's disappearance because I did not want to get him in trouble. Stable hands took our horses and we did not make a fuss.

But the next time I came for a ride, I was told Malek was no longer working there. And oddly, the owner of the stable wanted to ride with me. The stable owner hadn't ridden in over a decade, so this was a rarity. Abbas and I rode out to a familiar place where I had ridden many times. It has a magnificent view of the pyramids, high on a plateau. We got off our horses to rest them and sat in the sand enjoying the view of the pyramids for a while.

Abbas suddenly said to me, "Did you have orgasm?"

It had been a lovely ride. Who could not enjoy a ride in the Sahara with the pyramids by your side? But this idea of riding to achieve orgasm, by myself, like masturbating? "No, I did not!" I replied angrily. "And I never have!"

This was a mistake. I meant that I had never had an orgasm on a horse, not that I had never had an orgasm.

"Ohhh," he said. "Sex is your problem. You need sex."

What do I say to this? Sex talk with Egyptian men is difficult and odd. But more importantly, I suddenly felt frightened. My gut instinct said, "Go back right now." So instead of replying to his comment, I stood up and said, "Let's go back."

We got on our horses, but after trying several times, I couldn't make my horse go.

Abbas laughed heartily.

I tried again, but my horse would not move. Abbas laughed even harder.

Then I realized he had made that special sound. And I knew my horse would never go until Abbas allowed it to go. It was a very long way back to the stables, but I got off my horse and began walking. After about fifteen minutes I could hear Abbas slowly approaching with my horse in tow.

"Are you really going to walk?"

"What choice do I have?"

"You can ride."

"Will you believe me that I do not ride horses for orgasms?"

"Yes."

"Will you believe me that I am not looking to have sex with men in Egypt?"

He paused at that, not answering, but then motioned for me to get back on my horse.

We rode back, neither of us saying a word.

I felt massive relief as we entered the village where I felt safe again, but on the ride back I had wondered, had Malek told a lie about me to get himself out of trouble? Had he made me out to be one of those foreign women looking for sex?

Sadly, this would not be the only time this type of experience would happen—most all Egyptian men think foreign women are looking for sex.

Marriage in Egypt

For a short period of time I lived at a quiet, 3-star hotel. It offered extremely simple basics and the desk people were wonderfully sweet. They housed foreigners long-term and had a back room with office equipment available for our use.

The hotel was a short distance to the American University in Cairo (AUC), which was a major perk. By this time, I was enrolled in a Master's Degree program and I was sick of taking long bus rides to the AUC campus.

Within weeks I made friends with the two taxi drivers who took shifts in front of the hotel.

It was established that Muhammad would take me to AUC in the morning and Saeed would take me to wherever I might be going in the evening, which was usually the pyramids area where most of my friends lived. I became very close to Saeed because it was a long drive to the pyramids.

Pyramids Street starts at the pyramids and links to central Cairo. It started as a dirt road, but as part of the inauguration ceremonies for the opening of the Suez Canal, it was paved and trees were planted so that visiting dignitaries would have a lovely tree-lined avenue to drive on when going to the pyramids. Once we turned onto Pyramids Street, it gave us an hour or so to talk.

Once we got past the basics: Are you married? Do you have children? How many boys? How old are you? it didn't take long for Saeed to introduce some heavy topics. Saeed and I had serious, in-depth conversations about Egyptians, Americans, the cultural differences, and of course, politics, a favorite of all Egyptian men.

One night Saeed told me he wanted to take me to visit a friend of his, a lawyer. He said he had told his friend about me and that his friend wanted to meet me. When we parked in front of a bazaar and Saeed said, "This is my friend's shop," at first I was alarmed. I thought, "Oh no, he wants me to buy things!"

It is very common for a taxi driver to take you to a bazaar, whether you want to or not. Taxi drivers get a commission on whatever you buy, so many taxi drivers will take you to a bazaar, even though it's not where you told him to take you. But Saeed must have read my facial expression because he quickly said, "No, no, you are not here to buy, but to talk—law business is slow, Samir runs the family shop at night."

We entered and I was greeted warmly by Samir. He fussed over me and created a place for me to sit, brought me a soft drink, then proceeded to pick my brain about American politics and other serious subjects. We had an intense, but very enjoyable conversation. Then we began talking more personal.

It started with a joke about Egyptian wives. I had heard similar jokes about Egyptian wives many times. They open the door with their hand out when their husbands arrive home from work to take all the money earned that day. And other jokes about Egyptian wives picking the husband's pockets then shoving the husband out the door with just enough money for the coffee shop—wanting him to get out and leave her with the TV.

I laughed, but then asked, "Is this true about Egyptian wives?" Samir looked at me solemnly and said, "Oh yes, very true."

I looked over at Saeed and he nodded and said, "Yes, it's true."

This was to be the beginning of receiving insights into the average middle-class Egyptian, and most specifically, the city people who were not from a village.

The two of them proceeded to tell me how Egyptian men did not marry for love. Wives immediately had children as fast as possible and once the children start to come, the women just want money and for the husband to be away as much as possible. I was told that sex exists, the wife cannot refuse it, but it is a duty and it's just, "Ee, ee, ee" (their words). Quick and over with. "There is no real satisfaction in most Egyptian marriages," I was told.

Since that conversation, I found it to be true with most every married couple I talked to in Cairo. Egyptian women have openly admitted to me that they had as many kids as possible and as fast as possible to lock in the husband, so he wouldn't abandon them. But children are also insurance in case the men divorce them. Once they have male children, the husband cannot take the apartment from them until the male child turns twelve. So once the wives start having children, the whole world revolves around getting as much money from the husband as possible, before the last male child turns twelve.

This explained why, when asked if I was married, and I answered divorced, people always wanted to know if I had children, especially male children. As the years went by, I found this confirmed over and over by everyone I met—that very few marriages were happy—and that wives always tried to create "insurance" in case of divorce or abandonment.

Most married couples live very separate lives and see each other as little as possible. After work, the man goes to the coffee shop until the wee hours of morning, purposefully staying away. And often, tiring of this type of relationship, men will marry a younger woman thinking things will change with the second marriage. But it doesn't because they don't marry for love. The new bride immediately starts having children to protect her future and the whole cycle starts over again.

I do occasionally hear a story where a couple meets at university and marries, but only if both families agree to it first. The marriage must meet certain criteria. No one gets married without family approval. Therefore, this type of marriage, marrying for love, is rare.

Even my husband's family, who is more modern and more Westernized, continues to arrange marriages. Essam's niece, his twin brother's daughter, never met her fiancé. She didn't meet him until their engagement party and then didn't see him again until the wedding.

And my husband's unmarried brother continues to consult his brothers each time he wants to find a suitable wife, only to find a possibility, but then have one of the brothers say, "No, she's not a good bride for our family."

Marriage is all about marrying "up" or marrying a person of equal status. Or, at least someone with good family ties—someone whose family can improve your own family's connections or can offer some type of benefit or status.

Divorce, wife beating—and blaming the woman

One of the things I loved about First Lady Suzanne Mubarak was her work for women's rights, against female trafficking and slavery, and her work at trying to prevent visiting Gulf Arabs from buying young Egyptian village girls. Although the Arabs buy these girls for marriage, they are just using the child for her virginity. They marry her, have sex with her for a few weeks, and then abandon her. This leaves these girls with no choice other than a life on the streets. Their family is shamed, not only because she has been abandoned, but because she is no longer a virgin, and therefore, she is no longer marriageable in her village.

I also loved that the First Lady promoted the fact that headscarves are not a religious requirement. She also helped fight against female circumcising and helped to get laws passed that made it illegal. And, she promoted the passing of new laws that allowed women to initiate divorce. Previously, only men had the "right" to divorce. And they could do it easily, just by saying "I divorce thee" three times.

Over time, I became involved in women's rights in Egypt. I began to see many marriages in which the wife desperately wanted a divorce but could not. Women were not allowed to initiate divorce before the year 2000. Then, thanks to Suzanne Mubarak's work, a law was passed that women could initiate divorce in court proceedings.

But sadly, because of strict teachings of Islam, and the Muslim Brotherhood promoting these Islamic restrictions, it continued to be difficult. But also, if a woman initiated a divorce and had no children, she would have to give up her apartment and was not given any financial support. And even with children, there is often no financial support; her husband forces her to give up that right when she asks for a divorce. So, women are usually trapped in marriage. Even in abusive marriages.

I began supporting activist groups who were working on the issue of wife beating. At a conference I attended in Cairo, activists were focusing on the media and its role in abuse towards women. The media always sees the woman as the "cause" of the violence. If a man kills his wife, the media says she must have done something to deserve it.

The conference speakers referred to studies that showed that 63 percent of married women in Egypt had experienced wife beating and that over 50 percent of unmarried women reported physical violence from a brother or a father. Egyptian activists noted that many popular television dramas have scenes of violence against women and that these programs made violence towards women acceptable.

One study surveyed 18 television series and recorded 559 instances of violence against women. This raised the issue of how violence against women is promoted on TV. And, most horrifying, the men who commit the violence against women are the heroes of these programs! Therefore, many popular television programs play a role in making violence against women acceptable.

As I write this, my husband's niece is faced with big decisions. Her husband has been beating her. Soon after their marriage, her husband began to deprive our niece of food. Her husband would eat out after work and never gave her any money for food. That was the first problem she faced immediately after her marriage.

When she began to complain about being hungry, he would punch her. This went on for more than a year until she finally packed up her baby boy and went to live with her parents. My husband was consulted at this time. In Egypt, the males in the family are brought in when there's a problem.

If Mena, our niece, chooses to divorce her husband it will bring shame on the entire family. When families consider a suitable spouse for a family member, if the other family has even one divorce in the extended family history, this is often a reason for declining the marriage offer.

In other words, a divorce screws up the future for all unmarried members of the family.

Also, if Mena gets a divorce, she may face never marrying again. Being a non-virgin deprives a future husband of something all male Muslims feel is their right. And, that she has a child by a previous male is often met with stepfather abuse.

Although laws had changed so that a divorced woman with a male child could retain the apartment, the Muslim Brotherhood was in the process of changing this law. They were also making it difficult for a woman to initiate a divorce. There were still ways to make it happen, but it could take many years.

Meanwhile, complicating things further, a woman living alone, without a husband or male relative, would destroy her respectability, not only in her building, but in the entire neighborhood. There would be suspicion towards her, and many people would think she was a prostitute just because she was living alone.

Eventually Mena went back to her husband, feeling she had no choice. Being a "respectable" married woman was more important than being beaten—or being thought of as a woman of ill refute.

Added to the TV programs that promote violence towards women, there is at least one article per week in each of the main Egyptian newspapers that describes a situation in which the woman is blamed for a wrongdoing. Some of the situations are so blatantly not her fault yet she is blamed in a twisted way. These articles are obvious brainwashing tactics—and sadly, they work.

While I was at AUC, a student was attacked in the street just outside the campus gate. It was an extremely vicious attack, but the first thing people asked, her friends included, was: "What were you wearing?"

She was wearing a long, baggy, thick parka that camouflaged her body, and baggy balloon type khakis with baggy outside pockets. She had on sports shoes, nothing feminine or tempting.

She was tremendously shaken by the attack, but to then be repeatedly asked about what she was wearing and made to feel as if she had done something wrong, or was at fault in any way, traumatized her even further.

During the attack, people interfered and called the police. The witnesses verified her attire and said the man came up to her from behind; she had never even seen him. In other words, she did not "ask for it."

Some had asked her if she had made eye contact with the man—a no-no in Egypt according to "social rules" of chastity. Eye contact is considered flirting—an invitation.

The man grabbed her from behind, put his hands under her parka and began groping her crotch. When she resisted, the man grabbed onto her and began punching her hard in the face continuously to try to subdue her into submission. This went on for a while until people finally tore him away from her.

When police interviewed the attacker, he said he attacked her because, "She was asking for it—her hair smelled good—she put something in her hair." The police actually asked her, the victim, what she put in her hair to tempt the man! She told police that she used a common brand Egyptian shampoo and had put nothing in her hair.

The event was written about in the AUC newspaper. The following issue of the paper included feedback comments from fellow students who said things like, "She was probably wearing something inappropriate."

The girl who was attacked responded in the following week's paper with the details of the attack, including the eyewitness reports. She said the event itself was horrifying enough, but to have fellow students put the blame on her, and that she had to defend herself and have witnesses verify her clothing, was even more excruciating.

Still, even after her response, detailing what happened and what she wore, no one changed their opinions. The following week there was even more feedback, the most prevalent being: "She must have been asking for it." This response came from just as many female students as males.

And many said, "She should have been wearing a headscarf."

The remedy for the evilness of women—the veil and circumcising!

I have a friend who is a beautiful young woman, 24-years-old, who works at my bank and who does not wear a headscarf. She is well educated and knows that wearing a headscarf is not in the Quran and that she does not have to wear one. She is called a "slut" by all her male work colleagues and puts up with constant sexual harassment. Sometimes it gets quite nasty, and they even touch her inappropriately or grab at her body.

She is a virgin and has never had any sexual activity. She dresses very conservatively. She wears loose, hi-neckline, long sleeve blouses and full-length skirts (never wears pants; therefore no "V" of her crotch is shown). I mention this because she has not behaved or dressed in any way that could be called slutty.

They call her a slut and sexually harass her because she does not wear a headscarf.

They tell her that not wearing a headscarf is "against Allah." Even her female co-workers tell my friend that it is her fault she is harassed and that she is "asking for it" by not wearing a headscarf. But my friend knows she is not asking to be sexually harassed. She sits and does her work and never makes eye contact with her male colleagues.

Recently they have begun telling her she is an unbeliever. They are trying to terrify her into wearing a headscarf by accusing her of being an apostate.

Women in Egypt are not only faced with sexual harassment and social enforcement to force them to wear headscarves, they are brainwashed by television preachers and imams. They are told repeatedly that they must prove they are "virtuous." How? By wearing a headscarf or veil.

Women are also told by TV imams that they have no "worth" other than being a wife and mother. They are told that once those duties are achieved, they are worthless.

They are told there is only one way to achieve "worth" at that point in their lives, after they've had their children, and that is to prove they are "virtuous." Women are told they must wear the veil to prove their virtuousness to Allah.

These TV imams convince women that a woman's body is evil, and that their entire body must be covered to prevent evil from consuming them.

Women are told that their hands must be covered, because if a woman touches something without her hand being covered, she has then dirtied that object with her evilness.

Because of this emphasis that a woman's only worth is marriage and babies, marriage is stressed on very young girls. The pressure on girls to be married is extreme.

Most girls want to be married as soon as they turn eighteen, unless they go to university, but even then, most all university students want to be married by the time they graduate. Many are betrothed while in university or long before, and the marriage takes place immediately after graduation.

In villages, where education is not stressed, or where there are no local schools, girls marry well before the age of eighteen. To be unmarried causes great scorn from the entire village.

After marriage, the focus is to start having babies. To not get pregnant right away causes much embarrassment to a young village wife and can lead to the husband divorcing her or taking on a second wife. So, the wife's focus is on having children and trying to gain some feeling of security and worth.

Because they marry young, by the time the children are grown, women are still somewhat young. They then become vulnerable to the TV preachers who tell them their only worth is wearing the veil to prove their virtue to Allah and to guarantee entrance to Paradise.

My husband's youngest sister married young, had three children right away (boys), thereby fulfilling her "duties." When all three boys were grown, she had little to do with her free time. She had no employment skills because she had married young, and unlike her sisters, had not gone to university.

All Egyptians love television, and she, like so many wives, became consumed with TV and she watched the TV preachers. Soon after this exposure she began wearing the veil.

My husband has shown me photos of his family vacationing on the beaches of Alexandria. His family owned a summer home in Alex and spent their summers there for a period of about twelve years. He has four sisters. All four sisters, including the one who now wears the veil, wore two-piece bathing suits on the beach, as did most Egyptian women during the late 1960s and up into the 1980s.

My husband comes from a family of eight children. His family has told me that no girls wore headscarves while they were growing up, and not at college either. There was no sexual harassment—it was unheard of—and unthinkable. Yet today, sexual harassment is extensive and epidemic. So, what happened?

Islam happened.

The development of wearing headscarves and the enforcement of them began in the 1980s. Now, all my nieces and nephews, of whom I have many, tell me that all girls in school wear headscarves, and many are fully veiled. I'm told that to not wear a headscarf is an invitation for sexual harassment.

Part of this problem comes from the mosque, because this is what the imams are teaching. And part of this comes from the television preachers. But the headscarf and veil are also heavily promoted inside the universities. And since the latest generations of fathers grew up during or after the emphasis on headscarves, and since they hear the imams preach anti-woman propaganda, the latest generations of fathers do not teach their sons to respect women and do not teach their sons that sexual harassment is wrong.

Besides the headscarf and veil, imams also preach that all girls must be circumcised. They teach that uncircumcised women are highly sexed and therefore want sex more often, and that this high state of arousal from not being circumcised makes them desire sex with more than one man. They are insatiable. This idea of sex with more than one man terrifies both men and women. A woman's worth is being virtuous. A woman must be a virgin when she marries and then only have sex with one man—her husband.

The imams repeatedly preach: "Uncircumcised women are sexually out of control!"

Circumcising women is all about "control."

Many parents I've talked to say that although they are against it, they still circumcise their daughters so that the girl will not have the problem of being unable to control her sexual desire. If a girl cannot control her sexual desire, she will be undesirable to marry. Unmarried men looking for wives do not want a girl if she's not circumcised.

Yet what is really puzzling is that nearly all newly married men complain about their bad sex life! Everyone talks about it; it's no secret. They say their wives do not enjoy sex and prefer not to do it. And that the wife only has sex because it is her duty. This attitude eventually is a turn-off for the husband. So, it makes no sense for unmarried men to want their future wife to be circumcised but they do because they've been told their wives will be "out of control" if not circumcised.

I have become very good friends with a Christian doctor. He says that almost every week at least one Muslim woman comes to him and asks him to fix her vagina. It is usually because the circumcising was done poorly and the women still suffer from the botched job, have chronic infections, and can barely have sex without screaming in pain. Many women come to him because they believe their dislike for sex is due to being circumcised. They come to him because they want their clitoris back.

Yet these same women keep circumcising their own daughters!

There are always several sex cream ads in the newspapers. The pictures in the ads look like ads for pornography. Many of these creams are to be rubbed on a woman's vagina to help her enjoy sex. The creams are not for lubrication, but to give the sensation of having a clitoris.

These ads are so widespread that after I married Essam, I asked him about these ads. He told me that men always talk about sex, but not like Western guys do. They talk incessantly about "not having sex." Essam says once a month is considered a lot and a husband is lucky to get this.

Most husbands experiment with several brands of sex creams before finding out they don't work. The creams do not help the wives enjoy sex, nor want sex.

They circumcise girls to prevent them from desiring sex, but what happens is, women end up not being able to have sex comfortably, let alone be able to enjoy sex.

Circumcised women suffer chronic infections primarily because of the "at home jobs." Circumcising is usually done in the home, and in small villages, often done by a member of the extended family. It's almost always a hack job leaving the girl horrifically damaged because they often cut more than the clitoris.

In the last few years there has been much outrage regarding a sex therapist who was trying to help young couples have better sex. For a while she had a weekly column in a major newspaper, but it caused so much anger that the paper was forced to remove her column.

She offered some good basic advice, but quite honestly, judging by the questions she received, it was obviously hopeless. The men didn't have a clue as to how to please their wives, nor did they seem to want to. They just wanted sex more often.

Many of the wives said they refused to talk to their husbands about sex because they feared it would make them appear like a bad woman. They feared if they seemed interested in sex, the husband would be suspicious of them and possibly accuse them of wanting sex with other men—or worse, they'd be falsely accused of adultery. But mostly the women complained about the pain.

Another thing I found interesting is how many women complained that they considered sex an awful chore. This may be partly due to the fact they did not marry for love and hence have no attraction to their husband, let alone passion. Many marry a total stranger. And many young girls are forced to marry men twenty to forty years older than them, forced by arranged marriages. Because these older men have established an apartment, a business, or stable income, they are considered a great choice as husband. But these are not "sugar daddy" type marriages where a young wife is treated well. These young girls are often treated like slaves.

Besides sex creams, there is an overabundance of Viagra, especially free giveaway Viagra. Viagra is given as gifts, given to fellow employees, given as bribes during elections, and given out by taxi drivers. At least once a week Essam comes home with a Viagra given to him by a taxi driver. Essam always chats up a taxi driver and tells jokes the entire ride. His reward for being a fun customer? Viagra.

Most Egyptian men don't take Viagra for erection problems. They take Viagra thinking it will enlarge their penis to twice the size of their normal erection size. They think this supersize penis will excite the wife into wanting sex, without considering that a supersize penis would only hurt a young circumcised wife even more.

A very common theme in the Friday newspapers is a story of a girl who begs to be circumcised. The article will start by telling a story in which being uncircumcised causes a girl big trouble of some sort. Then, the story tells of her announcing to everyone that she wants to get circumcised. The end is always the same—she gets circumcised and lives happily ever after. She marries the most desirable man in her community, usually someone who is wealthy or important (or both). The moral of the story is that good things happen to girls who are circumcised!

One of the worse of these types of stories is about an uncircumcised girl who can't control herself from masturbating. Her state of horniness and desire for penis causes her to put all types of objects into her vagina. Because of this, she destroys her virginity and thereby destroys her chances of ever getting married.

These stories are always very sexy and titillating and I often wonder if they serve a dual purpose. Are they soft-core porn for the men, while simultaneously brain washing readers into condoning female circumcising?

Another popular type of story in the Friday newspapers is about an uncircumcised Christian girl who is having trouble with being oversexed. But it ends with a twist. The Christian girl converts to Islam! Islam is made out to be superior because it "protects" women from evil. These stories give the impression that Christianity is flawed.

I watched an Egyptian religious TV program about female circumcision one day. The host of the program explained that the small villages along the Nile circumcise all their girls.

The host interviewed various village women who stated they believe female circumcision is from Sunna, the religious practices established by

Muhammad. They also said they believe that if a girl is not circumcised "she can't bear it" (can't bear her horniness).

All of these village women were illiterate. The villages where these interviews took place have no schools.

While working with the Ministry of Culture I conducted research in small villages throughout Egypt. Even in villages where there are schools and women are taught to read, they don't learn to read well enough to read the Quran (more on this later). And, few villagers have access to books on Sunna.

These women rely on "religious men" to inform them of their duties. These village women were taught these beliefs about circumcising by their local imams.

In 2005, Ahmed al-Tayib, the Grand Imam of al-Azhar, stated, "All practices of female circumcision are crimes and have no relationship with Islam. It is not an obligation in Islam."

Al-Azhar is considered the most respected source on Islamic Law and its Grand Imam is seen as the highest authority in the Muslim world. But here we are, even after it was declared by the Grand Imam to be a crime, these villagers are still circumcising their girls because their village imams continue to preach it.

And, so are the TV imams, who millions of Egyptian women watch daily.

Once a prostitute, always a prostitute

One time Essam and I could hear yelling and screaming from outside in the alley behind the kitchen side of our apartment. Essam ran to the window to see what was happening. A man was standing by the door of a ground level apartment and he was holding his arm. Blood was beginning to show on his shirtsleeve and then began dripping to the ground. He was yelling and a woman opened the door and yelled back. A few people began to gather and they listened to his story, then hers. Suddenly Essam gasped and said, "She's a prostitute!"

Seems this woman had sex with this man once before. He came back for more sex and she said no. He refused to leave and then tried to rape her. She grabbed a kitchen knife and stabbed him.

I said to Essam, "That doesn't mean she's a prostitute. Soaphe (the doorman to our apartment building) often gets maids to have sex with Gammal (his helper) and they aren't considered to be prostitutes."

Essam answered, "But she had sex with him before, so she can't refuse him now!"

"Why not?"

"She just can't!"

Essam shushed me while he listened to more yelling. Then things quieted down and the man left.

The word prostitute had never come up between the man and the woman during the yelling, nor any reference to money. There was no mention of anything to make one think she was a prostitute.

People in our back alley are mostly maids and manual laborers. Many of the maids are foreigners, primarily Asian, who come to work in our area because it has several embassies. Foreign ambassadors and dignitaries prefer hiring Asian maids.

Our doorman often gets one of these maids to come have sex with his assistant. Gammal is always whining that he is horny. Gammal is very cute, so it's not hard to find a maid to service him—for free. These maids are not prostitutes. The difference here was that this woman in our back alley was Egyptian, and a Muslim.

My side of the argument was, what does prostitution have to do with it and where does choice come into it. Why does this woman have to have sex with this man just because she did once before? She was not a prostitute, but even if she was, why does she have to have sex with this man?

Essam's only argument was that the woman had to have sex with the man because she had had sex with him once before. He said the people in the alley who had gathered had yelled that out, too. So, he said, "Everyone agrees with me."

I said, "What about if she just didn't want to?" He said it doesn't matter what she wants. I said, "What if he was cruel to her or had goo coming out of his penis (a disease)—and she did not want to have sex with him?" Essam said she still had to.

Finally, after heated arguing I said, "What if she wanted to change, she wanted to be a good woman and virtuous, she wanted to be pure with Allah so she would be allowed into Paradise, and this was how she was starting her new way of life, by not having sex with men—why can't she stop having sex with men—starting with this man. Is your God not capable of allowing a woman to change into a good woman?"

Essam thought about what I said for a long time, then said, "Yes, I suppose Allah would allow her to change."

Sadly, I knew that all those people in the alley who thought the woman "had to" have sex with that man did not have me to change their minds. And I often wondered if the people in the alley would one day harm the woman who had stood up for herself.

Now, at this point, some of you who are reading this book may be curious about my marriage.

Essam and I met through my work as a researcher. He's intelligent and witty and we would have long, stimulating conversations regarding my work, but then began having conversations about most everything and we would talk for hours. We quickly became best of friends.

Though Essam was brought up in a wealthy family and was called Pasha by the time he hit his early teens, he did not treat the average Egyptian poorly as some wealthy people did. Upon entering their apartment building, wealthy people often hand off the shopping bags to the doorman, then point him to the stairs, while they take the elevator up several flights.

Essam on the other hand, will give the doorman a bag or two (holding some bags himself), give the doorman a large tip, invite him into the elevator, then tell jokes all the way up to his floor. Essam makes everyone laugh and treats everyone fairly.

Before marrying Essam, I spent much time at the homes of various members of Essam's family. I often spent the night at the main family home where the entire family would meet on Thursday nights, where all would spend the night in preparation for Friday—the main family day in Egypt.

I would help his female family members prepare the big Friday meal. I got to know their histories, how they met their husbands, and I learned that Essam had fought alongside them in all of their endeavors.

I learned that Essam was anti-headscarf and anti-veil. And he, too, admired the First Lady and thought highly of her endeavors at freeing the Egyptian woman from the abuses of an Islamic society. Essam never went to mosque and never prayed the five daily prayers. Why is this important? Mosques in Egypt had become brainwashing centers.

Over the years, I had noticed that the people I had become close friends with, and remained friends with, were Muslim in name only—they had been "born" Muslim, but they were not "practicing" Muslims.

The Islamic prayers said five times a day include derogatory statements towards Christians and Jews. Friday sermons given by imams almost always include Quran verses that include hatred and violence towards non-Muslims.

The verse from the Quran that is said five times a day is repeated more than once in each of the prayers. The Muslim who prays the daily prayers repeats these derogatory statements many times in a 24-hour period (see: Muslim Prayers).

The Quran contains at least 109 verses condoning and/or instructing war with non-Muslims. Some of these verses give commands to chop off heads, fingers, as well as killing non-Muslims wherever you find them. The Quran warns Muslims that Allah will send Muslims to Hell if they do not join the slaughter. The Quran encourages segregating oneself from Christians and Jews, encourages the belief that non-Muslims are the enemy of Muslims, tells Muslims to be ruthless to the infidel (non-Muslim) and that Allah intends for Muslims to triumph over non-Muslims (see: Hate and Violence in the Quran; see also, Berens "Inside the Quran").

My husband and my Muslim friends are not "practicing" Muslims. They do not say the Islamic prayers, nor do they go to mosque. They do not have this bias against non-Muslims drummed into them throughout the day, every day.

The Dancing Dick

Before my marriage to Essam, I had gone on a work assignment and had been given a driver/guide for the lengthy trip to Farafra Oasis. This driver/guide had somehow gotten the impression that I was looking for a husband. I was oblivious to this misunderstanding until night came. It was an extremely long drive, so we stayed at a village campsite one night.

That night, in an attempt to impress me, my guide did a "hard-on" dance. We had set up camp, cooked and eaten dinner, and were listening to music while tidying up when he began to dance. He removed his pants and began dancing in his underwear. He had an enormous erection. Though I had been assigned this guide through my work, and he should have been trustworthy, I was terrified.

I told him to put his pants on, but he explained that he'd make a good husband and that he was demonstrating his "strength" (his erection). I explained that I was not looking for a husband, and repeatedly told him to put his pants back on. I finally got him to stop dancing and put his pants on, but I stayed awake all night, frightened and wanting to stay alert.

The next day his advances started up again while we drove to our destination, a village where I'd be filming a festival. I threatened to tell the police at the village and this threat made him stop. But when we arrived at the village, I think he told a story to others to counter my accusation in case I told the police. Like I was asking for it, or was a bad woman looking for sex. Now I was going back on another assignment. And now married, Essam thought it would be fun to come along.

When we arrived at the village, Ahmed, the manager of the village campsite, took one look at me and said, "You've been here before, your guide was Mahmoud." I immediately knew this could turn into a very bad situation.

If Ahmed was just welcoming me back, he would have said something totally different and much more welcoming. Plus, he wasn't smiling. His eyes turned to slits when he looked at me and he looked rather sinister instead of welcoming.

Essam is a very jealous man. And even though he is more open-minded than the average Egyptian, because of his cultural upbringing, he has been brainwashed into blaming the woman.

The newspapers here always have reports of a husband killing his wife because she was unfaithful, and the husband never goes to prison even though there is no evidence that the wife was actually unfaithful. Essam and I have gotten into many a debate because he often sides with the man and thinks the husband had a right to kill his wife for adultery. But I eventually win the arguments because I point out there was no proof of her adultery.

Still, I was pretty worried about my experience with this guide, what he may have said about me, and whether Essam would believe me or him. I worried the rest of the day, not knowing whether to bring it up and prepare Essam beforehand, or to see how things went. I chose to wait and see.

That evening Ahmed decided he wanted to go with us to the oasis for the festival. He sat next to Essam all night and they constantly chatted while I filmed the festivities. I became even more nervous whenever I'd see them in an animated conversation. Nothing came of it luckily, and I finished my assignment without any trouble.

I waited until we were safely on our way home and close to Cairo before I told Essam the whole story. He gasped and said, "Mahmoud must have said you asked him for sex—or that you had sex with him!"

I said, "I think so, too."

I waited for his reaction as he sat there silently for a very long time and with a scowl on his face. He finally said, "I'm not happy thinking that Ahmed and others in the village think you slept with Mahmoud and that you are one of those foreign women looking for sex, but I believe you."

We didn't talk for a long time, but I could tell it weighed heavily on his mind. Then he said, "You should have reported Mahmoud to the police."

I said, "But Essam, do you know what a scandal that would have caused in that little village. Do you really think anyone would have believed me—a single, foreign woman—the way they always think foreign women are here to have sex? And I would have been kept at the police station for many hours and it would have been a big event and even written up in the newspapers, which means I'd probably be blamed for something I didn't even do!"

He thought about it, then nodded and said, "You're right."

Why did I even tell Essam about all this? Because I wanted him to know that men here lie. And that an innocent woman could be blamed for something she did not do—and possibly killed for it!

Removing culture

I had been to Bahareya Oasis a few times to document regional music and dance in traditional settings. I was sent again and to my shock, women were no longer allowed to dance at village festivals. In one traditional dance, the woman's role was performed by a man dressed as a woman because women were banned from participating.

Over the years, I witnessed this type of change in many villages. Some traditional dances had been in existence since Pharaonic times, handed down from generation to generation. There were dances celebrating the planting season, dances to celebrate the harvest, and so forth.

It was very disturbing to see these dances being banned. Egyptians have always had a strong sense of cultural identity through their music and dance traditions, but now, music and dance, most especially if it involved women, were being banned, thanks to the Muslim Brotherhood and Wahhabism.

The Muslim Brotherhood and Salafists (Wahhabists) want the Quran and *hadith* to be the base of all laws and enforced on all people. *Hadith* is the things Muhammad said and did, often called the "traditions" of Muhammad. Because of Islamic restrictions regarding music and dance, and restrictions on women, the Muslim Brotherhood and Salafists have convinced villagers to eliminate social activities and traditions that have been around for centuries.

Wahhabism is a belief that Islam is a complete way of life. The Muslim Brotherhood, ISIS, al-Qaeda, Taliban, and other Islamist groups are identical in ideology because they all believe in following the Quran and *hadith* to a tee.

Wahhabism got its name from Muhammad abd al-Wahhab, a religious preacher who lived in the 1700s. Wahhab preached that Muslims must follow the Quran and the behavior of Muhammad. The successors of King Saud of Saudi Arabia were Wahhabists. Wahhabism is the official state-sponsored form of Islam in Saudi Arabia. When the Saudis started making big bucks off their oil, they began using enormous sums of money to promote Wahhabism elsewhere to spread the Wahhabi system of Islam.

When the Muslim Brotherhood were banned in Egypt in the 1940s, many Brotherhood members moved to Saudi Arabia to help spread the system of *mutawwas*, proselytizing. The *mutawwas* system originally targeted the youth and nomadic Bedouin, but evolved into a tactical system of takeover. While Wahhab had used the *mutawwas* system to "purify" Islam, the Saudis used it to control the population and gain power.

The Egyptian Muslim Brotherhood helped create Islamic schools in Saudi Arabia during the 1940s and 1950s. After the ban against them was temporarily lifted, many Brotherhood members returned to Egypt, but went underground in order to infiltrate Egypt's universities. At this time, they began introducing the *mutawwas* system in Egypt. As in Saudi Arabia, where control of the population was created by proselytizing and brainwashing the youth, the Brotherhood in Egypt began focusing on the youth.

The Muslim Brotherhood surged in Egypt during the 1970s and early 1980s and grew stronger as the years went by. They purposefully gained a stronghold in villages where there was illiteracy and poverty—knowing they could influence the poor and illiterate more easily.

Additionally, many Egyptian men moved to Saudi Arabia to gain employment in the 1970s. Many of these men returned to Egypt in the 1980s and brought Wahhabism with them. They returned wearing the Wahhabi clothing and arrived with fully veiled wives in tow. These men called themselves Salafists, and like the Brotherhood, they spread Wahhabism in the poor, illiterate villages in the countryside. Salafi is a term for the first generations after Muhammad, and allegedly represent the true form of Islam.

Music and dance bans began in the countryside where illiterate farmers and country villagers trusted whatever their "religious" men told them. These religious men were purposefully placed in these villages by Muslim Brotherhood. They taught the villagers that a woman's worth was centered on her being a vessel for sex and for the production of children. Villagers were taught that women were a source of evil and must be veiled and kept restricted because of their evilness. Muslim Brotherhood and Salafists are obsessed with covering women's bodies.

During the 1970s in the cities, Egyptian women wore fashion that bared the arms and legs. Egyptian women wore miniskirts to work, to university, and on the metro, without any harassment. Men did not find them so tempting that they couldn't control their lust—this belief came with the Wahhabi beliefs of the Salafists and Muslim Brotherhood.

Villagers were brainwashed into thinking women are incapable of controlling sexual urges. Never is the responsibility placed on men to teach their sons that women should not be harassed. The opposite was being preached: men are *not* responsible for their lusts or desires. It is the woman's body that is evil and it is the woman's uncontrollable lust that tempts man to sin; therefore, rape is the woman's fault.

Women must be fully covered to "protect men" from a woman's evilness.

In ancient Egypt and during the Christian era in Egypt, women were equal to men. Written records show they owned their own property, they started their own businesses, and they formed partnerships with whomever they chose, with men or with women. They chose whether they wanted to marry, and whom. Islam destroyed equality for women in Egypt.

Right up throughout the 1970s, Egyptian women went to university in equal numbers as men. They drove cars and flew planes. They were scientists. This continued into the 1980s, but beginning in the 1970s, the Islamists began making enormous gains in the countryside. Around 25 million people in Egypt's countryside are illiterate. The Muslim Brotherhood strategically placed their preachers throughout the countryside to teach the villagers the Wahhabi form of Islam.

The Muslim Brotherhood also used the strategy of handing out free bread, rice, sugar, and other basic needs, and told them this was true Islam. They described Islam as a system where everyone would be taken care of. They propagandized a socialized system in which basic things would be given to them for free.

Then the Muslim Brotherhood began targeting the cities.

It was during this period that television stations run by Islamists began hosting tele-preachers who preached Islamist ideas about women. And, as they did in the countryside, they pushed the idea of socialism. Socialism would make people dependent, and thus, more controllable. They pushed socialism in the universities and by the 1990s, most all students at universities belonged to some type of socialist organization or political party.

Starting in the 1980s, the slow takeover of the villages in the countryside began to include banning music and dance. Since Egyptian festivities always included music and dance, these traditions were first "Islam-a-cized." Music was replaced with Quran recitation and a somber effect took over the once joyful events. And since women were considered evil and tempting, they were banned from festivities they had once participated in.

Within a period of years, women were no longer allowed to dance at weddings in the countryside villages and at the oasis villages of Faiyoum, Bahareya and Farafra. I was shocked when I had gone back to visit these villages and found dancing at weddings was now banned for women and that most all celebrations were segregated. Women who once wore colorful, flowered *galabeyas* and no headscarf, were now wearing full black veil. Women still danced in the privacy of their own home, or in a woman's gathering, but they could no longer dance at festivities in which for centuries they had mixed with men.

Egypt had regional traditions dating back to Pharaonic times. Desert activities and dances were different from farming activities and dances. Nile valley people had different traditions and dances than coastal fishermen, and so forth. Although all were distinctly Egyptian, there were variations in traditions between farmers, desert-dwellers and fisherman, and this was reflected in their dances and their festivals.

Coastal villages along the Mediterranean had fishermen's dances. There was the *Sahabah*, which represented the night of celebration after a good day of fishing, and the *Bambootee* dance, done by men who owned small merchant boats. But these various festivities included women, and so the dancing and festivities began to be banned.

In the Western Desert, there was a traditional dance called *el-Haggallah*. It consisted of three parts: the *Sheetway*, which consisted of singing and hand clapping; *el-Ghrineway*, where the unmarried men went out of the line and danced solo to impress the unmarried women; and *el-Magruda*, the female solo part, in which the unmarried women took turns dancing solo. This dance was done to help males gain insight into a girl's personality. Some males preferred a shy girl, and her shyness was visible in her dancing style. Some men preferred a bold, audacious girl, and this, too, would be expressed in her dancing style. But now this dance, all three parts, is banned.

Islamic Law: a female swimmer must be punished as an adulteress

After the Muslim Brotherhood took control of Egypt, the following *fatwa* (Islamic Laws) were made:

- A husband can have sex with his dead wife's body for up to six hours after her death.
- If a married woman goes swimming in the sea, she becomes an adulteress and must be punished accordingly.
- Women are forbidden to touch bananas and cucumbers.
- Women who go outside in public are offensive and thereby can be punished for doing so.
- It is forbidden for a woman to turn on the air conditioning during the absence of her husband.
- Marriage to ten-year old girls is permitted to keep girls from deviating from the right path.

- Women and children may be used as human shields during violent demonstrations.
- If a Muslim man is married to a Christian and she dies while pregnant, the baby must be cut out of the woman's body and buried in a Muslim cemetery and it is forbidden for the wife to be buried in a Muslim cemetery.

The reason why swimming is punishable as adultery is because the Arabic word for sea is masculine. The Muslim Brotherhood decided that because sea is masculine, when seawater touches a woman's body, she is an adulteress.

The ban on touching bananas and cucumbers was for the obvious reason of being phallic. A woman who touched one would make her go out of control sexually and thus her evilness may cause harm to men.

Essam had heard about this *fatwa* before I had. Right after this *fatwa* was declared we went marketing and I went to the produce section to buy fruits and vegies. Essam loves cucumbers and makes a special salad out of them. And we always buy bananas. All of a sudden I heard a commotion behind me and turned around. Essam was pushing people aside to get to me and people were letting out little squawks of disapproval at his rudeness. He had a look of total panic on his face. He looked to see if I had anything taboo in my hand or in my basket, and then sighed a loud sigh of relief.

When I was told about the *fatwa*, it was disturbing that women could be punished simply for touching a fruit or a vegetable. This was just one more Islamic excuse to abuse and hurt women.

Regarding women being "offensive," when the Brotherhood announced this *fatwa*, they stated that, "Women were created for sex only; therefore, their voices, their looks, and their presence outside the home, is an offense."

The reasoning behind the ban on women turning on the air conditioning was that turning on the air conditioning could be a signal to others that she is home alone and ready to commit adultery.

Regarding the use of women and children as human shields during violent demonstrations, the Brotherhood said violent demonstrations are jihad to empower Islam; therefore, to use women and children is a rightful tactic of jihad.

Regarding the *fatwa* that a Muslim husband could have sex with his dead wife, what I found especially troublesome, beyond the obvious horror of having sex with a dead body, is that Islamic doctrine states that the bodies of the dead must be buried immediately, within hours. So, the idea of a woman's dead body being sexually used first, means that women's rights don't exist at all, not even after death.

Kom Ombo Security Police

On the way to Kom Ombo for a field assignment we passed through a security checkpoint. Cars ahead of us would slow to a crawl before being waved on to pass. Occasionally someone was told to pull over for a more thorough check.

We slowed, were waved on, and made it through the checkpoint. My colleagues let out an audible sigh of relief. But suddenly there was yelling from behind us and a military officer, machine gun in hand, was shouting for us to stop. Our driver slammed on the breaks.

Three security officers approached and asked for ID and eyed my three companions in the front seat with great scrutiny. Two of the officers looked carefully at my passport, walked away and spoke to themselves for a moment, then returned and told me they knew who I was. They asked me several questions about where I'd be and for how long, then nodded and said, "Go."

After we pulled away and were out of earshot, my colleagues gave a loud hoot and a holler and gave each other a high five. A simple stop at a checkpoint can end up with a trip to the security police station and can last many exhaustive hours.

I am usually given a contact person for an assignment. This person is usually a sheik or a man who is trusted by the villagers. Most villagers in isolated regions would not like a foreigner filming their events and would not allow it if I did not have this person to pave my way. For this assignment my contact was a sheik from a village in Kom Ombo. He brought a friend, the driver, and one family member to escort me to Kom Ombo. All three men sat in the front seat and I sat alone in back. The car was tiny, and they sat crammed in front, but none of them wanted to sit next to a woman.

The sheik's village consisted of large compounds where several related families lived. The compounds were fully enclosed with tall brick and cement walls and the only entrance was a padlocked metal door. You couldn't see inside the compounds, or get in, without someone unlocking and opening the door. At one such compound, our driver got out, unlocked and opened the door, and I was ushered into a large courtyard. Off to one side was a pigeon coop, plus other designated areas for animals and poultry, and an area for slaughtering with a table and waterspout.

There were small doors lined along one long wall of the courtyard. Each door opened into a set of rooms where a family lived. I was invited into one of these rooms where seven women and five small children were gathered. Women sat on the floor along the walls. There was no furniture. Even though this was a private, locked compound, six of the women were fully veiled in black with only their eyes showing. The other was heavily head-scarfed, the kind that hides the forehead and neck, and she wore a tent-like, mud-colored *galabeya*.

The women were all curious about me and each took turns asking me questions. Of course I got the usual questions about my marital status and children, but I was also asked what I liked about Egypt, what I didn't like, what my favorite Egyptian songs were, and my favorite singers. And since I know Egyptian music and singers as well as any Egyptian, my selections made them happy, and many nodded in approval at my answers.

But then I was asked if I was a friend of Suzanne Mubarak.

This was a hard one. The First Lady and I had corresponded in writing about my work. She had even sent me a letter once via the Official Presidential Car, accompanied by Military Police, and it was handed to me personally by a member of her staff. This had given me fifteen minutes of fame in my neighborhood. Yes, Mrs. Mubarak paved the way for me to work with the Ministry of Culture, but we are certainly not friends in the usual sense of the word.

Thanks to Mrs. Mubarak's letters of recommendation, many Ministers and Vice Ministers in government knew who I was and I had met with several in person to discuss my work. There were many official documents in security and police departments all over Egypt allowing me into areas that foreigners aren't allowed into, thanks to Mrs. Mubarak.

I had also been mentioned twice in the main Cairo newspaper for doing a research and documentary project in cooperation with the First Lady. Even the officers at the security checkpoint had known who I was, so what the heck, right?

I answered the question with a yes.

This seemed to impress a few of them. But most looked uneasy. Were these women resentful of the modern reforms Suzanne Mubarak was making regarding women? Reforms that they could not partake in, like removing the veil, or not being forced to live in a locked compound?

A few uncomfortably quiet moments passed, then someone let out a loud *zaghareet*, which is a shrill yodel-like sound done at weddings and other joyful celebrations. We all laughed and the tension broke.

After a few hours of socializing with women from other parts of the compound, a male relative arrived and escorted me out, locking the padlock on the heavy metal door as we left. It was then that I fully felt the impact of being locked inside, and only able to get out if a male came to let me out.

I was taken to a shaded area where the sheik was smoking *shisha* with a group of men. As I was introduced to each man, I was careful about shaking hands. In villages like these, some men will willingly offer their hands, others hold back. There are those who think touching me would be *haram* (evil/forbidden).

The sheik then took me to his compound. His compound was much better off than the previous one and he was obviously proud of it. He had more animals and a larger enclosed reception area. Like the other compound, there were many rooms designated for different families.

I was escorted to a large, central room where I met the elder male members of the family. One of the sheik's brothers was sitting on the floor, leaning against a wall smoking hash. He was an obvious Muslim Brotherhood, complete with the short white *galabeya*, a long, untrimmed beard, and the purposeful scab on his forehead from rubbing it on the ground when he prayed.

Eventually children began bringing in platters of food. The sheik and his male relatives were proud to be feeding me, Egyptians are very hospitable. But as I ate I had a bad feeling. The meat tasted strange; it tasted off, not right. They had piled my plate full of it because meat is a big symbol of hospitality, honor, and affluence.

I always eat as much as possible when invited into people's homes because it means I accept their hospitality and appreciate their food. It's a compliment if I eat a lot, so I did. Plus, the male who was an obvious Brotherhood member was carefully eyeing me. I did not want him to have any reason to hate me any more than he probably already did, as I represented everything he hated: I wore no headscarf and I was free to roam the country and work independently among males.

It had been a long day, so after eating I thought I'd better use the bathroom while I was somewhere where I could. We'd be moving to a festival soon, an outdoor one, so who knows what I could expect as far as a toilet. Probably none. I asked to use the *hammam* and the youngest adult male looked embarrassed and left the room. When he returned, he apologized and said it would be awhile because they had to "prepare it."

While waiting, I watched as male children came in and ate the leftover food on our plates.

After about a half hour I was escorted to the bathroom. It was the only bathroom in the compound. Since there were so many people living in this compound, I'm guessing they also used potty pots, or maybe had a designated outdoor area.

The bathroom I was taken to was the size of a small closet, just barely enough room for one body. It had a hole in the ground and a small water tap with a hose connected to it. There was no window or vent. The temperature outside was around 100 degrees, this tiny enclosure felt at least 150, and airless. The bathroom had been rinsed down and water was still dripping from the ceiling and walls. Pieces of poop still stuck to the lower walls and floor. The odor almost made me lose it—and I am very tough.

When I came out from the bathroom, several of the men had gathered right outside the door. They had obviously come to see my reaction. Though their presence startled me a bit, I acted like all was well and that the bathroom experience was nothing new. Some sighed in relief and some nodded, and I noted that the Brotherhood member seemed almost disappointed. I think he was hoping my reaction would cause the others to think poorly of me.

After thanking everyone and talking a little with several of the children, who were in awe of my long blonde hair, we left for the "club." That's what they called it, but it was an open area in the center of the village.

A traditional band was tuning up and practicing a bit. A few chairs were placed in strategic spots for the dignitaries—the eldest males of nearby villages. All other males and male children sat on the ground. Women sat way off in an alley, kept totally out of sight. They would be unable to see the festivities about to take place, but would be able to hear the music.

As I walked by the alley where the women were kept segregated, I noticed that all the women were fully veiled, including gloves to cover their hands. Even toddlers, barely of walking age, were fully veiled. It was then that I looked around at the extremely large gathering of men and noted their clothing and the scabs on their forehead. The villagers were Muslim Brotherhood and Salafists.

The music started and a line of males began to do *el-Kahf*, a hand clapping dance. I had never gotten this type of *el-Kahf* on film before, so I was thrilled. Hand clapping as a rhythmic base came long before the invention of drums, so hand clapping dances are considered very ancient and handed down from one generation to another.

After about an hour of filming, I suddenly began to feel nauseated. I was pretty sure I had food poisoning.

This was a very big annual event. Leaders of local villages and important males from various villages were doing the dancing. We hadn't begun the most important part of the festival, but I was fearful I'd become more ill soon and might end up trapped in a locked compound (and spending most of that time in an odoriferous bathroom). My usual assistant at the Ministry of Culture was also on a field assignment and was not answering his cell, so I called Essam. I needed a story to get me out of there fast.

After speaking with Essam, the sheik ushered me to a car in one of the back alleys. We hit the road and made it out of the village and onto the dark country road. But soon afterwards, were stopped by an unexpected roadblock with a large number of security police.

After looking at my ID and then making a quick call, they said they knew who I was. At first I thought this was good, they'd release us quickly. After my call to Essam, he had arranged a hotel room for me in Luxor, about 100 miles from the village I had been filming in. I was anxious to get to a bed—and a bathroom.

But the officers would not let us go.

Essam is the only Egyptian I've ever met who does not fear police, military, or any authority. This is probably because he is manager of a company owned by retired EIA (Egyptian Intelligence) and many of his friends from childhood are now generals in the army. So once again I called Essam for help. After talking briefly, the officer handed the phone back to me. Essam said, "They are worried about your safety because there's been some terrorist activity nearby. They are going to escort you out."

Moments later a military truck arrived, with two officers in the cab and six soldiers in back carrying machine guns. They kept close to our rear bumper for about an hour, until my military escorts felt I was safely out of the terrorist zone.

Note: *Within a year after this visit, there were horrific attacks on the Christian villages in this area. Then later, after the Muslim Brotherhood took power, hundreds of Muslim Brotherhood and Salafists surrounded the main church in Kom Ombo and burnt it to the ground. Christian homes and businesses were attacked for three days. In Luxor, too, horrific attacks on Christians took place.*

Social Enforcement: An Islam-ization Strategy

When the 2011 "Arab Spring" protest began, the Muslim Brotherhood entered Tahrir Square as soon as they felt confident it was being reported by Western media as a young people's movement for democracy, and nothing related to an Islamist takeover.

Muslim Brotherhood Youth then worked the energy of Tahrir into a confusing frenzy of violence, making it easy to seize Tahrir without anyone being aware that the Brotherhood were inserting their own very different agenda.

Aided by Bedouin in the Sinai, members of Hamas, the Palestinian branch of the Muslim Brotherhood, crossed Egypt's border and were provided armored 4x4s. They broke into prisons that held key Brotherhood leaders.

Immediately following the prison breaks, police stations were attacked simultaneously throughout Cairo. Meanwhile, during the well-planned frenzy of violence, there were selected spokespeople in Tahrir lying to Western media to cover what was really taking place.

I had been witnessing a moderate society turning into a fully Islamic one, but I had also noticed an insidious strategy being used to enable these changes. Just prior to the "Arab Spring," men were being forced to go to mosque. They were being forced to listen to imams who preached strict enforcement of Islam.

On Fridays, mosques were becoming jammed full and men were spilling out of the mosque and into the streets, when previously mosques were moderately full at best. Many mosques in my area and those in the neighborhoods of my husband's family had been empty for years, so it was easy for me to notice the change and how it came about.

First I noticed that although most mosques were empty at prayer times and on Fridays, more mosques were being built. I would ask myself: Why build more when the existing ones sat empty and unused? But over the years I came to see that the Muslim Brotherhood had a plan. For several years they built mosques—whether needed or not. Then they placed their imams in those mosques—whether they had attendees or not. Then, over time, they began "socially forcing" men to attend those mosques.

The Brotherhood had been successful at placing their imams in the mosques in the countryside and had brainwashed the simple villagers. Through my work, I had seen many villages change drastically. Women had once been free to walk their streets, day or night, never wearing a veil or headscarf, and never harassed. Women danced at weddings, at all celebrations, and at festivals. Women were an integral part of village life. But this traditional way of life was vanishing, thanks to the imams placed in those villages. Once villagers received the brainwashing, they began oppressing their women and began living by the Quran and the traditions of Muhammad.

Now this same tactic was being placed in the cities.

Because it was Essam's only day off, we used to do our shopping on Fridays. Most everything used to be open on Fridays: markets, fruit and vegie vendors, almost all shops, whether for appliances, auto parts or furniture. But over the years, busloads of men from the countryside began to arrive on Friday mornings. They would plant themselves in front of mosques (not in them) and in the streets of busy shopping areas, blocking the entrance to shops.

Shopkeepers who arrived to open their shops in the morning were harassed and told they should be preparing to pray.

It didn't take long for the change to take place. Shops began opening later on Fridays, after the noon prayer and the lengthy sermon that followed.

But this success at preventing businesses from opening didn't stop the busloads of men from arriving on Fridays, and for these men to place themselves in the streets, starting at around 9:00 a.m., long before the noon prayer. It was a message to everyone that if you come out on Friday, you should only be going to mosque.

Essam and I used to do our marketing before lunch, drop our shopping bags at our apartment, then go back out and have lunch. No more. We had to wait in our apartment until after the noon prayer and lengthy sermons. Why? Because over time, nothing was open until later in the day. But even if we went out for a walk, we received threatening looks from the bus people. They were there to intimidate.

There are two mosques next to our apartment building. When not working in the field or at the Ministry of Culture office, I worked from my home. There I was forced to hear the loudspeakers blasting the call to prayer throughout the day, every day, and they cranked up the volume louder and louder as the years went by—to force men to go to pray.

One mosque, directly behind our apartment, began to conduct Quran recitations between the five calls to prayer. Thus I heard daily announcements of hatred towards Christians and Jews.

Then, one of the worse things that could happen, happened. Essam began to be socially forced to stop work during the day to go pray. He was being forced to pray by his co-workers. He had never done the five Islamic prayers. He never went to mosque. Now he was being forced.

I think of the apartment I rented where the owner of the building was so cruel to his employees and who espoused hatred towards Christians. He would go to mosque throughout the day and everyone in the neighborhood described him as a "good Muslim." When the 2011 "revolution" hit, he was among the first to crusade against Christians and he was one of those who encouraged the massacre that took place in Giza.

I think of another person who I had thought to be a friend, but who had fallen prey to forced prayers and forced attendance at mosque. After the Brotherhood took power, he handed out flyers in Christian neighborhoods that read: "Your businesses, cars, homes, schools, and churches will be torched." A Quran verse was included on these flyers: "Kill the disbelievers (non-Muslims) wherever you find them, capture them, lie in wait for them (ambush them)." (Quran 9.5)

The Brotherhood had built an excessive number of mosques and then forced men to attend on Fridays. Then a new campaign began, one of manipulating men to stop their work during the week to go pray. This social enforcement never used to be seen in Egypt. Now it was rampant.

It used to be a personal choice. Now it was forced.

Praying became more visible during the day. Bus drivers would stop, with a busload of tired, hot passengers, and get off the bus and pray on the street, often purposefully blocking traffic instead of moving to the sidewalk. Shopkeepers closed up shop and left to pray throughout the day—when previously they had never done so. Doctors stopped in the middle of an emergency and left to pray. We had this happen to us when my brother-in-law was taken to hospital for emergency treatment.

The call to prayer would blast on loud speakers and someone would plop themselves down blocking a cash machine, a phone booth, or the door to a restaurant or business, when they could have just as easily placed themselves elsewhere—out of the way and not hindering the activity of others. It was purposeful.

With this social enforcement of prayer and mosque attendance came a very visible growth of women wearing the headscarf and veil. And worse, the full black veil for toddlers began appearing in the window displays at children's clothing stores. People were being brainwashed into thinking a small child's body was so sexually tempting that it must be covered.

This, too, like forcing men to leave work and go to mosque, was social enforcement. It was an Islam-ization strategy.

Chapter 2. The Revolution: U.S. Involvement

The U.S. government uses Non-Government Organizations (NGOs) to interfere with foreign governments. An NGO is a government-funded organization set up to support "non-government" efforts.

In the 1970s, there were investigations into CIA attempts to destabilize foreign governments. As a result, to prevent future investigations, NGOs were created as front groups to fund and conceal CIA activity. These groups include the National Endowment for Democracy (NED), US Agency for International Development (USAID), the National Democratic Institute (NDI), Freedom House, and the International Republican Institute (IRI).

In the early 1980s, an organization funded by IRI called the Albert Einstein Institution (AEI) developed a strategy for removing governments. Modifying AEI technique, CIA operatives created seminars that taught paramilitaries how to create violent civil disobedience (called resistance) in order to provoke a response from police or security forces. Once police or security forces arrive, a false flag event is enacted, which provides pretense for government change.

These CIA coup training camps were partially funded by the IRI, which was chaired by John McCain from 1993 until 2018.

In 1999, this training was given to Serbian opposition, who called themselves *Otpor!* (Resistance!). USAID funneled millions of dollars to *Otpor!* through NED, NDI, IRI, and the Open Society Institute, a George Soros organization.

Otpor! was successful at removing the Serbian government, so the Center for Applied Non-Violent Action and Strategies (CANVAS) was created. CANVAS became the front for CIA coup training and went on to train coup leaders from the Ukraine, Georgia, Tunisia, Syria and Egypt.

In 2008, the U.S. State Department held an Alliance of Youth Movements Summit. At this summit were representatives from mass media giants such as Google, Facebook, YouTube, NBC, ABC, CBS, CNN and MSNBC (Cartalucci "Google's Revolution Factory"; Howley "Hillary Clinton Sponsored Secret"; Youth Movements 2008).

Various youth groups attended the State Department Summit, including members of Egypt's April 6th Youth Movement and Muslim Brotherhood Youth. The summit was a recruiting and coordinating center for revolutionists. It linked revolutionists with media giants and funneled the revolutionists to CIA coup training centers.

The principal strategy taught at coup training is to create a façade protest where a false flag event can be implemented.

Using bad economy, unemployment, or some other pretext, a protest is organized. Then, using media giants to promote the protest, and to propagandize and broadcast the protest, a false flag event is executed. The media giants display the event for millions to witness; the violence is blamed on "regime" forces, and, governments are removed.

To create momentum for a protest, the revolutionists were aided by Facebook, YouTube and Google, and this is why the State Department included these organizations at the Summit. The Egyptians who created the January 2011 protest had attended the Summit, met with Google, Facebook and mainstream media representatives, and were sent to a coup training center.

Members of the April 6th Youth Movement and Muslim Brotherhood Youth learned how to use social media to form a protest and to keep that protest going for days. CNN, MSNBC and other media promoted the protest and falsely portrayed members of the April 6th Youth Movement and Muslim Brotherhood Youth as heroes fighting for democracy. After the Muslim Brotherhood implemented the false flag event of violence, media went into high gear promoting anti-government propaganda.

A key player in the "Arab Spring" protests of 2011 was al-Qaeda. Historically, al-Qaeda has worked in tandem with the Muslim Brotherhood.

By 2009, the U.S. State Department was well aware that Osama bin Laden was only the figurehead of al-Qaeda and that Ayman Zawahiri was the group's strategic and operational planner (see: Counter Extremism Project). After the death of Osama bin Laden in May 2011, Obama began repeatedly stating that al-Qaeda was no longer a threat (Obama: al-Qaeda). But this was a deliberate lie, purposefully said to hide the truth behind the activities that were taking place. Al-Qaeda was involved in every Arab Spring country and was working in tandem with the Muslim Brotherhood in Egypt, Syria, Yemen, Iraq and Libya.

Obama told the lie at least 32 times (Lucas 2012), but the fact was, after bin Laden's death, under Zawahiri's leadership, al-Qaeda's calls to jihad for a caliphate intensified worldwide and al-Qaeda spread like wildfire throughout North and Central Africa, Yemen, Syria, Iraq, Afghanistan and Pakistan (see: al-Qaeda has intensified).

Starting in early 2011, the Obama administration fully backed the Muslim Brotherhood in Egypt and openly began supporting the "rebel" groups who were attempting to overthrow the Syrian government. These rebel groups were formed by the Muslim Brotherhood and al-Qaeda (see: Syrian Opposition Groups Defined).

In 2012, a memo and intelligence report were sent to Obama administration officials and government agencies stating that the Obama administration supported al-Qaeda in Iraq and that the Muslim Brotherhood and al-Qaeda were the catalysts behind rebel forces in Syria (2012 Intel doc; Dept. of Defense August 12; see also, Berens "U.S. trained and armed").

The Obama administration supported the terrorist "rebel" forces starting in 2011 when they were first created and continued supporting them throughout the Obama presidency. Millions of dollars were spent training, arming and funding al-Qaeda and Muslim Brotherhood forces (Berens "US trained and armed").

Al-Qaeda was also a major force in Libya.

Intelligence and State Department documents show the Obama administration was well aware of an al-Qaeda and Muslim Brotherhood terrorist group in Libya plotting an attack on American citizens before the attack took place. The documents also show the U.S. had been monitoring the movements of weapons from Libya to Syria starting in October 2011 (see: "Defense and State Department Documents").

Additionally, before his murder, a cable from Ambassador Chris Stevens was sent to the Secretary of State stating there were approximately ten al-Qaeda training camps and Islamist militias in Benghazi (FoxNews Exclusive; see also: The Arming of Benghazi).

Yet even after the Benghazi attack and murder of Ambassador Chris Stevens, when Libyan President el-Magarief, members of Congress, administration spokespersons, and several reports stated that al-Qaeda had played a role in the 2012 Benghazi attack that killed U.S. citizens, Obama continued to say that al-Qaeda had been decimated and was no longer a threat (Obama: decimated).

An Intel report had previously reported that the Muslim Brotherhood has branches in more than 70 countries and that the Brotherhood had "reached global status, wielding power and influence in almost every state with a Muslim population" (see: Roots of Violent Extremism).

According to Intel reports, al-Qaeda, too, had reached global status, with bases or a large presence in Afghanistan, Algeria, CAR, Chad, Egypt, Iraq, Kenya, Libya, Mali, Pakistan, Niger, Somalia, Sudan, Syria, Uganda, and Yemen (see: al-Qaeda has intensified; al-Qaeda Many Faces).

According to the Intel reports, the Muslim Brotherhood and al-Qaeda have the identical goals of restoring the historical Caliphate, expanding its authority over the entire world, and dismantling all non-Islamic governments.

The facts were: al-Qaeda had joined forces with the Libyan Muslim Brotherhood to overthrow the Libyan government; al-Qaeda had joined forces with the Egyptian Muslim Brotherhood to overthrow the Egyptian government; al-Qaeda had joined forces with the Syrian Muslim Brotherhood to overthrow the Syrian government.

Furthermore, the Islamic State of Iraq was created in 2010 from al-Qaeda in Iraq, and, the Islamic State of Iraq and Syria (ISIS) was the merger of al-Qaeda in Iraq with al-Qaeda in Syria.

Al-Qaeda was a very serious threat—and the Obama administration knew it and supported it.

Egypt's January 25, 2011 "revolution" originated under the façade of a protest against police brutality. An isolated case of police brutality was used to demonize *all* police.

A young man, Khaled Said, had died after being beaten by security police. Photos of Khaled Said's beaten face were robo-Tweeted incessantly and re-posted continuously on Facebook. But this protest campaign was not successful and would have fizzled except for two events.

In May 2010, a mob of more than 3,000 Muslims attacked the Christian area of the city of Marsa Matruh. Approximately 400 Christians barricaded themselves inside a church during which time Muslim mobs destroyed 18 Christian homes and 23 Christian shops.

This attack received very little attention from local media. And though Western media had representatives stationed in Cairo, Western media ignored it altogether.

Then, on January 1, 2011, there was a church bombing at Two Saints Church in Alexandria during a very large and well-attended service. Twenty-one Christians were killed and more than 70 were injured. Christians took photos of the carnage and posted them on their Facebook pages and on Twitter trying to get the world to take notice. But the church attack received very little media attention.

These two attacks weighed heavily on the minds of Egypt's Christians. They called for social justice on Facebook and Twitter. And even though there were very large demonstrations protesting the church attack, and crying out for social justice and equality, local and foreign media ignored the church attack and the protests.

Suddenly a new Facebook protest campaign called "We Are All Khaled Said" appeared and Christians were targeted to join this protest to boost numbers. This protest was allegedly against police brutality, but was now also to be for social justice and equality.

The protest kicked off to well-coordinated Muslim Brotherhood machinations and immediately turned specific. The creators of the protest announced their demands: end the Emergency Law and dismiss Habib al-Adly, who was Minister of Interior and in charge of Security Police.

The Emergency Law originated to combat terrorism. Arrests could be made for suspicion or ties to terrorism. The 1990s had been a period of endless terrorist attacks in Egypt which resulted in the deaths of more than 1,200 people. Habib al-Adly became Minister of Interior specifically to combat terrorism, and from 2000 to 2011, under his leadership, terrorist attacks dropped to an all-time low.

Who were the primary targets of the Emergency Law and the Security Police under Habib al-Adly? The Muslim Brotherhood and al-Gamaa al-Islamiya.

Terrorism and the Security Police

The Security Police System in Egypt was created to halt the growth of terrorism and prevent terrorist attacks. The use of Security Police against Islamist groups began during the Nasser period in the mid-1950s, but the 1970s were a period of massive growth in terrorist attacks, so in response, the use of Security Police intensified.

Because they used terrorism to achieve their goals, the Muslim Brotherhood experienced periods of being outlawed and banned in Egypt. In response, various groups emerged who were created by Muslim Brotherhood members, but these groups went by other names. Over time, these groups gained membership of their own and became offshoots of the Muslim Brotherhood.

At this time, the Brotherhood developed a strategy. They promoted themselves as "the peaceful moderates of Islam," but in reality, acts of terror were planned by Brotherhood leadership and the offshoot groups would carry out the attacks. The offshoot group would take credit for attacks, thus leaving the Brotherhood free from blame.

Most terrorist groups created in the 1970s and 1980s sprouted from the teachings and writings of a Muslim Brotherhood member named Sayyid Qutb. Qutb preached that Islam is a complete system that must extend into every aspect of life. He preached that Islam must guide social, private and political life. He taught that following *sharia*, Islamic Law, was mandatory and that Muslims must model themselves after the behavior of Muhammad.

One of Qutb's most devoted followers was Ayman Zawahiri, the current leader of al-Qaeda.

Zawahiri became a Muslim Brotherhood member at the age of fourteen and was a prominent activist in the Muslim Brotherhood Youth. At that time, there was also a discreet sector of the Muslim Brotherhood Youth called the Secret Apparatus, which were well-trained militia units. Zawahiri became obsessed with creating Qutb's vision of an Islamic State and co-founded a terrorist group called al-Jihad. Zawahiri's goal was to overthrow the Egyptian government and replace it with an Islamic State.

After al-Jihad conducted several terrorist attacks in the 1970s, Security Police rounded up members and put many in prison. At this time, al-Jihad split into two cells. Al-Jihad members who were from Cairo became the Egyptian Islamic Jihad, with Zawahiri as its leader. Members from southern Egypt became al-Gamaa al-Islamiya. Though they were now two cells, they co-conspired in terrorist attacks and had the united goal of overthrowing the Egyptian government and creating an Islamic State.

Because the Muslim Brotherhood was banned, al-Gamaa al-Islamiya membership grew during this period and Muslim Brotherhood leadership used al-Gamaa al-Islamiya as their front group for terrorist attacks. Throughout Anwar Sadat's presidency, 1970-1981, the Muslim Brotherhood and offshoot groups continuously plotted attacks and unrest.

The Muslim Brotherhood and their affiliate terror cells were outraged over the 1979 Peace Treaty signed by President Sadat and Israeli Prime Minister Menachem Begin. Omar Abdel Rahman, al-Gamaa al-Islamiya's spiritual leader, issued a *fatwa* ordering the assassination of President Sadat. Rahman, also known as the Blind Sheik, is now better known for his participation in the 1993 World Trade Center bombing.

Zawahiri's group, the Egyptian Islamic Jihad, participated in the planning and coordination of the 1981 Sadat assassination. Zawahiri was convicted for conspiracy in the assassination plot and spent three years in prison. After his release, Zawahiri travelled to Pakistan where he met Osama bin Laden. In 1988, Zawahiri co-founded al-Qaeda.

After evidence surfaced of how subversive and complex the Sadat assassination plot had been, there was a massive Security Police crackdown on all terrorist groups in Egypt. Because of this, many of Zawahiri's group left Egypt and went to Sudan.

Operating from its exile base in Sudan, the Egyptian Islamic Jihad joined forces with members of al-Gamaa al-Islamiya and members of the Sudanese intelligence. Sudan had large numbers of Muslim Brotherhood in its government. Together they created a plot to assassinate Egypt's President Mubarak.

The attempt was led by Mustapha Hamza, a senior member of al-Qaeda, who was also the commander of al-Gamaa al-Islamiya's militia in Egypt. Al-Qaeda, the Muslim Brotherhood, Egyptian Islamic Jihad, and al-Gamaa al-Islamiya shared membership and co-conspired in terror attacks and assassinations.

Because of Sudan's collaboration in the assassination plot, the UN voted to impose sanctions on Sudan. To reestablish itself in the international community, the Sudanese government forced Egyptian Islamic Jihad members to leave Sudan. Because of the security crackdown in Egypt, many members went to Afghanistan where they joined al-Qaeda.

From this point on, whenever the Muslim Brotherhood needed mercenary fighters, they called upon Egyptian Islamic Jihad members in Afghanistan, many of whom were now in collaboration with al-Qaeda, or had joined al-Qaeda, but continued to be part of the movement to take down the Egyptian government in order to create an Islamic State. And though Zawahiri no longer lived in Egypt, and was an al-Qaeda founder, he continued to plot against Egypt and remained one of the Egyptian Islamic Jihad's main organizers and recruiters.

Zawahiri's plan was to recruit Egyptian military officers and then wait for the right moment to launch an overthrow of the government. He planned to capture the Television and Media Complex, where he would then release false news of an "Islamic Revolution." Zawahiri would release false news that the Egyptian Army had defected. He believed this fake announcement would unleash an uprising against Egypt's government and he'd be able to implement an Islamic State using the Islamist militias already created by the various terrorist cells inside Egypt.

Zawahiri hoped that Egyptians would believe the Islamist militias were members of the Egyptian army (note: This is the identical strategy used by al-Qaeda and the Muslim Brotherhood in Syria in March 2011. They released a false news statement saying members of the Syrian army defected and had created a new army. In reality this army consisted primarily of Muslim Brotherhood and al-Qaeda).

The Sadat assassination had been organized from the al-Gamaa al-Islamiya headquarters in Assuit, a city in southern Egypt where the Muslim Brotherhood also had a headquarters, and where the two groups often worked in tandem. The two terrorist groups had created youth militias in Assuit. In conjunction with the assassination of Sadat, al-Gamaa al-Islamiya sieged Assuit and held it captive for three days. Sixty-eight police and army soldiers were killed in the fight to rescue the citizens of Assuit, where one of the largest communities of Christians also resided.

With help from the Muslim Brotherhood Youth, al-Gamaa al-Islamiya had become a powerful force in the student movement of 1976. The group's ideology spread in universities and members eventually gained one-third membership in university student unions. These unions formed movements that campaigned for Islamic dress, the short white *galabeya* for men, and the black veiling of female students. They also campaigned for separate classrooms for women.

By 1977, al-Gamaa al-Islamiya was almost in complete control at many universities throughout Egypt.

At first, university officials were very much against al-Gamaa al-Islamiya and their campaigns. Women were being trained in the advanced sciences, in aviation, and most any field they chose. Egypt was proceeding with women's rights and equality. Egyptians were very proud of their social advancements. Women did not wear Islamic headscarves, let alone the full black veil that was being encouraged by al-Gamaa al-Islamiya and the Muslim Brotherhood. Women were free to wear current fashions, short skirts, and sleeveless clothing without public harassment of any kind.

Al-Gamaa al-Islamiya and the Muslim Brotherhood took control of universities and targeted Egypt's youth, and this was the turning point in Egypt.

Al-Gamaa al-Islamiya handed out leaflets and newsletters at universities. They promoted the idea that the right to make laws and the right to govern people only belonged to Allah. They promoted the ideology that there is no need for a "man-made" government. They preached that only *sharia* was needed and that *sharia* is a complete system of laws and justice.

They emphasized that the unity of man via Islam was the only way to liberate oneself from all that is corrupt. They said that this included liberation from all things inherited, meaning the full removal of "heritage" and "nationalism." They wanted to end cultural behaviors that "separate" people from Islam. They abhorred nationalism. Their goal was a generic Muslim culture united under Islamic Laws.

They preached that all Muslims, no matter what country they lived in, should be united by having no separate distinction of nationality, nor any distinct cultural traditions that could separate them from their Islamic identity. Only Islamic culture, the traditions outlined in the *hadith* and *sunna* of Muhammad, should exist.

Their teachings meant that Egyptian traditions that had been passed down for centuries were against Allah. Egyptian music, dance, festivals, and even the traditional colorful clothing that village women wore, were against Allah. Women should only wear black to unify under Allah.

They believed the youth must be taught early that Islam is a complete and perfect system and that Islam "is" the government. Islam must be what regulates Muslims, not an elected government. They preached that democracy was evil and theocracy was salvation. They taught that Islam regulates war—that jihad must be used to spread and enforce Islam. They taught that Islam regulates the judicial system—by abiding by Islamic laws and administering the prescribed Islamic punishments.

They preached that the West was the most corrupt system and against Allah and stressed that Western influence should be avoided completely. They hated the Western attitude of equality among people, believing instead that only Muslims have rights, and that non-Muslims must be deprived of them. They quoted Quran verses which state that non-Muslims are not equal to Muslims.

They insisted that girls be married at a very early age and that girls should be betrothed at birth. They stressed that girls should be married before they could be educated. They preached that it is more difficult to make an older girl, or an educated woman, obey a husband. Girls must be taught early to be obedient and submissive to men.

These beliefs began to be promoted at all universities throughout Egypt in the late 1970s and early 1980s. By the 1990s, Quranic Arabic began to replace English as a second language at many universities. Islamic History began to replace Ancient Egyptian Civilization. Young people were led to believe they had no other culture or history other than Islam.

Over time, members of the Muslim Brotherhood and al-Gamaa al-Islamiya gained top positions at every university throughout Egypt. They held the majority of positions as faculty members. At Assuit University, Islamists gained positions as president and top administrators and began supporting segregation of classes and reduced female enrollment.

It was during this period that the quality of education began to decline in Egypt. Egypt's universities had once excelled in all fields and ranked equally to Western universities. By the 1990s, this excellence was destroyed.

At some universities, Islamists prevented the mixing of genders at films, concerts, dances and other social events by using violence. They would arrive in large mobs and used iron pipes as weapons. Assuit University had some of the most violent clashes that had ever occurred in Egypt. Islamists attacked police, liberals and Christians.

But massive, violent clashes quickly began to spread to other university campuses as well.

During this period, Islamists also began recruiting people living in the poor neighborhoods of cities. And later, after their terrorist behavior landed them in prison, they recruited inside prisons. Prisons became recruiting centers.

In the cities, they targeted the poor and the unemployed, as these groups were the easiest to propagandize and recruit. They gave out free food and medicine. During this period of recruitment, socialism was portrayed as a desirable form of government, but socialism was part of their strategy of takeover.

In April 1981, al-Gamaa al-Islamiya clashed with Christians near the village of Minya. Al-Gamaa al-Islamiya said that Christians must pay *jeezya* (the Islamic tax on non-Muslims). The Minya region has been the home of Egypt's Christians for centuries, long before the existence of Islam. This unlawful Islamic taxation on their own farmland angered Christians and they refused to pay the tax. Clashes erupted and resulted in the death of many Christians.

In June 1981, in a neighborhood of Cairo called al-Zawaiya al-Humra, Christians were brutally killed. Christian babies and toddlers were thrown out windows from high-rise apartment buildings. Many Christian homes and businesses were set afire. Various Islamist groups participated in the attack, including al-Gamaa al-Islamiya, Muslim Brotherhood, and Salafists. Al-Gamaa al-Islamiya had a logo and flag by this time, a sword on top of an open Quran; they waved this flag as they killed Christians in al-Zawaiya al-Humra.

Egyptians were shocked and angered. They wanted Islamist extremism stopped and fully supported the Security Police. Since so many terrorists had gone underground, the Emergency Law was created so that suspected terrorists could be arrested and investigated, and during this violent period of Islamist extremism, the Emergency Law was helpful in digging out terrorist cells.

But the terrorism continued.

Throughout the 1990s, Islamists murdered and attempted murder on well-known intellectuals and authors who criticized them, and they constantly targeted tourists and Christians.

After the attempted assassination of President Mubarak in June 1995, Security Police responded with a crackdown that the Egyptian people again supported wholeheartedly. Additionally, the various terrorist attacks had done serious damage to tourism—the largest component of Egypt's economy and employment. Egyptians fully approved of all efforts to squash terrorism.

Tourism was attacked by all Islamist groups, not only because they despised Western behavior and beliefs, but because Islamist groups knew that by destroying the economy, they could more easily remove the government. Destroying the economy meant higher unemployment and poverty. The unemployed and poor were the easiest to control and manipulate, and were the easiest to propagandize and recruit.

The Islamist strategies were to destroy the economy, take advantage of the poor and unemployed, take control of the youth, and use propaganda to cause unrest. Once unrest begins, bring in the Islamist militia.

Five months after the failed assassination attempt on Mubarak, under Zawahiri's leadership, the Egyptian Islamic Jihad bombed the Egyptian embassy in Pakistan, killing 16 and wounding 60. This attack became the "model" for al-Qaeda.

In November 1997, together with leaders of al-Gamaa al-Islamiya, Zawahiri helped organize an attack on tourists in Luxor. The attack angered the Egyptian people so monumentally, that at first, al-Gamaa al-Islamiya tried to deny responsibility.

As a cover, Zawahiri started up a propaganda campaign, blaming the police for the killings. But this propaganda did not succeed because the evidence against al-Gamaa al-Islamiya was overwhelming and horrific.

The Luxor Massacre resulted in the death of 62 people. The bodies of tourists, including the children, were disemboweled and Quran verses were written with their blood.

The previous attacks on tourists had slowed down tourism enormously and caused higher numbers of unemployment, but the Luxor Massacre halted tourism for a long period and all Egyptians suffered from the resulting effects. Egyptians were angry, and they wanted all terrorists arrested.

Once again, Egyptians fully supported the Security Police.

In July 1997, Islamist lawyer Montassir al-Zayyat had brokered a deal with the Egyptian government called the "Non-Violence Initiative." Several Islamist groups said they would renounce violence in exchange for the release of their leaders from prison.

But just four months after signing the "Non-Violence Initiative" and the release of their terrorist leaders, al-Gamaa al-Islamiya conducted the Luxor Massacre. The "Non-Violence Initiative" had been a ruse to free their leaders.

They had used *taqiyya*: lying/deceiving to achieve their goals.

In the 1990s, al-Gamaa al-Islamiya had risen against the Egyptian government repeatedly and had caused the deaths of more than 1,200 people.

During this period, al-Gamaa al-Islamiya was given full support from al-Qaeda and the Muslim Brotherhood and many of their members were interchangeable.

The 1990s were also a period of rising attacks on Christians.

On September 20, 1991, several Christians were attacked and killed in Imbaba, a suburb of Cairo.

On March 9, 1992, in a village called Mansheet Nasser, a young Christian farmer was shot after refusing to pay *jeezya*. After shooting the Christian, the Muslim mob then dismembered him.

On May 4, 1992, in the villages of Manshia and Weesa, thirteen Christians were killed.

On May 12, 1992, in the village of Manfaloot, a church was attacked. Six Christians were killed and more than fifty Christians were injured.

On October 15-16, 1992, in the village of Kafre Demian in the Nile Delta, Christians were attacked and their shops were looted and then burned. Forty-two Christian homes were set afire and many Christians were injured. The destruction of Christian property, merchandise, livestock and work places were estimated to be valued at five million Egyptian pounds.

On December 2, 1992, in the city of Assuit, Christians were attacked and many were injured. Also on this day, Christians were attacked in the village of al-Meer and four Christians were killed. Additionally, a Christian jeweler had his throat slit for refusing to pay the *jeezya* tax.

On March 13, 1997, in the village of Naklah, a train was ambushed and a Muslim mob boarded and murdered Christian passengers. Thirteen Christians were killed and six Christians were injured.

In February 1998, Zawahiri's Egyptian Islamic Jihad united with al-Qaeda, Jamiatul Ulemae Pakistan, and the Bangladeshi Jihad Movement to form the "World Islamic Front for Jihad against Jews and Christians." Soon after, there was a rise in the number of attacks on Christians in Pakistan, Bangladesh, and in Egypt.

For almost two months, from February to April 2001, attacks on Christians occurred daily in Assuit and 35 Christian houses were destroyed.

On April 19, 2001, a church was attacked in the village of Hegaza. Christians were hit with open fire as they exited the church. Two Christians were killed and many were injured.

The Egyptian government had tried peaceful solutions with Islamist groups, including the "Non-Violence Initiative," but all attempts failed. The result was that Security Police numbers were boosted and security intensified.

It had been well known that al-Gamaa al-Islamiya was allied with al-Qaeda, but in 2006 it was made official. Zawahiri, as deputy leader of al-Qaeda, announced al-Qaeda's official affiliation with al-Gamaa al-Islamiya. In a video released in August 2006, Zawahiri called al-Gamaa al-Islamiya "knights who had joined the fight against the Crusaders." An al-Gamaa al-Islamiya leader was also in the video announcement, to confirm the alliance.

This term "Crusaders" didn't only mean that Christians must be killed. It was during this period that Islamist groups began announcing that Security Police must also be killed, for not supporting an Islamic State.

In June 2011, Zawahiri officially merged yet another group with al-Qaeda, the Egyptian Islamic Jihad. Al-Gamaa al-Islamiya and the Egyptian Islamic Jihad were now officially al-Qaeda.

During the 1990s, many shootings occurred targeting tourists on trains, cruise ships and areas where large groups of tourists gathered. In April 1996, al-Gamaa al-Islamiya conducted a massacre at the Hotel Europa killing 18 tourists. Since the Assuit region was the main stronghold of both al-Gamaa al-Islamiya and the Muslim Brotherhood, Nile Cruises stopped sailing between Cairo and Luxor. It was too dangerous to dock and allow tourists to go ashore. Sadly, the Cairo-Luxor cruises were about to begin sailing again for the first time since the 1990s when the January 25, 2011 protest began.

After the Luxor Massacre, Security Police focused primarily on rooting out al-Gamaa al-Islamiya, as they were seen as the main culprits of terrorism. The Muslim Brotherhood took advantage of this focus, as this had been part of their strategy all along, to shift all blame to other terror groups.

During this period, while security forces were distracted, the Muslim Brotherhood intensified mosque building and thousands of Muslim Brotherhood mosques popped up throughout Cairo and Alexandria. They placed their imams in these mosques and continued preaching that Islamic Law must replace man-made government.

One other result of the 1997 Luxor Massacre was that Habib al-Adly became Minister of Interior and in charge of the Security Police. Adly reorganized the system and intensified security presence. From 2001, right up until 2011, under Habib al-Adly's management, the Security Police System had successfully squashed terrorist activity almost completely. There were few terror attacks in Egypt during the period in which Habib al-Adly was in charge.

For this reason, the Muslim Brotherhood and al-Gamaa al-Islamiya despised Habib al-Adly and wanted him removed. They needed to disrupt the Security Police System because it was so successful.

The first demands of the January 25, 2011 protest were the removal of Habib al-Adly and the Emergency Law. Then, after violence erupted, the protesters demanded the removal of President Mubarak and the State Security Service — the Security Police.

The Muslim Brotherhood and al-Gamaa al-Islamiya were behind the exaggeration of police brutality, and through their youth groups, they propagandized police brutality to the maximum. Yes, Khaled Said had died in police custody, but this isolated case was used to benefit Islamist groups who wanted the Security Police System removed.

Once the January 25th protest began, massive numbers of Muslim Brotherhood quickly infiltrated Tahrir Square and they proceeded with their goals of removing the police and the government. Western media did their job of promoting the falsity that the protest was about democracy and human rights.

The Muslim Brotherhood then began bussing in many thousands of villagers into Tahrir Square to give the illusion that the majority of Egyptians supported the removal of the president.

While Western media continued to feed the West false news, Muslim Brotherhood members were stating in speeches and on their official website that their goal was to unify the countries of North Africa under Islamic Law. Muslim Brotherhood had strongholds in the North African countries of Egypt, Libya, Tunisia, Algeria and Morocco — as did al-Qaeda.

Al-Qaeda too, made announcements. Zawahiri announced that the "Final Crusade" had begun and that the Caliphate would be reinstated. Zawahiri said the ruling capitals of the Caliphate would be Damascus, Syria; Baghdad, Iraq; and Cairo, Egypt—just as they had been during the "Golden Age" of Islam.

President Mubarak

Under President Nasser, a system of free health care and free university education was created and university graduates were guaranteed jobs in government and state-owned industries. Nasser also dispossessed large farm estates from the wealthy and divided the land.

Before Nasser took office, the majority of Egyptians were *fellahin*, peasant farmers. At least 60 percent of the *fellahin* were landless and they had hired themselves out to the large farm estates. Breaking up the large farm estates, which had provided the bulk of Egypt's food, caused Egypt to lose self-sufficiency in food production, but also, since most *fellahin* worked on large estates, they became unemployed when the estates were dissolved.

Those *fellahin* who owned farms split the land with each passing generation as fathers divided land to give to their sons. This caused the size of individual land ownership to become smaller over the years. In many cases, when families were large, the younger children received no land. By the 1980s, due to population growth and high inflation, small landowners were working at a deficit.

So, with free university and guaranteed government jobs, *fellahin* with several sons began sending one or more to university. And, with small farms working at a deficit, many farmers abandoned their farms and moved to the cities. This created the problem of overcrowding and the formation of ghetto areas in the cities.

This is also the period when poverty-stricken *fellahin* who had remained in their countryside villages fell prey to the Muslim Brotherhood. Poverty is a breeding ground for Islam.

During the 1970s, President Sadat implemented the "Open Door Policy." Investors received a ten-year tax holiday if linked with Egyptian partners and imports were duty-free. But only wealthy Egyptians benefited from Sadat's policy and this system also caused an enormous rise in corruption. Additionally, the cheap imported products flowing into Egypt caused the demise of many Egyptian industries, and thus, more unemployment among the lower and middle classes.

Also in the 1970s, Saudi Arabia's sudden wealth from oil had caused a great need for workers. Previous to the discovery of oil, there was no education system. Arabs were poor, unskilled, and most were illiterate. In order to develop schools, infrastructure and modernize, the Saudis called for foreign workers. Egyptians flocked to Saudi Arabia, but once Saudi Arabia was developed, men returned to Egypt—unemployed.

By the time Mubarak became president, with little food production and more food subsidies, there was severe strain on the government. The debt-ridden government had difficulty finding creditors to finance food and food shortages occurred. The Muslim Brotherhood took advantage of these shortages and began handing out free foodstuffs, claiming Islam provides for everyone.

When Mubarak took office, he called for a new era of production rather than importing. He forced dishonest officials from the Sadat era to resign and he fired members of the Ministry if suspected of corruption. He also boosted affordable housing, clothing and medicine.

Because of Sadat's treaty with Israel, Arab countries accused Egypt of being against the Palestinian cause and Egypt was thrown out of the Arab League.

The Muslim Brotherhood created ongoing violent protests over the treaty with Israel and in an attempt to calm unrest, Sadat had allowed Islamists more freedom. Amnesty was granted to leaders of the Muslim Brotherhood who had been imprisoned by Nasser and press censorship was relaxed a bit.

Under Mubarak, opposition parties were allowed to form and each created an affiliate newspaper that promoted their agenda. Political opponents jailed by Sadat were released. But by the time Mubarak took office, al-Gamaa al-Islamiya and the Muslim Brotherhood had control of the student unions, and their powerful activism had rallied "moderate" Muslims. This enabled the Muslim Brotherhood to infiltrate political parties, government, unions—and the press.

By the 1984 election, there were six political parties, and with the influx of Islamists into the political realm, there were demands made to implement *sharia*, Islamic Law. In 1985, Parliament rejected the application of *sharia*. As a result, violent protests broke out in Cairo, led by the Muslim Brotherhood. This was followed by an enormous wave of terror attacks on video shops and shops that sold Western items and assassination attempts on members of government who were against the application of *sharia*.

Under Nasser, controls over the Islamists were very tight. Sadat relaxed controls, but when Islamists became too demanding, he repressed them. Under the more tolerant Mubarak, political dissent was accepted, but when mass action occurred, such as Islamist street demonstrations for the implementation of *sharia*, or anti-Israel protests, they were repressed.

In the 1990s, security forces fought an insurgency of Islamic militants who were attempting to install an Islamic State. Not only had more than 1,200 people been killed, more than 10,000 had been wounded in attacks by Islamists. The struggle against Islamists characterized Mubarak's entire presidency.

The Mubarak government tried to boost economy and employment by removing some of Nasser's socialistic endeavors. Mubarak promoted privatization of state-owned industries and modernization of various industries in order for them to become more profitable and enable them to expand and hire more people. Various companies began eliminating costs by laying off workers who were part of the previous government system of overstaffing.

Starting with Nasser, whose program was to give every university graduate a job, even when there were no jobs, the government had been overburdened. University graduates had been absorbed into government jobs and state-owned industries for decades, and this resulted in an excessive number of unnecessary employees.

It was estimated that industries involved in this system had been overstaffed by at least 40 percent, and in many cases, up to 60 percent. Many were so overburdened by overstaffing, they were about to shut down permanently, which would have resulted in more severe consequences than temporary layoffs.

These industries laid out their plans to save money by removing the overstaffed, and then using that money to modernize and expand and create more jobs than before. But Islamist groups used the layoffs as a propaganda tool against the government. And since many had infiltrated the press, it was easy to promote this propaganda to the masses.

To help fight unemployment, Mubarak initiated new employment opportunities, and also implemented a project of irrigating large amounts of land and turning it into farmland. The goal was for the unemployed and poor to purchase and farm the land, instead of living in ghetto areas of cities. This farmland would also supply reasonably priced food products, something Egyptians were in need of, but would also help the government, which was being overburdened by food subsidization.

Divorced women and marginalized sectors of society could apply for free farmland. Many types of encouragements were offered to all Egyptians to own this land, including no money down loans and zero interest loans with low monthly payments. But anti-government propaganda convinced people that farming was for the very lowest class of society, and even the poor who were living in the city, and who had originally been farmers, refused to take advantage of this land.

These projects were promoted as failures by anti-government propagandists and the land was left abandoned. So, with cheap land for sale that the unemployed and poor refused, the rich began buying up the land and began making profits from it. Islamist groups then created propaganda about this, saying "the rich are getting richer—thanks to Mubarak."

This was when the *Keefeya!* party was created by Ayman Nour. *Keefeya!* means Enough! Nour took this slogan from the Georgian revolution of 2003, whose Youth Movement used the slogan *Kmara!* (Enough!). Members of *Kmara!* had been trained by CANVAS, the CIA coup training camp for revolutionists. Ayman Nour was a Muslim Brotherhood affiliate and heavily endorsed by the U.S. government.

Keefeya! officially emerged in 2004, but the group had originated in 2000 during the Palestinian Second Intifada. A solidarity movement for the Intifada began in the streets of Cairo where members of the Muslim Brotherhood Youth formed protests in support for the Palestinian "resistance." Members of this Intifada movement participated in the formation of *Keefeya!*

In 2003, the U.S. began condemning Egypt for not allowing the Muslim Brotherhood to run candidates in elections. Historically, the Brotherhood had committed terrorist acts and desired an Islamic State. Egyptians did not want a religious-based government and a law was made against forming religious-based political parties.

After *Keefeya!* was formed in 2004, massive propaganda against Mubarak began, as well as simultaneous pressure from the U.S. to allow the Brotherhood to run candidates in elections.

The system for presidency that existed under Nasser and Sadat was that the President served a term of six years and there was no limit to the number of times the President could be re-elected.

Up until 2005, the President was nominated by a two-thirds majority of the People's Assembly and then confirmed in a public vote. But because of pressure from the U.S., President Mubarak announced political reforms that allowed multi-candidate presidential elections.

Mubarak won the election of 2005, but immediately received protests from Ayman Nour and *Keefeya!* who claimed the election had been rigged. Ayman Nour was an operative of U.S. NGOs.

Muslim Brotherhood and other opposition, such as the activist group who later named themselves the April 6th Youth Movement, all immediately pushed the propaganda that the election had been rigged.

This strategy of accusations of voter rigging was used in Serbia, Georgia and Ukraine. Through NGOs, the U.S. spent $41 million dollars on the removal of Serbia's government. Many millions of these dollars were spent training "election observers" in Serbia. When the polls closed, these "observers" said that Milosevic had lost.

Officially, Milosevic had won by a large margin. These contradictions resulted in accusations of election fraud. Results were re-examined and the new results were practically the same, but this was not reported by the media, only the results made by NGO "observers."

Like Serbia, the 2003 Georgian revolution was also brought on by disputed elections. USAID spent $1.5 million dollars to computerize Georgia's voter rolls and other NGOs funded election "observers."

The Ukraine revolution, too, was funded and mobilized by U.S. NGOs. Yanukovych's party had won the majority of votes in the elections, but rumors started up that there was vote rigging. The organization creating these allegations was *Chesno*, funded by USAID.

Egypt's April 6th Youth Movement was formed in 2005, though the group didn't go by that name at the time.

Like the NGO-backed *Keefeya!* the April 6th Youth Movement included members from the Muslim Brotherhood Youth. Its founders based their activities on what their members had learned at an NGO-funded coup training camp. The group's leader was also a member of *Keefeya!* Members began organizing strikes, fully meant to further destabilize the economy.

On April 6, 2008, the group held a protest outside the Masr Spinning and Weaving Company. As the NGO-funded coup training instructs, the April 6th protest turned destructive in order to gain police attention. Police tried to break up the protest to stop the destruction of property, but it suddenly turned violent, leaving two dead. This was an attempt to use a false flag event that would enable them to use the other strategies learned at the NGO-funded coup training, but this first attempt failed.

The April 6th Youth Movement proceeded to become a well-trained "resistance" organization that promoted political disorder and violence and hatred towards police. And later, during the January 2011 protest, their leaders were promoted as "heroes" for democracy by CNN.

When analyzing the NGO-funded revolutions in Serbia, Georgia, Ukraine and Kyrghizistan, we see:

- All were presented as "spontaneous" revolutions, but all had ties to NGOs and had been in the planning stages for years
- NGOs were used to pay for and to mobilize the protest-revolutions
- All leaders of the protest-revolutions were trained at NGO-sponsored coup training camps
- NGOs trained "election observers" and interfered with the elections in these countries
- All used NGO-based accusations of election fraud as part of their anti-government propaganda
- NGOs spread anti-government propaganda via a wide variety of outlets to promote the protest-revolutions
- All used the NGO-funded strategy of "making the economy scream" (i.e. use bad economy to promote anti-government propaganda)
- All used the strategy of creating the "illusion" that the majority desired government removal

The coup training camps also taught the revolutionists to gain the support of the church, students, civil servants, or some other group that would make it appear as if average citizens were behind the protest and supported government removal. This is why Christians were targeted to join Egypt's January 25, 2011 protest.

In Serbia, the "illusion" that the majority desired the government removed was created by NGOs who gave $2.5 million dollars for stickers and posters depicting clenched fists and stating Resistance! These NGOs also gave 5,000 cans of spray paint. A small group of people posted stickers and posters and spray-painted anti-government graffiti in key spots throughout Serbia, thus giving media optics for the illusion that the movement was popular (see: Serbia Revolution).

The most important coup strategy taught is that nothing rallies people behind your movement more than an act of violence by police or authorities. This is the purpose of causing destruction and chaos during a protest. The destruction is meant to bring in police forces so that a false flag event can be implemented and blamed on police or authorities.

These were the strategies taught to members of the Muslim Brotherhood Youth and the April 6th Youth Movement who went to the State

Department's Summit and coup training camp. The Summit linked "Arab Spring" revolutionists with NGOs. The NGOs funded and mobilized revolutionists and sent them to coup training camps. The NGO front groups were: USAID, National Endowment for Democracy (NED), International Republican Institute (IRI), National Democratic Institute (NDI), Open Society Institute, and Freedom House (see: Seed "The Arab Spring US black ops"; Cartalucci "US Department of Imperial Expansion").

In 2008, Arab Spring revolutionists went to the State Department's Summit where they met with media giants and were linked up with NGOs to fund their revolutions. Google, Facebook, Twitter and the Obama administration's Internet team trained Arab Spring revolutionists in encryption technology and social media technique. Encryption was important during the early planning stages in order to communicate secretly so that intelligence agencies in the Arab Spring countries would not detect the plots. These revolutionists also met with Hillary Clinton, Condoleezza Rice, John McCain and Obama (Bensaada 2011).

In 2009, via NGOs, the U.S. State Department set up and financed fake "pro-democracy" organizations in Algeria, Bahrain, Egypt, Jordan, Kuwait, Libya, Morocco, Syria, Tunisia and Yemen. All were fronts for Islamists who wanted to remove their governments.

In December 2010, the Facebook pages "We Are All Muhammad Bouazizi" and "We Are All Khaled Said" were created by Muslim Brotherhood Youth members who had attended the State Department's Summit. "We Are All Muhammad Bouazizi" was the campaign that kicked off Tunisia's revolution and "We Are All Khaled Said" kicked off Egypt's.

Daily protests erupted in Tunisia, during which time, Facebook, Twitter and YouTube incessantly promoted anti-government propaganda and created the "illusion" that the majority wanted their government removed.

CNN and other mainstream media giants, whose representatives had been at the State Department's Summit, promoted propaganda to keep the Tunisian protests going. A key strategy taught at coup training is to remain in the streets for as many days as possible. This is meant to give the impression that the government is unable to govern; the premise being, if a government can't calm chaos in the streets, it should be removed.

The identical tactic was used for Egypt's "revolution."

All Arab Spring protests focused exclusively on removing leaders without any plans to replace them. The protests were meant to create a massive void—a void to be filled by Islamists.

In Libya, Syria and Yemen, when the protests and false flag events failed to immediately remove the governments, the U.S. funded mercenary armies to enter those countries. These armies were made up of Muslim Brotherhood and al-Qaeda.

Egypt's Protest

January 25, 2011: In the morning, I wrote in my daily journal: "Going to Kempinski to have lunch and then to Khan al-Kalili Bazaar." We did go to Kempinski, but didn't have lunch. The restaurant has enormous windows with wide views of the Nile and downtown Cairo. As we were choosing a table, we saw a large group of people walking along the Qasr el-Nil bridge heading for Tahrir Square. We had heard about the protest, but hadn't thought about the prospect of any bridges being closed off. Essam became concerned about our ability to get home later, so we decided to have lunch closer to our apartment so we wouldn't get trapped downtown.

The crowd in Tahrir was larger than expected, but as the days went by, the numbers grew dramatically as people were bused into Cairo from the countryside. The protest then quickly took on an entirely different dynamic.

Essam is from a large family of eight siblings, countless aunts and uncles, and an enormous number of cousins, each of whom have children. His family is spread all throughout Cairo and our many nieces and nephews and other relatives go to various different universities. Supposedly, according to the people being interviewed on CNN, university students had organized the protest and desired a revolution.

We were puzzled. None of our family members in university had heard anything about a revolution. And there had been no talk of any kind about ousting Mubarak. Everyone we knew was horrified at the idea. Everyone asked: Who will fill the void?

There were well-established political parties, and several socialist organizations that could form a new party, but none were prepared for a rushed, unscheduled election. And none had a candidate in mind for president. No one was prepared for a sudden removal of the president and government. Nor was the country prepared to be without police, which became another demand of the protesters just days later.

As various demands were announced, such as abolishing all police and ending the Emergency Law, we became more confused, but later we realized that having police around would have hindered the Islamist takeover.

The following was taken directly from my daily journal and from Facebook posts I wrote as I documented the days that followed January 25th.

January 28, 2011: The protest turned extremely violent. Protesters destroyed buildings, cars and other property. There was sniper fire into Tahrir and people were killed. There is total chaos and violence in the streets.

Local news is reporting that there have been several simultaneous prison breaks. Militants arrived in 4x4s and earthmovers. The 4x4s were equipped with machineguns and the earthmovers rammed prison gates and entrances. Guards were killed and prisoners were released, including leading members of al-Gamaa al-Islamiya, Muslim Brotherhood and Hamas.

Some protesters are on CNN demanding that President Mubarak step down. The protesters are also talking about the dissolution of the State Security System. They want to dismantle the Security Police.

January 31, 2011: The army was deployed today because some protestors continue to be extremely aggressive. Protesters have destroyed buildings and there has been a tremendous amount of smashing local shop windows, starting parked cars on fire, breaking into shops, and other types of violence. This type of violence is unheard of here! According to reports, a mob attacked groups of Christians inside Tahrir who were part of the original protest.

February 2, 2011: It was just announced that there are violent groups with bombs inside Tahrir and on the outskirts.

February 3, 2011: Thirteen people were killed at the Egyptian Museum. Protesters smashed into the museum and police responded. God, why smash up the museum? They smashed up the artifacts! They are destroying history!

I posted the following on Facebook to answer questions I was receiving:

What's unusual about the protests is that absolutely no one knows where they are going with it. Ousting Mubarak will throw the country into chaos and seems senseless.

When the protests began, they were originally controlled by crowd-control type of police. These are very young men, not trained in combat, and don't carry a weapon. They form lines and are used to block protesters from entering areas that will hinder businesses or block Cairo's busy main streets.

Security and other police were brought in when protesters turned violent and attacked the crowd-control police.

It was very odd that people were destroying other people's property. People here work a day-to-day existence in order to feed their families.

Everyone knows that to destroy a shop is to destroy a family, so no one would think of doing this to someone.

Once the violence started, people got killed. Policemen were the first to be killed—by protesters! Local news showed video of a mob of protesters attacking police.

After the deaths and immense amount of property damage, the military were called in. The military police are like our National Guard. The protesters were very aggressive and seemed to want confrontations.

February 4, 2011: A Facebook post:

I've been watching CNN and other Western news and they are all presenting this totally wrong. First of all, some of you have asked me about the embassy vans that mowed people down in the street. All embassy vans were stolen before they drove through the crowd. They were driven by whoever stole them—not by government employees or officials.

Mubarak is no criminal as Western media is portraying him. He has not committed any war crimes. CNN is not telling the truth.

I recently posted about the prison breakouts and you have all responded that you have heard nothing about them on your news. The people Hamas broke out of prison were Muslim Brotherhood leadership, and worse, members of al-Gamaa al-Islamiya, a terrorist group.

Hamas arrived at prisons almost simultaneously and released prisoners—members of the Muslim Brotherhood, Hamas and al-Gamaa al-Islamiya. Immediately after the prison breaks, almost simultaneously, the main police stations were attacked. Police were killed, prisoners were released, and police weapons were taken. The prison breaks and police station attacks were obviously well planned—these were not spontaneous attacks.

Many Egyptians right now are being called pro-Mubaraks, as if it's some horrible thing to be. People who do not want Mubarak to step down but want a transition period so that they can prepare democratic parties and candidates are being attacked violently, yet are being accused of being the violent ones!

This majority of people, the people who are being labeled pro-Mubaraks, are not being heard at all—they are being silenced by violence. The violence is said to have been done by pro-Mubarak "thugs," but it is the Muslim Brotherhood who are doing the violence! CNN is not reporting the truth.

The people the protesters in Tahrir are attacking are just regular people and business owners in Tahrir who are trying to talk the protesters into getting out of the streets and allow people to go back to work. All those businesses downtown are shut down for blocks. Everyone who has tried to talk the protesters into leaving and moving on with making changes are labeled as pro-Mubaraks and they are violently attacked and being beaten. Not the other way around.

The banks have been closed for a week and the cash machines, too. The protesters had been smashing bank windows and trying to break into the cash machines. No one has been able to get money for over a week. Ten days of violent demonstrations shutting down the city is just too much.

A lot of Iranians have entered the country this last week. A new Iranian news station has set up broadcasting here. It is filled with faked propaganda type docu-dramas with anti-West themes.

Members of Hamas, al-Qaeda, Muslim Brotherhood, and al-Gamaa al-Islamiya are out on the street in hordes. Many are attacking innocent people. Please, don't believe everything you hear on the news. The average Egyptian is being silenced.

February 5, 2011: A Facebook post:
I just saw a leader of the Muslim Brotherhood interviewed on CNN moments ago. When he was asked whether all religions in Egypt would be allowed, he said "of course." That my friends is baloney. That is a blatant lie—said specifically for Western media.

Also, why is it that only Muslim Brotherhood members are being interviewed by CNN and no "regular" Egyptian people? The average Egyptian is not being allowed to speak to Western media.

Other than Muslim Brotherhood, the people I see interviewed on Western news today are "experts" of some sort. But they are all saying they want to see Muslim Brotherhood involved in government! Why?

February 6, 2011: The protesters in Tahrir are telling CNN that their new demands are that Mubarak must resign immediately and the government must be dissolved.

February 8, 2011: Things are still bad, extremely violent. Twitter has been blocked because Muslim Brotherhood are using Twitter to encourage and keep the violence going. It was shut down in an attempt to curb the violence. Having no police at all, as the Tahrir protesters are demanding, and no president, seems insane, especially since they have no plan of any kind to replace the police or the president.

Note: *On February 10, 2011, the "Arab Spring" uprising began in Libya. Almost immediately, within a few weeks, Obama signed a presidential directive authorizing the State Department and CIA to begin an operation to arm the Libyan "rebels" (Hosenball 2011; see also: The Arming of Benghazi).*

February 11, 2011: Mubarak has resigned. Average Egyptians are at home watching this on local TV and are extremely saddened.

Our phones are ringing nonstop. Everyone is calling each other to talk about this horrible news. Our neighbors in our building congregate periodically in the hallways crying. Even the market delivery boys across the street were in a huddle crying when we went over to do some shopping. No one wanted this.

Why doesn't CNN walk around into any side street and interview regular people? They will find everyone sad and crying over Mubarak's resignation.

February 13, 2011: The protests continue. And I continue to be frustrated by CNN's coverage. There are approximately 90 million Egyptians. The extremists who wanted Mubarak removed do not speak for all Egyptians. Why doesn't CNN interview an average Egyptian on the street?

And now, what more can the people who remain in Tahrir ask for? They got what they wanted! It's time to get off the streets and begin preparing for elections. They are accomplishing nothing by staying in the streets. Old people cannot get their pension money. People cannot get food. No one can go to work. What good does this do?

The so-called "pro-Mubarak" people just want to begin organizing the new government and get protesters off the streets. They are not "diehard" Mubarak supporters like Western media is saying. This type of propaganda is just that—propaganda!

The following is an email response to a friend who asked me how I was feeling about the situation:

I lived in different parts of Cairo and made a lot of friends in each neighborhood. Men hang out in coffee shops and mostly talk politics. So, I called friends. Because of how men gather and talk, by speaking with friends in different parts of Cairo and the outskirts, I can gather the consensus of many others. They all said the same thing: no one wanted Mubarak to resign.

After Sadat was assassinated, Mubarak kept peace with Israel, even with threats from other Muslim countries telling him not to. And, if he wanted to leave the country right now to escape these threats of being hanged, he could. He's done nothing wrong and refuses to kowtow.

As far as what's going on in Algeria, Yemen, etc., as you have asked, the Western news reports are very one-sided. They only report the Islamist side to everything.

Iran sent a plane to Cairo and about 100 Iranian officials are now here doing...what? The rumor is that they are meeting with Muslim Brotherhood leaders. But why?

February 14, 2011: AUC is in Tahrir Square and I've been worried about that building. It was originally a palace. Inside those walls are ornate water fountains and beautiful wooden oriental rooms. AUC has been like a second home to me and I continue to use their research facilities. I've been so concerned that AUC may have been trashed during the protests I went to see for myself.

As soon as I saw that AUC had not been destroyed like so many other buildings downtown, I was relieved and we left. I did not want to linger because I fear the ongoing chaos.

To cheer us up we took a horse carriage ride home and guess what? The carriage driver said he did not want Mubarak to step down either! He is 32 and said all of his friends and the people in his entire neighborhood feel the same way. It's so confusing that none of the regular folks get to voice their opinions.

February 15, 2011: A Facebook post:
I live near a main road and bridge that connects to Tahrir Square. Gangs of bearded men have come over to our street and have been beating up neighborhood people. Police came by our apartment building today and handed out police sticks to defend ourselves with.

With the universities closed because of ongoing violence, one young man in our building went door to door asking if anyone wanted to join him to protect our building. About twenty young men, who would normally be in classes, now take turns camping out in the lobby. Some stand outside in front of the entrance keeping an eye open for anyone suspicious, or a mob, or bearded men. They will then inform those in the lobby to prepare themselves with the clubs given to them by the police.

We have a 6th floor corner apartment so we have a wide view of our surrounding neighborhood. From my living room window I videotaped a gang of bearded Islamists breaking into the local police station. The police fought back but lost the battle. They were out-manned and out-gunned.

All the markets around us are now closed because of looters and violence.

February 16, 2011: Today I received an official letter from AUC. It said the sniper fire into Tahrir came from the rooftop of AUC. The gate was broken down and AUC guards were attacked by armed bearded men.

Police, security police, and the military, are not allowed to grow beards. They have never been allowed to grow beards. And the majority of Egyptians do not grow beards. Traditionally, since Pharaonic times, Egyptians have hated body hair and the majority of men here are clean shaven. Beards are not popular. Only extremists grow beards.

The letter went into great detail, but it was made clear that the shootings from the rooftop of AUC that killed people in Tahrir were not done by army members, nor by police or security police, nor any government type. The sniper fire was not done by "regime forces" as CNN has been reporting. CNN is only reporting what the Muslim Brotherhood tells them to say.

It had never made sense to me, nor anyone here, that "old regime" members would do it. First of all, there is no "regime," so I hate using that word. This word "regime" is being used by Western media to fool Westerners.

But the bottom line is: the snipers who fired into Tahrir were not police, security, military, or government-related.

They were bearded Islamists.

Mubarak and security forces got blamed for something they did not do.

February 17, 2011: Four groups have organized, each over 10,000 strong, and are planning peaceful marches to Tahrir tomorrow. The groups announced their purpose, each one noting that they want to express gratefulness to Mubarak and what he's done for Egypt and the region, but also to express sorrow that he was forced to resign.

The problem is, the people who are camped out in Tahrir are now trying to silence people who want to honor Mubarak. The Tahrir protesters say they will be holding another protest in Tahrir to combat the marches being held by regular, average Egyptians.

The Tahrir protesters are calling their protest "Martyr Day" for those who died in the sniper attacks. The Tahrir people say that the "pro-Mubaraks" should not be allowed to gather. But isn't this the opposite of what they tell CNN? They tell CNN they want democracy, equality, and social justice, but they are denying the majority of the Egyptian people from expressing their opinions.

Busses full of people from the countryside have begun arriving into Tahrir, so now there is a risk of violence against the people who want to honor Mubarak.

We were planning to attend one of the marches to Tahrir, but with this threat of violence from the bus people, plans began to change. The groups are now meeting in different public squares. Each group rallying in metro Cairo have been estimated to be much larger than those gathered in Tahrir (who have to pay and bus in people to make their rallies large). There are also other extremely large rallies happening throughout Egypt, not just in metro Cairo, to pay respect to Mubarak.

Oh, and get this, speakers on stage in Tahrir right now are demanding a war against Israel!

Note: *We went to the rally and it was enormous. Videos from people who went to the other rallies showed those were enormous, too.*

But when we got home and turned on the TV, Western media was only reporting the demonstration in Tahrir. We flicked channels all night and into the next day and not one word about the rallies regular Egyptians showed up for throughout Egypt. Western media was making it out as if the regular people, the majority, didn't exist.

February 18, 2011: One of the Muslim Brotherhood's top spiritual leaders, Yusuf Qaradawi, who is against the existence of Israel and openly says so, has been invited by the Muslim Brotherhood to lead a Friday prayer and sermon in Tahrir Square. This man has been in exile in Qatar because of terrorist activities.

It's been reported on local news that many throughout the Arab region are now talking about starting a war with Israel.

Why isn't any of this being reported on CNN? Their reporters are here and are witnessing these developments.

Note: *Previous to Yusuf Qaradawi's return to Egypt, he had issued fatwas calling for the murder of Americans and Jews. After his Tahrir sermon, Qaradawi issued a fatwa to blow up churches and kill Christians. This fatwa inspired al-Qaeda to conduct terror attacks on churches in Minya.*

Qaradawi had been exiled in Qatar because of his affiliation with al-Qaeda and participation in the assassination plot on President Mubarak in 1995.

Qaradawi is a chief funder of terrorism. His "Union of Good" is a coalition of 57 Islamic charities in 21 different countries. The 57 charities can make financial transfers between coalition members in the 21 different countries. This charity is used to fund terrorism worldwide.

One of the most prominent supporters of the Muslim Brotherhood is the Brookings Institute, a U.S. "think tank." In 2017, Brookings "experts" testified against declaring the Muslim Brotherhood a terrorist group in America.

Qatar, where Qaradawi resides and organizes his "charities," donates enormous amounts of money to Brookings every year. In 2013 alone, Qatar donated $14.8 million dollars to Brookings (see: Emerson, Rossomando & Yonkman 2014).

Brookings holds its annual conferences in Qatar where global leaders, including U.S. heads of state, top members in U.S. armed forces, and influential politicians, schmooze and listen to various Islamist speakers, including Yusuf Qaradawi (see: Berens "Who are the experts").

Brookings "experts" also urged against designating Ahrar al-Sham a terrorist group, even though the group fights with ISIS and al-Qaeda. Ahrar al-Sham is an Islamist mercenary army backed by Qatar and Turkey. Its founder was a senior al-Qaeda operative (Emerson, Rossomando & Yonkman 2014).

February 20, 2011: Muslim Brotherhood and other extremist groups are now forming religious-based political parties. Religious-based parties are illegal in Egypt—but they are forming them anyway. It seems they are above the law.

Local news reported that Obama has made several calls to the Supreme Council of the Armed Forces (SCAF) stating that the Brotherhood must be allowed to participate in the formation of government. Is this the reason why Islamists are being allowed to form political parties?

The Muslim Brotherhood made a statement today saying they will only leave Tahrir Square after the release of hardcore Muslim Brotherhood leaders, including Khairat El-Shater (Deputy Supreme Guide of the Muslim Brotherhood). The prison these men are being held in is a maximum-security prison. Hamas didn't attempt a prison break at the maximum-security prison.

The new Iranian news station that just started up here continues to air what they call "documentaries." Some are on the Holocaust. They say the Holocaust didn't happen. It's obvious these documentaries are not real; they are dramatized. But Egyptians are falling for it. Essam came home last night telling me that everyone in his office thinks the Holocaust is a Jewish lie.

February 21, 2011: This morning we got two text messages on our cell phones from the "Armed Forces." One was regarding today's demonstration and said: "Be careful of bad influences and bad people trying to infiltrate the demonstration."

Who do they mean by bad people? The Brotherhood? Salafists? Al-Gamaa al-Islamiya? I can think of no other bad people except them. But I'm thinking they mean foreigners! The Muslim Brotherhood have begun a big campaign against talking to Westerners. There are rumors that all Westerners in Egypt are spies. There's a commercial on local TV channels that is creepy and very anti-Westerner. They run it constantly.

February 25, 2011: Schools have been closed for a month due to violence. It's hard to get anywhere with Tahrir and the main side roads blocked with protesters. The bridges are closed and half the city can't get anywhere, let alone to work. These daily protests have put the city of Cairo at a standstill.

The Pyramids and the Egyptian Museum finally reopened this week, but because there are no police, no one went. Islamists have been warning people not to go or they will be attacked. People were too scared to go.

February 28, 2011: Local media reports that approximately 30,000 criminals are on the loose from the prison and police station breakouts. Many of those who had been in prison have been radicalized and have been fed promises of a grandiose system of Islam. There is a visible presence of these bearded extremists on the streets.

Note: *Right after making that post in my journal, the ongoing Tahrir protest turned extremely violent. For ten days, mobs of protesters smashed cars, broke into businesses and attacked innocent people.*

Everyone asked: Why? After all demands had been met? But it became clear that this was part of the plan. Disabling the police made it possible for the Muslim Brotherhood Youth to distract the public with chaos and they used violence to silence the views of others. Meanwhile, the Muslim Brotherhood moved forward with their takeover.

March 2, 2011: Today the Deputy Supreme Guide of the Muslim Brotherhood was released from a maximum-security prison. Official reports say his release was part of a deal made with SCAF. The rumor continues that Obama is pushing SCAF to allow the Muslim Brotherhood to be involved in forming the new government.

March 4, 2011: In a village just south of Cairo, a Muslim mob attacked the Church of the Two Martyrs and set it afire, damaging it extensively. Twelve

Christians were killed in the attack and several Christian homes and businesses were destroyed.

March 5, 2011: Several State Security offices were attacked. These offices keep files on Islamists and their activities. There was a battle with guards at some locations, but the attacks were so well orchestrated the attackers won the battles and got inside.

The security headquarters in Nasr City was attacked (a city with large numbers of Muslim Brotherhood). The main security office in Alexandria was also attacked and so was the security headquarters in Assuit (a city where the Muslim Brotherhood and al-Gamaa al-Islamiya have their headquarters).

According to local news, the attacks were meant to destroy files on Islamists and their leaders, but what's interesting is the Muslim Brotherhood immediately began making announcements that they confiscated documents at one of the security headquarters that they say prove the security police were involved in the January 2011 church attack.

In other words, they are admitting that they were the ones who conducted the attacks on the security offices.

Note: *The Brotherhood never produced any documents of any kind regarding this accusation that security police attacked a church. It had been a lie meant to fool people into distrusting the Security Police System.*

March 8, 2011: Today, al-Gamaa al-Islamiya, the terrorist group responsible for the Luxor Massacre, formed a political party. Its members can run for President!

~~~~~~~

By this time, three hardcore Islamist organizations had formed political parties—the Salafists, al-Gamaa al-Islamiya, and the Muslim Brotherhood.

The Muslim Brotherhood said they would never run a presidential candidate, but quickly broke their promise and began promoting their presidential candidate, Khairat el-Shater, Deputy Supreme Guide, second in command of the Muslim Brotherhood, and who had just been released from a maximum-security prison.

Shater was later disqualified, so Muhammad Morsi, known for his unquestioning loyalty to the Muslim Brotherhood, and who would obey Brotherhood leadership unconditionally, was chosen as the Brotherhood's presidential candidate. Morsi was one of those criminals busted out of prison by Hamas.

An escaped convict was running for president!

While the Muslim Brotherhood kept the public distracted with ongoing chaos and violence, they simultaneously campaigned for fast elections.

When people tried to organize and create new democratic political parties, the organizers of these parties received death threats and their newly opened headquarters were torched. By the time the elections came, there were no real opposition parties to run against the Brotherhood and Islamist parties.

Meanwhile, the Brotherhood opened headquarters in all 29 governorates throughout Egypt. No other party had this type of power and this amount of financial backing. And during this period, before the elections, Muslim Brotherhood senior leaders were invited by the Obama administration to attend meetings in the U.S.

Via threats to remove military aid to Egypt, Obama had advised SCAF to allow the Muslim Brotherhood to participate in establishing the new government. In return for allowing Muslim Brotherhood to run for government, the Muslim Brotherhood said they would uphold the Egypt-Israeli Peace Treaty. But just as Islamist groups had signed the Non-Violence Initiative in 1997, then broke the agreement once their demands were met, the Muslim Brotherhood used *taqiyya* when they agreed to uphold the Egypt-Israeli Peace Treaty. In reality, they were plotting against Israel.

Rage, chaos, and violence against Christians

Violence against Christians broke out April 18, 2011 and lasted several days in Abu Gerkas el-Balad, in Minya. One Christian was killed and ten Christians were seriously injured. During the attack, Muslims threw an elderly Christian woman from her apartment balcony. Christian homes, shops and businesses were looted and burned, and their fields and livestock were destroyed.

May 7, 2011: Today Salafists started a rumor that a Muslim woman was abducted by Christians and was being held captive in a church in Imbaba, a suburb of Cairo. Tweets from Salafists told people to head to the church because Abeer, the kidnapped woman, was begging to be rescued. These Tweets caused a Muslim mob to form at St. Menas church. Christians created a human barricade around the church to protect it and clashes erupted. Local Salafi sheiks and more Muslims soon joined the clashes.

The Muslims broke into the church, but found no Abeer being held hostage. But that didn't stop them from continuing their attacks on Christians in the neighborhood. Christians hid inside buildings while Muslims outside chanted, "With our blood and soul we defend you Islam." The Muslim mob then torched the church and many Christian homes and businesses.

The army came and the Muslim mob began throwing Molotov cocktails at the army. The army then used tear gas to break up the Muslim mob.

It turned out there was no kidnapped woman. The rumor was started purposefully to incite an attack on Christians. It was a lie. Twelve Christians died and 232 people were injured, mostly Christians.

May 8, 2011: Muslims destroyed a church in Sole, a village just outside of Cairo. Because of this, thousands of Christians began demonstrating against the attack. There were ongoing clashes in Sole for more than 48 hours, resulting in many deaths. Then, during a Christian funeral, Muslims attacked the funeral. There were twelve deaths and at least 238 people were injured, mostly Christians.

May 10, 2011: It was reported in a local paper that there have been about 1,000 rapes per month in Cairo since the revolution. Most victims have been seriously injured and one has died. Before the revolution, rapes were rare.

May 18, 2011: A Church in Ain Shems, a suburb of Cairo, has been attacked and set on fire. Many Christians have been injured.

May 30, 2011: Protesters attacked a Military Armory. Some of the protesters were armed with machine guns and began shooting at the military guards. Western media reported it as the military attacking the people—a lie!

For ten days the protesters in Tahrir have been smashing up shops and parked cars. These so-called protesters continue to harm regular working people's property.

And now, today, after all this violence and destruction caused by protesters, the protesters in Tahrir are asking for the military to step down!

June 19, 2011: We've had enormous riots in the streets for days. Mubarak stepped down right away. The military did not attack people. The police disappeared pretty fast, too. So why keep having these extremely violent protests—and now riots? What exactly are they protesting?

Tahrir Square and the surrounding downtown streets are closed off again and all business has stopped.

The Pyramids have been closed since February. Everything is closed. Life here is hell.

July 25, 2011: The protesters in Tahrir are there every day, but they continue to make Friday the "big day." They usually name their Friday protest the "Day of Rage." Buses filled with people from the countryside start arriving early in the morning and continue arriving for hours. Many spend the night in Tahrir.

On Saturday, the mob in Tahrir decided to march to the Military Headquarters. A suburb called Abbisaya is on the path to the Military Headquarters and when the people of that area heard about the protesters coming their way, they decided to form a blockade to stop the Tahrir protesters from going to the Military Headquarters. People fought each other with fists, rocks, sticks, guns, and knives. Unfortunately, it was the Tahrir people who had the guns and knives.

Over 300 were injured and many were killed.

The rumors (lies) have started up again. This rumor was that a Christian woman wanted a divorce, but since divorce is not allowed in Coptic Christianity, she became a Muslim so she could divorce. Muslims said they heard a woman convert to Islam and said she was then kidnapped and was being held captive in a church. A Muslim mob decided to take action against the Christians and attacked the church.

It turned out that no woman had converted to Islam, nor had there been a woman kidnapped. It was a lie told as an excuse to attack Christians. Many Christians were injured.

The people living in the Pyramids area are starving. Their whole existence relied on tourism. They are horse and camel people and trinket salesmen. There have been no tourists for six months.

Those who owned small stables have had to let their horses die because they have not rented out a horse in six months and cannot feed their family, let alone the animals. My friends in the Pyramids area have told me their horses have all died from starvation. They have dragged the bodies into the desert. The desert around the Pyramids is covered in dead horses.

July 30, 2011: I read a blog by one of the protesters in Tahrir who is among those who pitched a tent in Tahrir. He said he has learned a lot about "starting a new country." Without police, they formed their own police and when they capture someone, they strip him naked and tie him dangling from a tree. People walk up, pick up sticks placed by the tree, and beat the person. Some people walk by, not even knowing why the person is hanging, and beat the person. This is their new "justice" system.

August 2, 2011: The military finally dispersed the protesters who've been living in tents in Tahrir. They asked them to leave via loudspeakers from military vehicles for two days, but the protesters wouldn't budge. When the military announced they would use force, the business community around Tahrir came out onto the street and cheered!

Though no one was harmed in the dispersal, the tent people are claiming their human rights have been violated.

What about the people they hanged on trees? Or the business owners who've had their windows smashed and shops destroyed? Or the people who had their cars smashed or set on fire? What about their rights?

September 30, 2011: Though the tents in Tahrir have been removed, violent protests in and around Tahrir continue.

October 9, 2011: The St. George church in a village near Edfu was set on fire and demolished by a Muslim mob. Christians organized a protest against this attack, demanding equal rights. The protest was held in Cairo.

Though the protesters consisted of some Muslims, the majority were Christians. The protesters brought their families, as this was a peaceful protest asking for equal rights. Suddenly there was rock throwing from a Muslim mob and then machine guns shot into the protest from the outskirts. Hundreds were wounded and at least 28 Christians were killed.

November 19-21, 2011: Clashes broke out in Tahrir as protesters are now demanding the removal of the military police. These so-called protesters then started burning churches and attacking Christians.

November 25, 2011: A large group of protesters from Tahrir gathered on a side street next to Tahrir. Violence broke out and clashes erupted between various groups within the protest. 42 people died and more than 1,000 people were injured.

December 1, 2011: Islamists won more than 60 percent of the vote in the first round of Egypt's parliamentary elections. As a result of this win, the Salafists made a statement demanding traditional Islamic punishments be implemented, such as stoning. The leader of the Salafist party said: "Citizenship shall be restricted by Islamic Sharia. Freedom shall be restricted by Islamic Sharia. Equality shall be restricted by Islamic Sharia."

December 17, 2011: Protesters in Tahrir set fire to the Egyptian Institute early this morning. The protesters started the fire at several spots on the ground floor of the building. They also blocked street entrances so that fire trucks could not respond. The fire engulfed the entire building without hindrance. Most all of its valuable collection of history has been destroyed.

The complex housed ancient maps, manuscripts, books, journals and other writings. More than 50,000 manuscripts were destroyed. Members of the Museum Commission made a statement saying it was obvious that the protesters "wanted to erase all aspects of Egyptian culture" and that "this act was committed by people who want to remove the history of Egypt."

When neighborhood people tried to save some of the books, the protesters then destroyed the books and manuscripts that had been brought out from the burning building and placed on the sidewalk.

December 23, 2011: Many thousands of Islamists gathered in Cairo demanding that the Military turn their power over to the people. But I wonder, who are the "people" they are talking about?

And what will happen with no police and now no military police? Are we just to have Salafists and Brotherhood "policing" the streets? Will they hang innocent people on trees?

January 17, 2012: The final election totals are in: 75 percent of the Parliament are hard core Islamists.

June 23, 2012: At a rally for Morsi, an imam gave a speech introducing Morsi. He said that with Morsi as president, "the capital of Egypt will not be Cairo, Mecca, or Medina, it will be Jerusalem. Our cry shall be: Millions of martyrs march toward Jerusalem. The United States of the Arabs will be restored by Morsi and his supporters. The capital of the Caliphate will be Jerusalem. Morsi will liberate Gaza tomorrow. Brandish your weapons. Banish the sleep from the eyes of all Jews. Come on, you lovers of martyrdom, you are all Hamas. We say it loud and clear. Yes, Jerusalem is our goal."

Egypt's first "free and fair" presidential election?

Ahmed Shafik, who ran against Muhammad Morsi, had been a fighter pilot, squadron, wing and group commander, and a General and Commander of the Egyptian Air Force from 1996 to 2002. Egyptians have a long history of preferring army and air force members in their government. It is mandatory that every Egyptian male serve a minimum required time in the army, so all

Egyptians have members of their family in the military or who have served in the military. Most Egyptians a have a very high regard for members of the military and Shafik was the favored choice.

Yet Muhammad Morsi "won" the election. How?

There were eyewitness testimonies, video, photos, TV coverage, and other evidence attesting to the fact that Egypt's first "democratically elected" president was not freely nor fairly elected as Western media continuously stated.

Two female neighbors of mine came home after an attempt to vote. Their clothes were torn; they were dirtied from falling after being shoved to the ground several times; and, one's face was already beginning to swell and get colorful. They never voted. Many women shared similar experiences on Twitter and Facebook.

Bearded men wearing the short white *galabeya* were allowed into voting stations, but clean-shaven men wearing Western clothing were not allowed in at some voting stations. They were chased away by bearded men with clubs.

After hours of allowing only bearded men in, some voting stations closed early. Working men do not go vote until after work, hence why voting stations do not close until 11 p.m. Shop owners especially do not vote until after they close their shops, which is usually around 10 p.m.

Many men were prevented from voting by this scam of closing voting stations early after the bearded men had voted.

Men in cars with megaphones drove through the Christian villages saying if Christians came out of their homes to vote, they'd be killed.

A very conservative estimate was made that approximately 30 percent of the poor in the southern villages were paid to vote for Morsi. When interviewed, many villagers openly admitted that they had been paid to vote for Morsi.

In many villages where there is high illiteracy, people were handed ballots that were already marked for Morsi.

The voting took place on June 16 and 17. We all watched results coming in on live TV. Ahmed Shafiq was winning and was well ahead right to the very end. On the night of the last voting day, several news stations announced that Shafiq had won. The few remaining voting stations that hadn't reported their final results were small communities and trivial in number.

But suddenly it was announced that the winner would not be "officially" announced until June 24. A full week away! We could understand waiting until the next day, but an entire week?

During the first few days of waiting came reports that Obama was having talks with Brotherhood leaders and SCAF. For days media and other reports came in stating that a deal was being made.

During those days, before either candidate had been declared winner, the Muslim Brotherhood began bussing in enormous numbers of people from the countryside and they filled Tahrir with a massive, violent crowd.

Then came announcements made several times a day. Men in cars with bullhorns drove through the streets of Cairo saying that all of Cairo would be burned unless Morsi is declared the winner.

As the following days progressed without news of who won, the threats of violence grew: if Shafiq won, they announced there would be mass killings.

By this time, several hundreds of official complaints against the Muslim Brotherhood had been officially filed with the Supreme Court Judges for various types of ballot rigging, violence, and bribing with large sums of money. It was verified that there were 456 *different types* of voting violations. There was also sufficient evidence videotaped and photographed to call the election invalid.

Bearded men continued to drive through the streets announcing: "There will be blood in the streets of Cairo" and "Cairo will be set afire."

The bused in people from the countryside waited in Tahrir Square for days. They got louder and scarier by the hour because Brotherhood members were on stage giving speeches inciting violence. These speakers were waiting for the announcement that either Morsi had won, or, to give the order for the violence to begin. We all knew they'd start by destroying all businesses in the nearby streets adjoining Tahrir. But we also knew that violence would break out everywhere.

When it was finally announced on June 24, after days of negotiations between the military and the Muslim Brotherhood, and allegedly Obama, it was announced that Muhammad Morsi won.

But we all knew he hadn't.

June 30, 2012: On this, Morsi's first day in office, Morsi made an official statement that he will work to free Omar Rahman. Rahman was convicted in the 1993 bombing of the World Trade Center and was being held in an American prison.

Rahman was the spiritual leader of al-Gamaa al-Islamiya and had issued the *fatwa* to assassinate President Sadat for making peace with Israel.

Note: *An Intel document dated the day after the Benghazi attack in Libya on 9/11/12 gave specifics about the Benghazi attack including that it had been planned in advance and executed by the al-Qaeda and Muslim Brotherhood group called "Brigades of the Captive Omar Rahman."*

This is the Omar Rahman who was convicted for the plot of the 1993 World Trade Center bombing.

The Intel document was sent to Hillary Clinton, the Defense Secretary, the Joint Chiefs of Staff and the National Security Council. The Intel doc explains that the leader of the group had been sent to Libya to set up al-Qaeda bases.

The report detailed their weapons supply and that they had been training every day and that the U.S. had been aware of this training before the Benghazi attack.

The Intel document and another sent by the State Department make it clear that not only did the Obama administration know about the al-Qaeda and Muslim Brotherhood plots in Libya long before the attack in Benghazi took place, the Obama administration also knew about the Muslim Brotherhood and al-Qaeda shipping weapons from Benghazi to Syria.

The U.S. had begun monitoring weapons moving from Libya to Syria starting in October 2011. (see: "Defense and State Department Documents")

Days of Wine and Roses? Or, days of no wine and no noses!

Extremism escalated and I was constantly harassed in the street. Muslim Brotherhood women, called sisters, and wearing the full black veil, would viciously yank my hair as I walked down the street.

An imam on a popular religious TV station declared that any American woman found in Cairo should be killed. Just days after that announcement, two British women were attacked and beaten severely, almost to death. They were mistaken for Americans.

Rapes and violent attacks on women became commonplace.

Churches continued to be burned, and many Christians died in attacks.

Nightclubs were burned and gutted. Islamists went out nightly "cleansing" Pyramids Street, which had more than 2,000 nightclubs. Atrocious things were done to dancers who made their living in these nightclubs. Islamists went into the nightclubs, attacked the dancers, and cut off their noses.

The few liquor stores that existed struggled to stay in business, not for lack of customers, but because they were torched repeatedly and shops with glass windows had their windows smashed and inventory destroyed.

Employees at these liquor stores had their lives threatened and feared going to work.

Taxis began to be monopolized by Islamists who made sure they were recognized by wearing a beard, a short white *galabeya*, and the scab on their forehead. They blared the Quran so loudly it truly hurt your ears. Since there were no police, a taxi driver would veer off to a side street where he'd rob you. Or worse things, if you were a woman.

There was an epidemic of men killing their wives without any evidence of the wife's wrongdoing. The wives would be accused of adultery, then killed—no witnesses—no trial.

Islamists decided that couples seen together in public is against Islam. In Egypt, there is a tradition of using crowded shopping areas as "chaperones" for engaged couples to meet and get to know each other. But after Islamists made their announcement that this was against Islam, attacks on couples became frequent, most especially knife attacks.

In one particular case where the boy was beaten and knifed to death, his fiancée was also knifed. She did not die, but she is hideously scarred from knife wounds to her face. They purposefully knifed her face to disfigure her for life.

Right down the street from our apartment, a nineteen-year-old had his hands chopped off for buying wine. A foreigner had asked the young man to buy a bottle and bring it to his hotel. It was an easy way to make some money during this terrible period of unemployment, so why not? As the young man was walking out of the liquor shop with bag in hand, a group of Muslims grabbed him, held him down, and chopped off his hands.

The young man hadn't consumed the wine. He hadn't committed a sin. He was simply trying to earn some money. But the young man's screams, saying it wasn't for himself, and that he hadn't touched the bottle or consumed the wine, were ignored.

During this period of lawlessness, or should I say, mob-mentality Islamic Law, the Sinai began filling up with militants. They announced Islamic Law would be enforced in the towns they held control over. They declared that cigarettes were against the law and the punishment for being in possession of even one cigarette was having all your fingertips chopped off.

A man was accused of looking at another man's wife while she was out marketing. She was fully veiled with only her eyes showing. But her Muslim Brotherhood husband decided that this man had looked at his wife and that this was against Islam. He and a few friends cut the accused man's testicles off.

There weren't any witnesses that the accused man had looked at the other's wife. But later, neighbors told authorities that the two men had had business disputes. This leads me to believe there were other motives behind the accusation. But see how easy it is to use Islamic Law ideology and turn it into an easy way to kill or maim someone?

More and more of this type of Islamic Law "justice" was taking place instead of using a courtroom, with witnesses and a judge. To me, it seemed that Islam was just a way to kill or maim and get away with it. It certainly wasn't how I would define "justice." Yet even "moderate" Muslims began saying Islam is the perfect justice system.

When Essam and I were first married, we began the habit of doing all shopping together, whether for food, clothing, medicine or household items. Because I had frequented Christian areas before our marriage, we began including a few Christian shops in our shopping excursions. Previous to our marriage, Essam had never shopped at Christian shops. Not long after our marriage, and these shopping excursions, Essam said to me one day: "You know what I like about Christians? They never lie or try to cheat you."

I began to think about the fact that during all the many years I've lived in Egypt, I've never met a Muslim who saw anything wrong with lying. And if they can get away with cheating you, or stealing from you, most will.

I thought about the taxi drivers who robbed people. And how some would take women to an alley and rape or injure them.

I thought about the wives who were being murdered.

Lying. Cheating. Stealing. Murder. Rape. Maiming.

These behaviors were being done by "good Muslims" who prayed five times a day and who went to mosque faithfully. These behaviors were being done by Muslims who quoted verses from the Quran and who were devout practitioners of Islam.

I thought about how Muslim children are not taught a Ten Commandments type of ethics. No, instead they are taught that Muhammad was the ideal Muslim, and therefore, they should strive to emulate his behaviors.

According to *hadith*, which is based on things Muhammad said and did, and which much of Islamic Doctrine is created from, Muhammad was a liar, a thief, a murderer, a torturer, a rapist, and a pedophile. Muhammad broke treaties after gaining trust from his opponents.

Yet Muslims are told to emulate Muhammad.

Where was their common sense? Where was their sense of decency?

How can Islam be the fastest growing religion in the world?

How did Islam become so powerful?

3. The Christian Origins of the Quran

During those years I witnessed changes in Egypt, I tried to find answers to the questions I just asked. Through my work, I had access to scholarly research, ancient manuscripts and historical archives that described the early years of Islam in the Near East. The more I researched, the more I came to believe that the stories we've been told regarding Islam's history didn't have any factual evidence to support them. In my search, I discovered:

There was no mention of Muhammad, or any information on Muhammad, until about 200 years after his death.

There was no Quran until about 200 years after Muhammad's death.

There was nothing written about what Muhammad said or did, what is known as his "traditions" (and from which much of Islamic history is *created* from), until about 200 years after Muhammad's death.

There is no evidence of any kind that Islam existed during the Arab conquest.

Yes, "Arabs" took power in the Levant, but the evidence shows these Arabs were not Muslims.

The version of the origins of Islam taught in our schools and universities as if it were fact is not based on any facts or any evidence.

Islam developed as a political system of control, but in order to implement this control, it had to include a religious source in order to compete with the religious influences and leadership already present in the Levant. Thus, it took about 200 years to create a prophet, a holy book, and a history. And then, it took several more centuries to become the system of control that we find today.

It wasn't until the Abbasid Empire that Islam began to be created and codified. And it was during the Abbasid period that books began to be destroyed if they contradicted the Abbasid version of their newly written history.

Due to forced conversions during the period we now call the "Golden Age of Islam," Christians were *forced to take on Muslim names*. Important achievements in architectural design, science, math and medicine, were thus reported as being Muslim achievements when they were not.

The Abbasid Empire originated in Persia. When Islamic history was created, Persian names were changed to appear Arab-like. Persian names were turned into patronyms, names based on the name of one's father. In this way, Persian names were Arabized (see: Popp 2010; Popp 2013 "From Ugarit to Samarra"; Popp 2013 "The Influence of Persian").

Right now, in our present decade, blasphemy laws are being put in place in Europe and in Canada to prevent people from questioning Islam.

Anything that contradicts the Muslim version of Islamic history is being systematically removed from the Internet, from libraries, and from university research programs.

Each time a country is taken by an Arab Spring or an Islamic Revolution, that country's museums, its history, and its archives, are destroyed. This is being done because if the truth becomes known, Islam will lose the control it has over people.

The Near East before, during, and after Muhammad

In the fifth and sixth centuries, Monophysite Christianity was established as the religion of the Levant (the Levant included modern day Syria, Israel, Lebanon, Jordan, and parts of Iraq). But while the majority of churches in the Levant accepted the doctrine of Monophysitism, Byzantium's base in the West and its capitol, Constantinople, accepted Dyophysitism.

Dyophysitism follows the doctrine that Christ had two separate natures, the divine and the human. The Monophysite view is that Christ had one nature; the divine and the human were miraculously joined.

In 622, unity was established between the two churches in order to fight the Persians. Byzantine leadership proposed a compromise, accepting that Christ had two natures, the human and the divine, but only one "mode of activity." The various patriarchs, both in the East and the West, agreed to accept this doctrine and united to fight Persia.

The *year 622* is considered to be the date of the Islamic *hijra*; i.e. when Muhammad migrated from Mecca to Medina, where he allegedly united Arab tribes under Islam. But there is no evidence that Medina or Mecca existed during the lifetime of Muhammad. As we shall see more thoroughly in a moment, Muslim sources purposefully chose important dates when creating their history and based many of their Islamic battles on the campaigns that were conducted by Heraclius, the Byzantine emperor and head of the Byzantine Army.

In 622, Heraclius officially pronounced the unification of the churches, rallied his army and left Constantinople towards Persia. This is Heraclius' famous *Campaign of 622*. At that time, the Arab transition to power was in its first stage. The borders of the Byzantine's Near East province had been turned over to Arab chieftains to help protect the borders and to help fight the Persians.

In 632, after ten years of intense battles with Persia, and financial exhaustion because of it, Heraclius ended the system of subsidizing the Arab tribes who were entrusted with border defense (called foederati).

Here again, we see another important year that Muslim writers later incorporated into their history: 632 is the year Muslim sources say Muhammad died and the Muslims found themselves without leadership. But this was actually the year the foederati system died and the Arabs found themselves without "Byzantine" leadership.

This was the period when Arab tribes began to take power, first over the borders in which they had been paid to protect, and then later, after a Christian Arab became governor of Syria, they took control of the Levant.

By 680, Christians in the Levant had been living under Christianized Arab rule for forty years. According to all evidence, the lives of the people living in the Levant had not changed. But in 681, the Sixth Ecumenical Council convened and reverted to Dyophysitism. The Levant was abandoned by Byzantium and Monophysite Christians began to be heavily persecuted by Dyophysites in eastern Syria and Iraq.

The Muslim account that Arab tribes had previously united and converted to Islam under Muhammad, and had become an army, and that this army "conquered" the Levant, does not match the actual evidence.

In-depth studies of manuscripts and documents written in the 600s and 700s (the period when Muhammad allegedly lived and the 100 years or so after his death) conclude that writers, historians and theologians had no idea that the Arabs had a prophet, a sacred book, or a religion of their own (see: Mingana 1907; 1998). The writers of that era wrote nothing about Islam, nothing about an Arab prophet, and nothing about an Arab holy book (see: pgs. 176-242, Ohlig 2013 "From Ugarit").

Coins and inscriptions during the first century of Arab rule show that the Arab rulers were Christian (for details on coins and their continued depiction of Christianity, see: Popp 2010 and Popp 2013 "From Ugarit").

Christianity thrived and spread during the first century under Arab rule and an abundance of convents, monasteries and churches were built during that time.

An enormous amount of literature appeared during the first 100 years of Arab rule in the form of archives, journals, theological treatises and other literature. Yet Islam was never mentioned in this literature.

If a Christian population had been subjugated by an Islamic empire, you would think it would have been mentioned in this literature. People were openly debating religion, yet there is no mention of Muhammad, of Islam, of an Arab holy book, or of the Arabs being Muslim.

While Christianity, Zoroastrianism, Judaism and Samaritanism were discussed and debated in the literature of the first 100 years of Arab rule, the one religion the texts of that time period do not describe or mention is Islam.

Throughout the 600s, during and after the period in which the Arabs came into power, Arabs entering the Levant were called *hanpe*, which means "pagan." Never were the terms "Muslim" or "Islam" used, nor anything related to them. A review of the literature produced at the time of the Arab takeover and the first century afterwards, establishes that people did not see any elements of Islam around them, in the Arab leadership, nor in the Arab tribes.

Mecca

Before and during the period of Muhammad, Mecca sat isolated in an infertile, uninhabitable depression between ranges of hills. Miles to its west was the blistering Red Sea coast, with extreme desert temperatures compounded by suffocating humidity. To Mecca's north, south and east was the Rub al-Khali, or the Empty Quarter. The Empty Quarter is the largest continuous body of sand and desert on the planet.

Mecca is one of the hottest locations on earth.

Compounding the extreme heat, there were no reliable water sources before or during Muhammad's lifetime. There are no perennial lakes or rivers in Arabia. According to official climate data, there is virtually no rainfall in Mecca. The average rainfall *per year* is 5.8 mm, or 0.22 inches (see: Mecca Climate). Some years there may be a short, sudden rain that causes deadly flash floods, but these are unpredictable and rare with years passing between occurrences.

In certain months, though extreme temperatures continue to plague the daylight hours, nighttime temperatures suddenly drop so low, that even a modern-day traveler risks death.

In 1931, an American named Karl Twitchell and a team of geologists went to Saudi Arabia to do exploratory work in the Hijaz where Mecca lies. "On the subject of water, they brought disappointing news to [King] Abd al-Aziz: There was none...there was no possibility of large-scale development of water resources because they didn't exist." (Lippman 2004, p.19)

At the time this exploratory expedition took place, water was being imported from Egypt. But this import of water hadn't begun until after the invention of the steamship.

Besides extreme heat and lack of water, violent winds are frequent in the Hijaz region of Arabia. Hammering 40-100 mph winds are common and cause deadly sand storms that can bury people alive. Settlement in an area lying in a barren hollow, such as Mecca, would have been avoided.

The Hijaz was not an adaptable environment for permanent settlement, yet according to Muslim writers of their history, in the 500s and 600s Mecca was a grand city with public buildings, temples, and magnificent houses belonging to wealthy traders, houses that included elaborate gardens.

There is no archeological evidence of a trade center or trade routes in the Hijaz or in Mecca during or before the period of Muhammad. There are no remains of any Arab cultures in the Hijaz during the sixth and seventh centuries of which was supposedly the grand period of Mecca and Muhammad (see: Winnett & Harding 1978).

Extensive archeological surveys of the Hijaz region conducted in the 1900s uncovered no pre-Islamic pagan sites, nor any pagan sanctuaries such as those described in the Muslim sources. Many scholars believe the Muslim writers of "Islamic History" invented these stories in order to support the Arab ruling powers and to give them a history (see: Crone 1987; Crone & Cook 1977; Crone & Hinds 1986; Wansbrough 1977, 1978).

The Muslim sources of Islamic history state that Mecca was a wealthy trading center with enormous numbers of merchants who exchanged goods with Yemen to the south and Syria to the north. Yet oddly, in the literature written by the people living during those centuries, there is no mention of a trade center in the Hijaz or Mecca.

According to Crone (1987), "if" the Meccans had been middlemen in long distance trade, as described by Muslim writers depicting their history, there would have been mention of this in the writings and documents of their "customers."

Greek and Latin authors had written significantly about the people of Yemen who traded in frankincense and myrrh. Writers gave details about Yemen's cities, their tribes, their political organizations and their trade. In the sixth century, Greek and Latin authors wrote extensively about the Ethiopian trade. Egyptians wrote about trade in Yemen, Khartoum and Ethiopia.

There are no writings about Mecca or a trade center, not in Greek, Latin, Aramaic, Egyptian Coptic or any other literature.

These stories of a trading center in Mecca began to appear some 200 years after the death of Muhammad—and were written by the Muslim authors who created Islamic history. These stories were written during the period when the ruling powers desperately needed a "backstory" to validate their rule.

Densely populated areas did develop in Yemen, thanks to farming, fishing, and tradable resources. Yemen's mountains provided a natural border dividing it from Arabia. Yemen traded extensively with Egypt and Ethiopia.

Yemenis crossed over to Ethiopia at Bab al-Mandab—a distance of only 20 miles.

Crone (1987) examined the documented evidence on the spice trade and showed that Mecca could not possibly have been a trade center. Crone points out that Mecca was not situated at any crossroad of any trade route. Nor was it a natural stopping place, nor was it a place on the incense route from Yemen to Iraq. Mecca was not a natural crossroad between a north-south route, nor a crossroad between an east-west route.

The only underground water that existed in Arabia, and where it surfaced high enough to be extracted by well, was in the eastern region, hence why the only trade route that did erupt from Yemen was on the eastern coastline to Iraq. The eastern region also benefitted from a small annual rainfall.

There is no evidence that the advanced culture of Yemen had any influence on the Bedouin of Arabia. The Arab's primitive lifestyle was a completely different phenomenon from the sophisticated Yemeni civilization.

The Arabs were also unrelated linguistically from the Yemeni people, furthering the evidence of no north-south trade route through the Hijaz towards Syria.

It wasn't until the eleventh century and the full creation and development of Islam that professional caravan trips to Mecca began to be more organized. But the trip to Mecca, no matter how organized and well planned, was treacherous and deadly. In 1183, one traveler wrote that many died along the way and that "many hells…strew the road to Makkah (Mecca)." (Tschanze 2004, p.6)

The trip to Mecca was "an extraordinarily long and difficult marathon across often unforgiving terrain, and an individual's travel could take years…The land routes were often littered with the remains of caravans…stricken by disease, short of water, or just plain lost." (Tschanze 2004, p.4)

Many died from contaminated food and water carried with them on the long journey through the vast inhospitable desert. They died from "exposure, thirst, flash flood, disease... In 1361, 100 Syrian pilgrims died of cold, and in 1430 some 3,000 Egyptians died of heat and thirst. In 1757, virtually the entire Damascus caravan was lost…" (Tschanz 2004, p.7)

Sketches, drawings and photos made by travelers in the 1700s and 1800s continue to depict a relatively barren Mecca. It wasn't until the invention of the steamship in the 1800s that water was made more available through a system of cisterns and importation of water.

Traveling the Red Sea before the invention of the steamship was deadly (see: Lippman 2004). It wasn't until the creation of the Hijaz Railway in 1908 did travel by caravan end, and travel to Mecca became less deadly.

There was never a trade route through the Hijaz to Mecca.

There was never a Mecca before or during Muhammad's lifetime.

The word Mecca has never been explained etymologically on the basis of Arabic. Etymology is the study of the history of words, their origins, and how their form and meaning have changed over time. The word Mecca did not originate from any Arab dialect, nor any Arabic word.

Mecca is not an Arabic word.

Mecca is an Aramaic word. The word Mecca is an Aramaic adjective that means "the lower one;" i.e. topographically, it describes the physical feature of a land area. This adjective is used to designate a place located "in a valley."

As explained more thoroughly in a moment, this valley called Mecca was in the Negev Desert of Israel, and not located in Saudi Arabia.

Additionally, the etymological origin of the word "Arab" shows that starting in the 9th century B.C. *arab* originally meant "those from the West as seen from the Tigris [Iraq]." West of the Tigris is the desert regions of Syria, Jordan and Israel. Even more specific is the etymological origin of the word *araba,* which referred to the desert tract of the Dead Sea area of Israel. (p.178, Ohlig 2013)

In the Old Testament, the word *arabi* meant "inhabitants of the steppe" and was the word used to designate non-Jewish tribes who inhabited the steppes of the Negev Desert highlands of Israel (p.178-9, Ohlig 2013).

The Arab transition to power

The Syrian Desert merges into the borders of what is currently Iraq and Jordan. Starting from the third century, the Syrian Desert and this border region became a center for Arabs who became Christianized.

The Ghassanids were an Arab tribe who lived in the Syria-Jordan border region. Most were Monophysite Christians; they had converted to Christianity in the 300s and by the 500s they were allies of Rome and received fees for defending the border (Popp 2010; Popp 2013 "From Ugarit").

But in 581, the Ghassanids were accused of treason during a battle against Persia, and because of this, the Ghassanid buffer state was dissolved in 584 (Popp 2010, p.21). At this time, the Ghassanids broke into fifteen small tribes, but they continued to hire themselves out as mercenary fighters.

The last period of the Persian Empire is called the Sasanian Empire, so the end battles of the Byzantine-Persian Wars are often called the Byzantine-Sasanian War. But for sake of simplification and clarification, I will continue to use one term, the Byzantine-Persian War.

The Byzantine policy was to hire Arab tribes to patrol the border with Persia and these tribes became the border defense system. Most of these Arabs had converted to Christianity but kept many of their own customs and laws. The Persian policy was similar to the Byzantines; they used Arab tribes to secure their border with the Levant.

While the Ghassanids were Christianized Arabs who patrolled and protected the buffer zone along the desert region of Jordan and Syria, the Lakhmids were an Arab tribe that patrolled the buffer zone along the Persian border of what is currently Iraq. The Ghassanids and Lakhmids were two unrelated tribes. The Ghassanids protected the Byzantine border and the Lakhmids protected Persia's border.

By the year 600, the Lakhmids were a mix of pagans and Christians and their base camp was in the Christian city of Hira near Kufa in southern Iraq. The Lakhmid tribe originated in the desert border area of southern Iraq around the year 300 and developed into a Persian vassal state that provided military aid to the Persians. They occupied southern Iraq from about 300 until the year 602.

The last Lakhmid leader, Noman III (r.580-602) was Christian, and by 602, the Lakhmid tribe was rapidly converting to Christianity. Persia's King Kosrow II, as defender of the Zoroastrian state, saw the growing Arab Christian state in Hira as a threat. Kosrow ordered Noman III killed in 602, the Lakhmid buffer state was abolished, and the Persians took full control of Hira, Iraq.

In all likelihood, Hira was the inspiration behind the story of a trading center in Mecca. Hira became the primary long-distance trading center between the East and the West after the cities of Palmyra and Hatra were destroyed. Palmyra was a trading center situated in the Syrian Dessert and Hatra was a trading center in northern Iraq. The civilizations of Hatra and Palmyra ended when they were captured by the Romans in the 270s.

After Palmyra and Hatra were destroyed, Hira, Iraq became the center for long distance trading and matches descriptions of Mecca, including its public buildings, temples and magnificent houses with elaborate gardens owned by wealthy merchants and traders.

After the dissolution of the Ghassanid buffer state in 584, and the dissolution of the Lakhmid buffer state in 602, remnants of these two Arab tribes remained in the border regions of Syria, Iraq and Jordan. The Arabs who eventually took control of the Levant did not come from Mecca or Medina in the Hijaz region of the Arabian Peninsula as claimed by Muslim creators of their history. They came from the desert regions of the Levant where they had resided for centuries.

The settled inhabitants of the Lakhmid buffer state had been a mix of people. The administration consisted of Persian upper elite, but most of the populous were Aramaic-speaking peasants. The Persian official state religion was Zoroastrianism, but the majority of the people in the Iraqi territory were Christians.

The majority of Christians under Persian control were Nestorian Dyophysites, but the southern territory of Iraq continued to include adherents of Babylonian paganism and Arab paganism.

The Lakhmid family had become powerful around the year 300. At one point, the tribe's leader, Amr Adi, tried to extend his power across the Syrian Desert into Ghassanid territory. During this period of attempted expansion, Adi's son converted to Christianity and went over to the Byzantine side. Some members of the tribe split and followed him, but the majority remained loyal to the Lakhmids. A border between the Ghassanid and Lakhmid buffer states was drawn at that time. When the Lakhmid buffer state was abolished in 602, the Lakhmids were a mix of pagans and Christians.

The towns that grew along the Byzantine side of the border with Persia built large, elaborate churches. All towns on the edge of the desert had watchtowers and border patrols (King 1991; Negev 1986). The Romans had previously built defenses along this same border. This border defense ran northeast from the Gulf of Aqaba in southwest Jordan for about 900 miles and reached northern Syria. Along the entire way, the Romans had built forts and watchtowers.

Archeological evidence shows that the settled Christian Arabs who lived in the fringe area towns separated themselves from the Arab tribal population. The evidence shows the nomadic Arabs who were hired to patrol the desert borders were pagan; they left thousands of pagan rock inscriptions in this area (Nevo & Koren 2003).

According to extensive surveys and excavations of the border forts and watchtowers, the archeological evidence shows that the Byzantine military began abandoning the fortifications along the border by the end of the sixth century. They left their frontier defenses in the hands of the Arabs. Byzantine legionary camps, sixteen forts and all twelve of their watchtowers were handed over to the Arab foederati by 590-600 (see: Parker 1979, 1987).

Then later, after the final battles of the Byzantine-Persian War, and financial devastation due to them, in 632, the Byzantine Empire stopped making payments to the Arabs. This resulted in the Arab chieftains emerging as the ones who collected taxes from those living in the border towns in return for continuing to protect the borders.

In 632, the majority of the Levant consisted of settlements of Greek and Aramaic speaking Christians, most of whom were Monophysites. But along the desert borders, there were two main types of populations, the Christian Arabs who lived in the border towns, and the nomadic Arab pagans, who had been receiving payments for patrolling and protecting the borders.

As the Byzantine army was withdrawn, Arabs began filling the role of the Byzantine army on the borders with Persia.

According to archaeological and other evidence, the lives of the local populations did not change. The only difference was that instead of Byzantium paying the Arabs for border protection, the Arabs collected taxes from the locals. Previously, Byzantium had collected the taxes, now the Arabs did.

This was the beginning of "*jeezya,*" the tax, only it had nothing to do with Islam. The concept of a tax on non-Muslims evolved later.

The archaeological evidence shows no destruction of towns during this transition of power, nor was there any abandonment of towns. Journals and logs depict no disruption of daily life. The populations did not diminish during this transition to Arab rule. The literature and documents written during this time period show the standard of living not changing.

In other words, there were no signs of a "conquest." The power and control simply changed hands.

New churches continued to be built throughout the transition and after the transition. In fact, more churches were built after the transition of power to the Arabs, possibly due to increased conversions to Christianity as the pagan Arabs began to have more contact with the Christians they collected taxes from.

This first stage of the Arab transition to power soon led to another stage: fighting among the Arabs for dominance.

Enter Mu'awiya, a Christian Arab.

Mu'awiyah gained his power base from the desert border Arabs and in 639 he became governor of Syria. When Mu'awiya took power, local Byzantine leaders, mostly Bishops, continued business as usual, but formed treaties with the desert Arabs and paid them for protection from invasion. The Arabs received their money and in return they agreed not to interfere with the administrative system (see: Hill 1971; Shaban 1971).

The traditional means of authority at that time was to become a protector of a holy place. Mu'awiya declared himself the official protector of John the Baptist's tomb and basilica in Damascus.

When Mu'awiya became governor, it did not occur from an offensive coordinated from Medina, as Muslim accounts claim. Muslim sources say Muslims rallied an army of 10,000 Meccans to attack Medina, then left to fight for Islam in the Levant (through the largest continuous body of sand and desert in the world).

Not only is this claim illogical, archeological and other evidence prove this isn't true.

Chalcedonian, Monophysite and Nestorian Christians provided accounts of the events that took place during the transition of power to the Arabs. None of the written works from local sources mention the battles that Muslim sources describe. Moreover, the Islamic conquest as described by Muslim sources cannot be proven archeologically. At the locations where the Muslim sources say battles took place between the Muslim army and the Byzantine army, there have been no archeological findings. No Byzantine uniform buttons, no weaponry, no coins from the war chest, nothing has ever been found (Popp 2010, p.100).

Information about Muhammad and the battles his armies fought did not begin to appear until 200 years after Muhammad's alleged death. Biographical information on Muhammad comes only from Muslim sources, and not until the ninth and tenth centuries. This includes a history of Islamic military campaigns written by al-Waqidi (d. 822); the *Sira* of ibn Hisham (d. 834), which is a biography of Muhammad; a book titled *Generations* by Ibn Sa'd (d. 845); and a book called *Chronicles* written by al-Tabari (d. 923).

Current Islamic "scholars" rely heavily on al-Tabari for historical Islam without analyzing how al-Tabari's works originated. Al-Tabari is taken to mean "the one from Tabaristan." Tabaristan was an area in northern Persia, what is currently Turkmanistan. The works of al-Tabari were written by a team of writers, representatives from the political ruling realm who were chosen to create a history compatible with the new ruling powers (see: pgs. 104-109, Popp 2013 "From Ugarit").

Political Islam was created as a control mechanism and a "history" was needed to validate it in order to enforce it.

Muhammad allegedly died in 632. The histories, biographies and stories of Muhammad's military campaigns, and those of his Muslim army, were all written some 200 years after Muhammad supposedly lived, and most importantly, these writings appeared without any other previous writings on the subject.

There is another Muslim "source" for their history, called *hadith*; i.e. the collections of the traditions and habits of Muhammad (the things he said and did). These were written in the late ninth century, some 230-280 years after the death of Muhammad. These collections are from Bukhari (d. 870); Muslim (d. 875); Maja (d. 886); Dawud (d. 888); Tirmidhi (d. 892); and Nasai (d. 915).

Bukhari is most cited for *hadith*. Muslim accounts say Bukhari examined more than 600,000 traditions of Muhammad. Some 200 years after the death of Muhammad, Bukhari gathered more than 600,000 stories about Muhammad? How can this be possible? After a 200-year void of nothing written? Where is the evidence to support these stories?

There is none.

Muhammad's history, and Islamic history in general, is a product of the age these "histories" were written—which was the ninth and tenth centuries, and not the sixth or seventh centuries in which Muhammad allegedly lived.

There was nothing written about Islam or Muslims by the adversaries of the Arabs, nor anything written by the Byzantines, who were well known for their vast literary output.

There was nothing written about Islam or Muslims by the Jews or Christians who would have been living under "Islamic" rule, both of whom were also known for their literary output.

Rock inscriptions and the story they tell

Extensive studies were conducted on rock inscriptions dated at the fifth, sixth and seventh centuries in Iraq, Syria, Jordan and the Negev Desert in Israel (see: Nevo 1985; Nevo, Cohen & Heftmann 1993; Nevo & Koren 2003).

Before around 650, the rock inscriptions were either non-religious or they were pagan. After around 650, the majority of rock inscriptions continued to be non-religious or pagan, but a simple monotheistic type of rock inscription began to appear.

Nevo, Choen and Heftman (1993) categorized the non-pagan rock inscriptions that began appearing after 650 as either Basic, Muhammedan, or Muslim. The Basic texts were the earliest to appear, about 40-60 years after the alleged death of Muhammad, and they did not exhibit any creed that would designate them as being any specific religion. Muhammad is not mentioned, nor is there any reference to Islam. But when the concept of God was mentioned, it was: "Lord of Moses and Jesus," which is unspecific as to whether this was referring to Christianity or Judaism.

The Muhammedan category began to appear approximately 100 years after the alleged death of Muhammad, as well as 100 years after Arab rule had begun. The inscriptions added the "word" muhammad, but lacked any aspect of Muslim theology, which only appeared in the very latest classification of the study, categorized as "Muslim."

As we shall see in a moment, the "word" muhammad was originally a Judeo-Christian term, and had nothing to do with Islam.

The inscriptions categorized as "Muslim" appeared in the 800s, about 200 years after Muhammad's alleged death. The Muslim category was then divided into two groups according to their dates. Early Muslim inscriptions were dated in the 800s, approximately 200 years after Muhammad's death, and the later Muslim inscriptions, that were more distinctly "Muslim" in character, were dated at around 900 or later, more than 300 years after Muhammad.

Why did it take so long for Islam to appear? The magic number seems to be 200 years. Consider the following:

It took about 200 years for a biography or any information on Muhammad to appear.

It took about 200 years for the "traditions," i.e. *hadith*, to appear.

It took about 200 years for rock inscriptions to begin appearing that had Muslim characteristics.

And it took written Arabic, the one used for the Quran, about 200 years to appear.

The Quran gets a bit tricky because it began as a Christian liturgical book and changed and evolved over time, but once again, it took about 200 years after Muhammad's death for the Quran to appear in Arabic and become the Arab holy book.

No matter how you analyze it, there is an enormous gap in time before anything "Islamic" appeared. And if there had been a conquest as the Muslim sources describe, that was based on religion, as they state it was, you would think that those living at the time would have documented it in some way. Or at least have mentioned it.

And remember Mu'awiya, who became governor of Syria right after the Arabs began taking control? According to Muslim-written "history," Mu'awiya was Muhammad's scribe. The "traditions" of Muhammad, written some 200 years after the events allegedly happened, say Muhammad saw that Mu'awiya "had a pen behind his ear" and Muhammad said to Mu'awiya, "What is this on your ear?" Mu'awiya responded, "A pen which I have made ready for Allah and His Messenger." Muhammad then said, "May Allah repay you well on behalf of your Prophet! By Allah, I will only ask you to write down revelations from heaven (referring to the Quran)." (see: ibn Kathir)

So, if Mu'awiya was a scribe, and Muhammad gave him revelations to write down (i.e. the Quran), and if Muhammad was accepted as a full-blown Prophet at the time, why is it that Mu'awiya didn't write down the revelations?

Why didn't the Quran appear until 200 years later?

Why didn't Mu'awiya persuade the tribes or their chieftains to stop being pagan? Pagan cult centers were built and experienced an enormous growth in the Levant *after* the Arabs took power (see: Nevo 1985).

Why was there an increase in the building of churches, monasteries and convents during the first 100 years of Arab rule if the Arabs conquerors were Muslim?

Because this story about Muhammad was made-up—like all the stories about Muhammad.

Islam is the fastest growing religion in the world. Muslims today, even in Western countries, are trying to implement Islamic Laws. To stop this, we must begin to spread the truth, via the facts and the actual evidence that exists.

The transition to Islam

The Umayyads are considered to be the first Arab dynasty to rule the Levant, starting with Mu'awiaya, who first became governor of Syria in 639, and who then became ruler/caliph in 661. Life basically remained the same under the Umayyad rulers and the administration continued to be run by Christians.

At the time of the Arab transition to power, the Arabs migrating into the Levant from the desert border patrol areas were pagan. They remained pagan until well into the mid-eighth century as the archeological evidence proves (see: Nevo 1985; Nevo, Cohen & Heftmann 1993; Nevo & Koren 2003).

The urban Arabs who inhabited the region had become Byzantine in culture. They had begun converting to Christianity starting in the 300s. The texts they left behind reflect this as well as archeological evidence from churches, tombstones, inscriptions and papyri (see: Negev 1981).

Archaeological evidence demonstrates that starting from the fifth century, Christianity was the observable faith in the towns and urban centers of the Levant. But paganism continued just outside the towns among the Arabs. An extensive study conducted by Yehuda Nevo in 1985 provided evidence that this Arab population was worshipping pagan shrines and stones and continued to do so without interruption in the Negev well into the eighth century (see: Nevo 1991).

These pagan cult centers grew larger under Abd al-Malik (r.685-705). More than fifty pagan cult centers were built during al-Malik's rule and continued to be actively used until approximately 743 (Nevo 1985). That's more than 100 years after the death of Muhammad, when one would have thought, according to Muslim sources, that all Arabs in the region, especially the "invaders," were practicing Islam. Instead, when Arabs began ruling, Arab paganism grew and intensified, as shown by the growth in the numbers of Arab pagan cult centers.

There is a total lack of archeological evidence for a Meccan pagan cult center as the Muslim sources describe in their "history" of Islam, but the pagan Arab cult centers found *in the Levant* exactly match the descriptions of the Meccan and Hijaz pagan sanctuaries described in Muslim sources (see: Nevo 1985).

It was not in Mecca and the Hijaz that large pagan cult centers were built; they were built in the central Negev Desert of Israel.

And it was not during pre-Islamic times that these cult centers reached their peak, as Muslim sources state. Arab pagan cult centers reached their peak during the 700s, well within the time that Muslim sources say Islam was being practiced by the Arabs—but wasn't.

Some of these pagan cult centers were still being used in 770. Arab pagan cult centers were active, and pagan rituals were being performed in them, throughout the first 150 years of Arab rule.

Nevo and Koren (2003) point out that these pagan cult centers, especially since they were very prominent architecturally, could not have existed without the Arab ruling powers' knowledge. These active cult centers, with many centers of worship, continued to exist openly (see also: Nevo 1985, 2002; Nevo & Cohen 1993).

Why were these cult centers built during the first 100 years of Arab rule? Because there was no Islam. There was Arab rule, but the Arabs were not Muslims. The Arabs living in the towns and urban centers of the Levant were Christian, but the majority of Arabs in the desert border patrol regions continued to be pagan.

Brock (1982) examined historical references to the Arabs in Syrian documents during the period of Arab takeover, the alleged Islamic Conquest. These writings were written by people who witnessed the Arab transition to power. He concluded that these writers experienced no "conquest."

Furthermore, there was no reference to Islam in the writings by the Christian inhabitants who lived side by side with the Arabs. Brock also states that there was no mention of Muhammad and concluded that the authors of literature written during that period did not see an Arab religion during the first century after the Arab takeover.

By the mid-sixth century, the Christian Near East had divided into several national churches: Nestorian Iraq and Persia (Dyophysite); Western Syria (Monophysite); Coptic Egyptian (Monophysite); and Armenian. The

Armenian Church was Monophysite, but had discrepancies over the formula defined by the Ecumenical Council. Monophysite Christianity was also the national religion in Yemen and Ethiopia.

During the last phase of the Byzantine-Persian Wars, two religions co-existed in Persia. Though Zoroastrianism was the official religion of the state, much of the ruling class and aristocracy were Christians. According to Popp (2013), by the 600s, Persia was on its way to full Christianization (see: "From Ugarit" p.43).

Nestorian Christianity was fully accepted under the Sasanians, the last dynasty of the Persian Empire. Nestorians were Persian in culture and the chief Nestorian Church stood right next to the Persian royal palace (Popp 2010, p.19).

Abd al-Malik became ruler/caliph in 685. Coins and inscriptions show that al-Malik was Christian (Popp 2013 "From Ugarit").

In 747, there was a revolt against the Umayyads that resulted in the Abbasid Revolution of 749-750. The Umayyads were defeated and the Abbasids of Persia took power.

After assuming power, the Abbasids established their capital in Kufa, Iraq. They relied on Persian viziers to help them govern and their administration consisted primarily of Christians.

After 809, the Abbasid Empire fell into a two-year civil war and became divided. By 820, the Samanids of Persia had taken control of parts of what is now Turkmenistan and Afghanistan and the Hamdanids took control of Syria. The Hamdanids were Christian, but they were Dyophysites. This caused much unrest because the majority of Syrians were Monophysites.

It was during the 800s that we begin to see the creation of Islam, and with its creation, we see changes in the meaning of Christological terms as the Abbasids re-wrote history in order to enforce their rule.

The history of the word *caliph* is Christian-based. Byzantine emperors called themselves "Servant of Christ" on their gold coins. Battles on doctrine, specifically whether Christ was divine or whether he was human, caused great division between the patriarchs in the Christian West and the Christian East.

Instead of calling themselves "Servant of Christ," Christian patriarchs in Jerusalem began calling themselves "Speaker for God" (*khalif-at allah*) to separate themselves from the idea of Christ being the son of God. There was only one God, and Christ was his Servant and Messenger.

This is how the word khalif/caliph began being used for rulers in the Levant. The original use of this word had nothing to do with Islam.

It is the same with the "word" muhammad. The word's meaning changed over time (see: pgs. 131-141, Luxenburg 2010 "A New

Interpretation"; pgs. 252-4, Ohlig 2013 "From muhammad Jesus"; p. 15, Popp 2013 "From Ugarit"). Historical literature shows the word muhammad originally meant "desired." Literature and texts show that over time, the word evolved and took on religious meanings. The word transitioned from God's desired one, God's chosen one, God's praised one, and God's messenger.

Rock inscriptions also prove that the word muhammad was not originally a name for a person, but was a word used to describe a religious attribute (see: Nevo & Koren 2003).

It is the same with the word abdallah (which means Servant of God: abd allah). Abdallah did not become a name until much later, long after Islam was created. Over time, Muhammad the man (or should I say, the myth), became the son of a "person" called Abdallah (also spelled Abdullah).

The Quran mentions muhammad four times. Compare that to various people mentioned in the Quran: Aaron is mentioned 20 times; Jesus 24 times; Adam 25 times; Noah 33 times; Mary 34 times; and many others are mentioned more times than muhammad. The term *rasul allah* (messenger of God) occurs at least 300 times, yet *rasul allah* is never attached to muhammad.

Nevo and Koren (2003) point out that when the word muhammad is mentioned in the Quran, there is no personal information included. There is no mention of family, ancestry, lineage, or deeds. But when the Quran mentions other people, the deeds they've done or their lineage or affiliation with people or a tribe is always mentioned.

People are mentioned in the Quran in a way that tells of their ancestry or of their affiliation with people or a tribe. Since muhammad is never mentioned in that way, and mentioned so few times, the use of the "word" muhammad in the Quran, as in the early days of the use of the word, is a religious descriptive word, and *** not the name of a person***.

The *al-Magazi wa al siyar Sirah* is the first account of Muhammad's life in writing. Unfortunately, it disappeared. The only form of this alleged biography is given to us by ibn Hisam (d. 834) around 200 years after the alleged death of Muhammad.

During those 200 years, there was no written history or biography of Muhammad. Nothing about Muhammad was written during those years. Muhammad's birth and death dates have never been established, let alone verified, because there are no records, no documents, nor any evidence of any kind that show Muhammad existed.

So, we have a "biography" which disappeared, and then, Hisam miraculously comes up with this missing biography, around 200 years after the death of Muhammad, but Hisam only refers to it.

Conrad (1987) collected scholarly assessments on the subject of Muhammad's biography and all came to the same conclusion: the Muslim accounts of Muhammad are impossible to accept as true.

The *Sirah*, as Muhammad's biography is often called, is questionable regarding Muhammad's date of birth, his age at the time of various events, and, his life in general. According to Conrad, after viewing all the written works by Muslim sources, the whole chronology of Muhammad's life is contradictory and totally unsubstantiated.

One must wonder why Western universities continue to teach the *Sirah* as fact.

After giving evidence as to why Muhammad was probably a mythical figure and not a real person, Wansbrough (1977) points out that "if" Muhammad actually was a real person, he could not have possibly lived during the period that Muslim sources say he lived.

Wansbrough further points out that when reading the *Sirah*, it gives one the impression that the sole reason for writing the *Sirah* was to create and establish the existence of an Arab prophet. And, not only was this "backstory" needed to support the existence of an Arab prophet, a history also had to be created to back up the Quran.

Although the words "messenger of God" appear in the Quran, those words do not refer to Muhammad. Neither is Muhammad a central figure in the Quran. The central figures in the Quran are Moses and Abraham. Moses is mentioned in 502 verses and Abraham is mentioned in 245 verses.

Wansbrough (1977) demonstrates that the Quran fully supports the position that Moses was a prophet, but the Quran does not support the position that Muhammad was one. And as mentioned previously, muhammad is mentioned in the Quran in a way that appears to be a descriptive word, and not a man.

There is no information about Muhammad in the Quran; therefore, information on Muhammad had to be supplied separately. This was the sole purpose of the sudden appearance of the *Sirah*.

Hadith and Islamic Law

Most Islamic Laws do not come from the Quran, they are created from *hadith*, the traditions of Muhammad.

Wansbrough (1977), a reputable source of scholarship on this subject, concluded that the *isnads* (the chains of transmission of the traditions of Muhammad from person to person ***orally*** over a 200-year period) are impossible to accept as fact.

The "stories" of the things Muhammad said and did allegedly come from "direct sources" from the seventh century, via chains of oral transmission. Supposedly, people told other people, and those people told other people, and so forth, for 200 years.

Earlier I mentioned that the source of *hadith* came primarily from Bukhari, who allegedly examined more than 600,000 traditions of Muhammad, but that others were also known for their collections as well. The reason why Bukhari is cited the most is because the others often referred to Bukhari as their source. They also used one another as sources.

So, what we have is a circular pattern of sources, each claiming the other as their source.

Cook (1981) also demonstrated that the *isnads* are inadmissible and cannot be considered factual. Cook's research showed no historical authenticity of any kind. Cook points out that the "traditions" should be dated on external criteria, that is, external to the *isnads*. In other words, any other type of evidence besides this sudden appearance of *isnads*.

Since there are no external sources or evidence in existence (no writings, documents, or other types of evidence), the *isnads* cannot be considered factual.

Joseph Schacht spent the greater part of his life researching Islam and is considered a leading expert on Islamic Law and its origins. Schacht (1967) concludes that most of the traditions were put into circulation in 820.

According to Schacht, every tradition of Muhammad should be taken as fictitious. Schacht could not find any tradition of Muhammad that could be considered authentic.

Schacht ascertained that the laws that were thought to have been developed out of the traditions of Muhammad were actually practices of the rulers of the early 800s, and had nothing to do with Muhammad (Schacht 1967, 2000; see also: Wansbrough 1977, 1978).

Wansbrough (2006) also confirms that the stories of Muhammad could not possibly be based on fact and confirms through scholarly research and analysis that these stories originated out of the period of which they were written—the 800s. The stories reflect the political situation of a later time, and not Muhammad's.

Hadith has nothing to do with Muhammad.

Muslim sources say the "traditions" were told to close family members and allies of Muhammad and then handed down "orally" throughout the 200 years that followed Muhammad's death.

This would be similar to the telephone game where you stand in line and say a sentence to the person next to you, and then that person says the sentence to the person next to him, and so forth. When the very last person in the line says the sentence, it is nothing like the original sentence.

Imagine after 200 years how much the stories about Muhammad could have changed. Yet we are to accept these stories of Muhammad as factual.

But the core problem with the "traditions" is their sudden appearance after 200 years of non-existence.

Now open up any textbook on Islam or Islamic history in any university throughout America, or open any Islamic history book in your local library, and you will find that *hadith* and Islamic history is presented in our textbooks and history books as if this information is fact-based.

Classes in Islamic Studies and Middle Eastern History offered in universities throughout America teach this information as fact-based, when none of the information is based on fact or any kind of real evidence.

Additionally, there are no books, research studies, or reading lists recommended by college professors that offer information to the student which present the questionable aspects of *hadith* and Islamic history that I am presenting in this chapter. There is only a one-sided presentation of Islam, and it is not one based on any fact-based evidence.

Keep in mind, the majority of Islamic Laws forced on people today are created from the "traditions" of Muhammad. And these are the laws Muslims living in the West want to begin enforcing on us!

In his most well-known work, *The Origins of Muhammadan Jurisprudence,* after examining the evidence, Schacht (1967) concludes that the system of "transmitting traditions" of Muhammad does not meet the requirements for a legitimate system of laws.

Moreover, Schacht points out that these claims of Muhammad's "traditions" were accepted without any investigation of any kind. Schacht demonstrates the traditions of Muhammad could not have survived an investigation back then, and most certainly, not now.

But therein lies a significant problem. In universities throughout America, research and investigation on Muhammad, *hadith*, and Islamic history are prohibited. Students are only allowed to re-hash the Muslim sources—sources that have no evidence to back them. Students are not allowed to investigate and analyze the questionable aspects of Islam.

Why do we continue to teach the "traditions" as if they are based on facts?

Why is scholarly research on Islam banned?

Because powerful Muslim organizations and various governments and countries run by Islam do not want you to know the truth. The truth negates the validity of Islam and would hinder the control these organizations and governments have over people. It would also hinder the spread of Islam.

Islam will disintegrate if the truth about Islam is told.

During the period of the creation of Islamic Jurisprudence from the 900s to the 1200s, there became a compulsory "status" attached to *hadith*. The laws attributed to Muhammad via *hadith* ("stories" of things he said and did), were considered authoritative and could supersede all other sources of legal authority.

Laws that had been created by the local or regional community were abolished as "man-made" and replaced with Islamic Laws, created mostly from *hadith*.

Hadith details very abusive ways to treat women, condones and promotes slavery, and includes numerous outdated, archaic behaviors. Many Muslim majority countries today, who have experienced a recent "revival" of Islam, such as the Iranian Revolution, the Arab Spring, or some other Islamist takeover, have had their governments replaced with Islamic Law.

The laws previously created to provide justice and more equality among people, reflected in more modern times, have been replaced with archaic laws—simply because we've been told Muhammad was the last prophet and his behavior is therefore ideal.

Islamists say governments must be taken down because they create man-made laws.

Yet *hadith* is purely man-made.

Hadith not only is man-made, it was created during an archaic period of inhumane practices. It should not be promoted as a way of life to be practiced in the modern era. Yet more and more Muslims throughout the world, and most especially Muslims in the West, are demanding that Islamic Laws, created primarily from *hadith*, be enforced on all people.

~~~~~~

Most of the Arab populations already existing in the urban centers of the Levant had fully converted to Christianity, but on the borders and in the desert regions, most Arabs remained pagan. They built pagan cult centers and these pagan centers grew in size and in number during the first 100 years after Arab rule began.

Over time, some Arabs who settled in the border towns began to adopt a basic form of monotheism. This is apparent in their rock art, which first consisted of pagan inscriptions, but then began to exhibit a slow transition to some inscriptions stating "Lord of Moses and Jesus" (see: Nevo, Choen & Heftman 1993).

The Jews had national and religious leaders and they had a holy book and prophets. The Christians had powerful religious leaders, a holy book, and they defined themselves through their belief in Jesus.

The Arabs on the other hand, had no prophet, no holy book, and no religious leaders. They had no ancient history and they had no nation.

Arabs lived in tribal societies, divided into clans. Clans and tribes organized around elders and the sons of elders. When a clan or tribe grew too large, they often had leadership disputes and would divide and move to separate territories. Clans were tied by immediate kinship and members often did not know their distant ancestral history.

During the period of transition, nomadic Arabs lived in the desert outskirts where there were reliable water sources. Arab mercenary armies resided in encampments away from cities and the populous and they remained committed to their clan or tribal chieftains. They hired themselves out as mercenary fighters or as border protectors.

The Arabs who migrated into the Levant and Persia from these border areas had no collective identity. They had no shared history, no common language between them, and no written language. They consisted of members of individual tribes who often spoke different dialects. Many of these dialects were incomprehensible to one another. Historically, Arab tribes fought one another, which kept them alienated from one another.

As the first stages of the transition to power in the Levant began, the leaders who surfaced recognized that to remain in power, they needed some form of unity.

The Arabs had no ancient lineage, only immediate kinship ties; whereas, the Jews had a long history, documented in the Old Testament, and they followed their descent from Abraham. They had occupied the land from the time of Moses and considered it their divine right.

The Christians thought of themselves as the successors of the Jews and many traced their roots to the ancient Greeks. There had been a Greek presence in the Levant starting in the 7th century B.C. and this presence had grown during the Hellenistic period.

The Arabs had no ancient history and they had no roots.

Wansbrough (1977) demonstrates that from about 750 on, the development of the Quran was in a constant flux, and that the central purpose of the Quran's development was to establish the Hijaz origins of an Arab prophet.

Bashear (1989) also analyzed the Quran and Islamic history and confirms that during the period from roughly 750-800, the Hijaz was purposefully chosen and placed into the historical background for Islam.

Bashear concluded that Mecca was created as Islam's religious base in order to give the Hijaz a location for the Arab identity.

Islam: Fact or Fiction?

By examining the archeological remains of the early Islamic period, and thoroughly noting the total non-existence of Islam, prominent archeologist, Yehuda Nevo, and researcher Judith Koren, questioned the "Muslim" conquest cited as fact in the history books of today. Their conclusion was that Islamic history has been created and that it cannot stand up to "non-Muslim" sources and the actual evidence (Nevo & Koren 2003).

Nevo and Koren concluded that during the Arab conquest, the Arabs were pagans. These Arabs slowly, over time, took on the Jewish and Christian beliefs they encountered in the Levant. They argue, using real evidence, that Muhammad was not a historical person, but a mythical figure.

In another study, Nevo (2002) details seventh and eighth century religious inscriptions on stones and rocks in the Negev Desert. Nevo concluded this evidence causes substantial difficulties for believing the traditional Muslim account of Islamic history.

John Wansbrough, expert in Quran and Islamic Studies, demonstrated that the traditional accounts of Islamic History and the Quran are inaccurate (Wansbrough 1977; 2006).

Wansbrough also demonstrated that the Quran evolved and was under continuous change for well over a century. The text of which is now the Quran, and even the concept of Islam itself, didn't occur until more than 150 years after Muhammad's alleged death, and some 200 years after Muhammad's alleged lifetime (see: Wansbrough 1977; 2006).

Ohlig (2013) notes that the Islamic Empire did not leave behind any literary evidence during the first 200 years of its existence. But during those 200 years, there were extensive writings by historians and other writers. There were serious religious debates going on, also in writing. Yet there was nothing written about Islam.

The Christians in the regions under Arab control wrote copious amounts of literature. There was a thriving intellectual life, with fluid debates and literary conversations. Yet never was being under Islamic rule, or having an Islamic ruling regime, ever mentioned.

During this period of 200 years, Christians conducted extensive and far reaching missionary work, including into the Arabian Peninsula. Never did they mention coming across Islam or Muslims in their travels.

Religious writers of that period, many of whom travelled extensively into neighboring regions, debated Monothelitism, Monenergism, and other concerns at the time, but never that there was a new religion in existence, let alone a religion being propagated by the new rulers.

If there had been a new religion belonging to the Arab rulers, wouldn't it have been mentioned? Or wouldn't it have been debated along with the other religious issues of that time?

The words Islam and Muslim were never used in any of the writings during those first centuries after the Arabs took control. The Arabs were mentioned and written about, but they were referred to as pagans, Ishmaelites, Hagarenes or Saracens (people who came from desert regions), but they were never referred to as Muslims.

Jacob of Edessa (d. 708) was a Syrian theologian and a fruitful author and scholar of that time. Neither Islam nor Muslims were mentioned in any of his vast number of writings.

Coptic sources (Egyptian Christians) mentioned the Saracens (desert people) in their writings, but only that they oppressed, killed people, and practiced prostitution (see: Ohlig 2013).

John of Damascus thought of the Ismaelites as heretic Christians and accused them of "maintaining their pagan traditions." (see: Ohlig 2013, p.236)

After analyzing the Christian literature of the first 200 years after the Arab takeover in Egypt and the Middle East, Ohlig (2013) states: "Islam is not named ...The Arabs/Saracens/Ismaelites/Hagarites are not perceived as Muslims ...If the Arabs should really have been Muslims and propagated a new religion ... as the traditional reports want to make us believe, then these authors must have completely failed to notice it." (p.235)

Ohlig asks: "What should have prevented them from mentioning a new non-Christian religion or from fighting against it with theological arguments? ...As numerous theologically highly sophisticated books about Monophysitism, Diphysitism, Monoenergetism, Monotheletism and so forth demonstrate, these authors possessed considerable literary and linguistic abilities." (p.235)

The archeological and other evidence shows that the Arabs living on the desert borders of the Levant were pagan, but that the Arab ruling elite already established in the urban areas of the Levant were Christians.

Ohlig (2013) points out that Christian symbols were on the coins of the early Arab rulers, and that according to everything we have in literary form, the ruling Arabs were Christians. He points out that this was most true of the Umayyad rulers (r. 661-750).

"Islam can first be spoken of as a new religion in the 9th century...The mention of a prophet called Muhammad are even rarer and later. This name [muhammad] which was originally a Christological title, was given to the prophet over time, in the last decades of the first half of the 9th century." (Ohlig 2013, p.237-241)

While analyzing the literary evidence that was written during the first 200 years of Arab rule, Ohlig discovered that after Islam did begin to make an appearance, he found that older manuscripts which had used the words Hagarene or Saracen *were re-written using the word Muslim* (see: Ohlig 2013, p.177).

Give that some careful thought.

There were no printing presses during that time. Men made handwritten copies of books. They copied books and other literature by hand. As Ohlig went through the original manuscripts and compared them to later *copies* of them, he found that when manuscripts were copied centuries later, *the men who copied them used the word Muslim.* Copies of these manuscripts replaced the original words with the word Muslim.

History had been re-written.

~~~~~~

By 621, the Persians had captured the major cities of the Levant and also Alexandria, Egypt. In 622, the Patriarchs of Antioch, Alexandria and Constantinople agreed to end the division between their churches in order to fight the Persians. This unification of the churches helped Byzantium recapture the territory lost, and most importantly, recapture Jerusalem.

The loss of Jerusalem had been a devastating blow. Jerusalem was Christianity's most holy city. It was where Jesus ministered and where he was crucified, died, and rose again. It was the site of the most important churches of Christendom, churches that commemorated the events of the life of Jesus.

When the Persians took Jerusalem, they plundered the city and destroyed the Church of the Holy Sepulcher, which marked the crucifixion and the tomb of Jesus, and they prevented Christians from making pilgrimages to the city.

There is no evidence to support an Islamic *hijra*, the Muslim migration to Medina, but there is written documentation, archeological and other evidence, showing that in 622, there was an "Arab" migration as mercenary Arab fighters living in the desert regions of the Levant joined the final battles of the Byzantine-Persian War.

When Muslims began creating their history, they chose this year, 622, as Muhammad's alleged migration to Medina. It is there, according to Muslim writers of their history, that a tribe of Jews joined the Muslims. As we shall see more thoroughly in a moment there was indeed a uniting of Arabs and Jews, but it did not take place in Medina, it took place in Jerusalem. Muslim writers took real events, but altered them to make them "Islamic."

The claim that the birth of the Islamic community began with the *hijra*, the "migration" of Muhammad's followers to Medina, and that later, Muslim armies then left to conquer the Levant, has no evidence of any kind to back it.

Instead, this period, known as Heraclius' *Campaign of 622*, was the period in which pagan Arabs migrated from the border region of Syria, Iraq and Jordan to hire themselves out as mercenary fighters. They joined Christian Arabs in the final battles of the Byzantine-Persian War.

During the various battles that took place, some Arabs fought with the Persian army and others fought with the Byzantine army. Arabs fighting with the Persians fought Arabs who were fighting with the Byzantines. It was tribe against tribe, just like the stories of Muhammad in Medina and Mecca.

Muslim writers of their history created the story of the *hijra* and the battles that followed out of factual events: after uniting Christians, Heraclius rallied an army and left Constantinople in 622. His key battles took place from 622-629 and culminated in the recapture of the holy city of Jerusalem. Muslim writers chose these same years and battles as inspiration for Islamic history.

The final series of battles fought between Byzantium and Persia left both armies financially devastated. After recapturing Jerusalem, the Byzantine army withdrew from the Levant. This withdrawal opened the door to the Arabs to take power.

The stories of Muhammad's campaigns and battles, created by Muslim authors in the 800s, were inspired by the campaigns and battles conducted by Heraclius, the Byzantine emperor who recaptured the Levant and Jerusalem from the Persians.

Early Islamic history did not originate in Mecca and the Hijaz of Saudi Arabia, but instead, Islamic history was created from events that took place in Jerusalem and the Levant during Heraclius' *Campaign of 622*.

~~~~~~

After centuries of conflict between Byzantium and Persia, by the year 600, the Persians were ruling east of the Euphrates River and Byzantium ruled to the river's west. Many of the end-game battles took place in the Levant, in which the desert areas were a buffer zone of sorts, and hence why Arab mercenary fighters were useful.

In Persia, Zoroastrianism was the official religion of the empire, but many of the aristocracy and administrators under the King of Persia were

Christian. Additionally, many of the Arabs residing in Persia had converted to Christianity. Most Christians in Persia were Dyophysites.

The Euphrates River runs through Syria and Iraq. Dyophysites were predominant to the east of the Euphrates River and Monophysites were predominant to the river's west.

The Byzantine army had been drastically weakened from years of battles, thus, in 604, the Persian army was able to cross the Euphrates and capture towns in western Syria.

In 610, Heraclius became emperor of the Byzantine Empire. He was a charismatic leader who fueled his army with religious passion and his braveness in battle generated enormous loyalty.

Heraclius summoned a priest named Pilipikos, who had previously been in the military and had fought in many battles against Persia. Heraclius made Pilipikos a general and dispatched him from Constantinople to the Levant with a large army. Wearing his priestly garb, and calling himself a Soldier in the Covenant of the Church, Pilipikos led the battles of 610, and thus gave this last phase of the Byzantine-Persian Wars the tone of a religious war.

> *According to Muslim sources:*
> *In 610, Muhammad was commissioned to be the "Messenger of God" and begins the process of conducting holy wars.*

In 613, a Persian general named Shahrbaraz invaded Syria and captured Damascus and Homs, enabling the Persian army to strike further south towards Jerusalem. The Jews, who had long been oppressed by the Byzantines, sided with the Persian army and joined them in the battle for Jerusalem.

In 614, Jews from Tiberias, Nazareth and Galilee joined together with tribes of Arabs and marched on Jerusalem with the Persian army. Customary to Persian military tradition, when the Persians arrived on the outskirts of Jerusalem in 614, Shahrbaraz offered a peaceful transfer of power if the city would surrender. But the Christians of Jerusalem refused.

In response to this refusal, and with help from Jews, the Persian army killed many hundreds of Christians.

> *According to Muslim sources:*
> *In 614, Muhammad advises the Meccans to accept Islam. The Meccans refused and killed many hundreds of Muslims.*

After the Persian army captured Jerusalem, Nehemiah ben Husheil, who had helped rally large forces of Jews to fight with the Persians, was handed control of Jerusalem. Husheil immediately began making arrangements to build the Third Jewish Temple, as instructed in the book of Ezekiel.

In the book of Ezekiel, the prophet Ezekiel is transported in a vision from Babylon to Israel where he envisions a temple to be built (*this is similar to the Muhammad myth in which Muhammad is transported in a vision from Mecca to Jerusalem and thus begins the belief that Jerusalem belongs to Islam*). According to Ezekiel, the Third Jewish Temple is to be built on the Temple Mount and the land will then be restored to the people of Israel.

Christian interpretation of Ezekiel's temple is that it is the temple to be built during the millennial reign of Christ and a symbol of the future and eternal reign of God. The temple to be built on the Temple Mount, and the beliefs attached to it, crossed the realm of both Christianity and Judaism.

After Nehemiah ben Husheil began making arrangements to build the Third Jewish Temple, a Christian revolt occurred in Jerusalem. Nehemiah ben Hushiel and his council members were killed and an intense battle took place among the inhabitants of Jerusalem: Christians vs. Jews.

The number of Christians joining the battle grew very large and they killed many Jews. The Persians eventually regained control of the fighting and they in turn massacred many Christians. In this battle, the Church of the Holy Sepulcher (which was annexed to the tomb of Christ) was destroyed and the True Cross, which Jesus was crucified on, was taken and carried to Ctesiphon, the Persian capitol.

Shahrbarāz allowed thousands of Christians to be tortured by his Jewish aides in the battle at Jerusalem and many Christians converted to Judaism at this time in order to escape death by torture.

Within a year, *in 615*, Persian troops took most of the Levant. Arab tribes in the region were divided, some fought with the Persians, and some fought against them.

The Persians in Jerusalem soon realized there was little to be gained from siding with a small local minority and the attitude towards the Jews quickly changed. The Persians in Jerusalem began persecuting the Jews.

According to Muslim sources:
614-615 *was a period of battles conducted by the Muslims. In 615, fed up with the Muslims, the Quraish tribe of Mecca began persecuting the Muslims.*

The Jews had hoped the Land of Israel would be given to them in exchange for their support. But *in 617*, the Persians fully sided with Christians over the Jews, even though the Jews had helped them capture Jerusalem. The Persians executed the Jewish governor and expulsed all Jews from Jerusalem.

> *According to Muslim sources:*
> *In 617, Arab tribes went to war against each other in Medina. Jewish tribes in Medina split and took different sides. Though some Jews had fought and helped them capture Medina, the victorious Arab tribe turned on the Jews and expulsed all Jews from Medina.*

Records show that the Jews debated the meaning behind the events that had just taken place in Jerusalem. They interpreted that Nehemiah must have been Messiah ben Joseph. This meant that the King Messiah, Messiah ben David, was sure to follow. Jewish leaders declared: "A Prophet is about to arise."

According to Jewish beliefs, Messiah ben Joseph will appear just prior to the coming of Messiah ben David, who will gather the children of Israel, march to Jerusalem, and reestablish the Temple. Prior to this, those in Jerusalem will wage war against Joseph and slay him. But it would then be Messiah ben David who would appear and be the one to bring in the Messianic Age.

This presumption of a coming Messiah caused a flurry of anticipation throughout the Jewish community, but also among the Christians. Christian interpretation of Ezekiel's temple was that it is the temple to be built during the millennial reign of Christ.

As emperor of Byzantium, and protector of holy places, Heraclius made the decision to conduct a campaign against the Persians himself and to recapture Jerusalem. This was historic, as no emperor had gone personally onto the battlefield since Theodosius the Great (r. 379-395).

In 622, after taking a few years to reorganize and train a new army in a way that could better fight the Persians, Heraclius rallied his troops. Dressed in a penitent's attire and bearing a sacred image of the Virgin Mary, Heraclius left Constantinople with tremendous fanfare.

The first battle between the two armies took place in Armenia and ended with an astounding victory over the Persian general Shahrwaraz. Since the Byzantine army had previously been in a fifty-year lull, void of any great success, the news of this victory quickly spread and became legendary.

To facilitate the success of the *Campaign of 622*, Byzantium had proposed a version of monothelitism that **united the Christians** under one doctrine. This unification helped Heraclius recapture Jerusalem and regain control of the Levant.

According to Muslim sources:
In 622, *Muhammad takes his army to Medina. But first, Muhammad* **unites the Arab tribes** *under Islam in order to conquer Medina and take control of the Hijaz.*

In 623, with help from Christians in Armenia who joined his army, Heraclius entered Persia and carried out an attack on the chief holy site of the Zoroastrians (*this is similar to the story of Muhammad smashing the pagan idols in Mecca*).

In 624, Heraclius offered peace to Persia's King Khosrow II, threatening otherwise to invade the heartland of Persia, but Khosrow rejected the offer. Heraclius proceeded to attack the Persian heartland, and using Arab mercenary fighters, captured King Khosrow's military guards, collapsed the Persian army in their heartland, and paved the way to victory in the Levant and in Jerusalem.

According to Muslim sources:
In 624, *Muhammad and his army take part in a series of battles which resulted in the victory over the Hijaz heartland and paved the way for victory in Mecca.*

Heraclius' campaigns of 624 and 625 raged across northern Syria and Iraq where Heraclius engaged in many famous battles. He fully recaptured the territory the Persians had previously taken. Then, following a victory in Nineveh in 627, Heraclius besieged the Persian capital of Ctesiphon where the Persians had taken the Holy Cross. Heraclius then took possession of the Holy Cross.

The "Jewish Revolt against Heraclius" took place from 614-628. This Revolt was a major component of the end-game battles. During those years, the Jews fought alongside Arabs who were fighting with the Persian Army. The creators of Islamic history used many of the Jewish Revolt battles as a source of inspiration, most especially the battles that took place from 625-627.

In 628, Heraclius and his army were victorious in many important battles resulting in the Persians agreeing to a treaty. In 629, the Persians withdrew from the Levant and Heraclius regained full control.

In 629, Heraclius began making his way to Jerusalem, the leader of a conquering army.

According to Muslim sources:
In 628, Muhammad is victorious in many battles resulting in the Quraish
tribe agreeing to a treaty.
In 629, Muhammad begins making his way to Mecca, the leader of a
conquering army.

In **March of 630**, Heraclius marched into Jerusalem.

According to Muslim sources:
In March of 630, Muhammad marched into Mecca.

Heraclius' successful *Campaign of 622* and the battles that followed ended with the recovery of the Levant and Heraclius returned the Holy Cross to Jerusalem. But by 631, the war had left the Byzantine army financially devastated and the Byzantine army withdrew from the Levant.

In 632, Heraclius ended the subsidization of Arabs who were in charge of border defenses. The Arabs were allowed to collect taxes in return for continuing to protect the borders. But the Arabs were at a loss. Byzantine army units were no longer left behind in authoritarian roles. The border Arabs suddenly found themselves without leadership.

According to Muslim sources:
In 632, Muhammad dies, leaving the Muslims without leadership. Just
before his death, Muhammad orders his companions to rally his Muslim
army and go to Syria to fight for Islam. Thus, the armies of Islam
marched out of Arabia in 633 with the goal of spreading Islam, by force if
need be.

In 633, Arabs began settling in the Levant, remnants of the Byzantine-Persian War. These Arabs were primarily pagan and built large cult centers, as the archeological evidence proves.

In an effort to unite the churches once again and settle doctrine disputes, Sergius, Patriarch of Constantinople, endorsed the concept of Monoenergism, which proposed the two natures of Christ had one energy. While this was received favorably at first, Monoenergism soon gathered opponents, among them, the Patriarch of Jerusalem.

The opposition to Monoenergism led Sergius to then propose a new doctrine of Monotheletism, the belief in a single "will" in Christ. Sergius declared the prohibition of the term "one energy" as well as the doctrine of "two wills."

Heraclius supported this new doctrine and put it forth in an edict that was posted in the Hagia Sophia Cathedral in Constantinople in 638.

But the doctrine of Monotheletism was rejected by Christians in the Levant and the edict caused great hostility towards Byzantine leadership. Meanwhile, things in Persia had been in great upheaval and had reached a peak.

Christianity had been recognized by Persia's King Yazdegerd and was fully accepted by the Sasanian dynasty. But in 431, there had been a break with mainstream Christianity due to the announcements of the First Council of Ephesus.

The Council condemned Nestorius, archbishop of Constantinople, for refusing to call Mary "Theotokos" (God Bearer). This condemnation of Nestorius was accepted by the Roman Empire, but the Persian church disagreed. When Nestorius was deposed in Constantinople, a very large number of his followers fled to Persia.

Persian emperors used this opportunity to strengthen the Nestorian position within the church in Persia by eliminating pro-Roman clergymen and replacing them with Nestorians. This was done to make sure Christians in Persia would be loyal to the Persian Empire, and not to the Romans.

Persian King Khosrow (r. 531–579) was tolerant of all religions. Zoroastrianism was the official religion of Persia, but Khosrow was not bothered when one of his sons converted to Christianity. This was the period when Persian rulers began welcoming Christians into their court. After Khosrow, Hormizd IV took the throne, then his son Khosrow II.

Khosrow II's generals had been the ones who began taking control of the Levant starting in 613, but Heraclius' *Campaign of 622* then successfully regained control. After Persia's loss to Heraclius, Persia fell into a period of economic decline, heavy taxation, religious unrest, extreme class division, and large landowners gained increasing power.

The final blow was in 632, when Yazdgerd III became king of Persia. He was very young and never held authority. Persia found itself without leadership.

Again we see the importance of the year 632, the year Muhammad allegedly died, and when the Arabs found themselves without leadership.

In 632, the Arabs in Persia found themselves without Persian leadership. By 636, Christianized Arabs filled the leadership void and took control of Ctesiphon, capitol of Persia. The young king fled Persia and was later killed.

After Heraclius supported the new doctrine and posted it in the Hagia Sophia Cathedral in 638, Christians in the Levant were once again at odds with their Byzantine overlords. It was during this period of intense disputes on doctrine, but also lack of leadership, that Mu'awiya took control and became governor of Syria in 639.

Then, in 641, as Christians were protesting the edict and prohibitions placed by Sergius, Heraclius died.

During this period of transition and turmoil, debate on the nature of Christ intensified. The final decision on doctrine was to be decided at the Sixth Ecumenical Council, but the Council did not meet until the year 680, during which time the debate festered, unresolved.

During this period of division between Christians on the nature of Christ, an Arab Civil War over leadership took place from 656 to 661.

> *According to Muslim sources:*
> *This Arab Civil War is called fitna. Muslim sources say infighting and division caused the split in Islam.*

At this point, Monophysite Christian Arabs were ruling in western Syria and the northern region of today's Israel and Jordan and Dyophysite Christians were ruling in eastern Syria and Iraq. There was a massive divide in the Levant among Christians.

According to Muslim writers of their history, the Arab Civil War began as a series of revolts fought against Ali (Ali ibn Abi Talib). When Ali was murdered in 661, Mu'awiya became ruler/caliph.

> *According to Muslim sources:*
> *The "traditions" of Muhammad say that after Ali ibn Abi Talib migrated to Medina with Muhammad he married Muhammad's daughter, Fatima. Because of this marriage, Ali began taking part in Muhammad's caravan raids and robberies and became like a son to Muhammad. Then, years later, after Muhammad's death and after Uthman was murdered, Ali was chosen caliph by Muhammad's followers and Ali moved the capital of Islam from Medina to Kufa, Iraq.*

Muslim writers of their history had to create a solution to the fact that Medina and Mecca did not exist at the time their version of Islamic history supposedly began. So, they created the story of Ali moving the capital of Islam from Saudi Arabia to Iraq.

Allegedly, according to Muslim sources, Muhammad and his followers fought enormous battles ending with the conquest of Medina and Mecca and the unification of Arab tribes under Islam.

Allegedly, according to the Muslim creators of their history, the men in Muhammad's army had all converted to Islam before invading the Levant.

But according to actual evidence, the Arabs who entered the Levant in the 600s came from the desert borders of Syria, Jordan and Israel and were pagan. The Arabs who originally took control over these Arabs were Christian Arabs like Mu'awiya.

In 680, the Sixth Ecumenical Council met and the doctrine of Christ's "two separate natures" was decreed. The Monophysites, who believed the two natures were miraculously joined, were considered to be *religiously misguided*.

In 680, Mu'awiya died.

According to Muslim sources:
In 680, Hussein ibn Ali, son of Ali, was killed. Hussein ibn Ali's son, Ali ibn Hussein, claimed he was the rightful caliph. The followers of Ali ibn Hussein declared Mu'awiya and his son Yazid "religiously misguided," thus causing a split among the Muslims.

There were battles for power taking place between Arab Christians to the east of the Euphrates and Arab Christians to its west. Because of doctrine disputes, some refused to pledge allegiance to Mu'awiya's son Yazid. The Dyophysites of Iraq and Persia considered Monophysite Christians to be religiously misguided.

The refusal of allegiance to leadership is allegedly what caused the finalized "split" in Islam, but the split was the disagreement over Christian doctrine.

In the sixth and seventh centuries, there were seven Nestorian-based provinces in Persia and a few bishoprics on the Iraqi desert border. The Nestorian church had legal protection in Persia and Nestorians played an important role in the formation of Arab culture in Persia, most especially in Hira, Iraq where the Christianized Lakhmid Arabs had their base.

During al-Malik's rule (685-705), the coins he produced continued to include Christian symbols, crosses, and depictions of Christian rulers. Later, but still during al-Malik's rule, the "word" muhammad slowly began to appear on coins, but the word continued to remain a Christological term.

Popp (2010) gives various evidence, including inscriptions on coins and their history, showing that al-Malik held the concept that the second coming of Christ was about to take place. Al-Malik supported a new Christian movement that he had hoped would unite all Christians and end the division. According to Popp, this movement was "to be an imperial church in the Iranian [Persian] sense, following the example of the Nestorian Church." (see: pgs. 52-57)

Historically, Byzantine's capitol at Constantinople minted gold coins while Byzantium's Near East province minted coins in copper. With Heraclius deceased, and his heirs banished in 695, al-Malik minted his own gold coins, coins with depictions of Christ. Al-Malik considered himself the rightful successor to the dynasty of Heraclius (see: Popp 2013, p.99, "From Ugarit").

Al-Malik struck coins in Jerusalem, Baalbek (Lebanon), Edessa (Iraq), Aleppo, Homs and Damascus (Syria), Amman (Jordan) and elsewhere in the Levant—all depicting Jesus the Messiah (Popp 2013, p.118, "From Ugarit").

Al-Malik ruled the Levant from 685-705. Muslim sources of Islamic history say he was the 5th Umayyad Caliph, and therefore a Muslim. But the evidence shows al-Malik was Christian.

Al-Malik built roads leading to Jerusalem, including the road from Egypt to Jerusalem. He did this so Christians could more easily make pilgrimages to Jerusalem where the Second Coming of Christ was to take place. Al-Malik commissioned no roads leading to Mecca because there was no Mecca and there was no Islam.

The Abbasids took power in 750, and in 762, they established a new capital in Baghdad, not far from the former Persian royal residence in Ctesiphon. The Abbasids had a close relationship with Buddhists, who were the powers that carried weight in the eastern portion of Persia (in what is now Afghanistan and Pakistan). Up until 809, Buddhist temple leaders held positions of high authority as viziers to the Abbasid caliphs in Baghdad.

We see no evidence of Islam up until this point in time.

The creation of the Quran was a process that didn't begin until after the Abbasids took power. This is confirmed in 813 when the seventh Abbasid caliph Ma'mun (r.813-833) mandated a doctrine stating that the Quran was "created." The Quran had been going through a period of development during Ma'mun's lifetime. He recognized the Quran was not the "words of God" — which is the doctrine that would be declared later to help enforce submission to Abbasid leadership.

Arabic as a written language had been going through a long process of being created and codified, and Ma'mun was aware of this also; the process was taking place during his lifetime. It wasn't until after Ma'mun that rulers began implementing the power of a new religion and a new holy book.

In the 800s, the biography of Muhammad suddenly appeared, and then, Muhammad's "traditions."

> *According to Muslim sources:*
> *Abraham was one of the first Muslims. Abraham and his son Ishmael built the kabba in Mecca, which is a shrine built upon a rock. After Abraham consecrated the kabba as the spiritual center of monotheism, the first custodians of the kabba were pagans. The pagans made it difficult for Muslims to make the pilgrimage to Mecca during the early years of Islam.*

Both Jewish and Christian scholars have traced the movements of Abraham. Abraham is firmly established in Mesopotamia and Canaan, never in Saudi Arabia.

As far as why Muslims did not make pilgrimages to Mecca, it was not because pagans prevented them from doing so; it was because Mecca did not exist at the time Muslim writers of their history say it did. This story of pagans preventing Muslims from making pilgrimage is yet another "backstory" created to explain why no one made pilgrimages to Mecca.

But we do see that the creators of Islamic history used some fact-based events when creating Islamic history. When the Persians took control of Jerusalem in 614, the Persians made pilgrimage *to Jerusalem* difficult.

Muslim sources of Islamic history created Mecca as their site of Islamic pilgrimage, but this idea of pilgrimage was based on traditions that were occurring in the Levant.

The rituals now associated with the *haj* at *mecca* (*mecca* being the Aramaic word for valley) are remnants of the pagan water cults in the Negev Desert of today's Israel. The word *haj* is a Hebrew word that means feast. The water cult rituals culminated with a feast.

The pagan Arabs chose a valley (mecca) in the Negev of Israel where annual rains occurred as the location for their water cult rituals. Arabs had been residing in the Negev of Israel for centuries.

More pagan centers were built after the final stage of the Byzantine-Persian Wars. During Abd al-Malik's rule, more than 50 pagan cult centers were built and they were actively being used until the year 770 (Nevo 1985).

It was not in Mecca in Saudi Arabia that the Arabs created a large pagan center, it was in the Negev Desert of Israel. Annual rains would flood the valley (*mecca*) and form a temporary lake. Pagan Arabs made pilgrimages to celebrate this temporary water buildup. They would circle a stone, drink from the water buildup, and they would run between the hills to simulate and celebrate the water runoff.

The authors of Muhammad's traditions and Islamic history took these pagan rituals when they created their backstory for the Haj in Saudi Arabia, but these rituals began in the Negev where large pagan centers were built. These rituals were incorporated into Islam as Islam was being created.

Today, Muslims who do the Haj do the same rituals as the Arab pagans did for their rain cults in the Negev. They circle the *kabba*, the cube-shaped shrine that covers a stone. They run the *wadi* to represent a rush of water from a rainstorm. There is a pause, the "halting" until dawn at the hill of *Quzah*. The halting represents the culmination of water runoff. *Quzah* is the name of the pagan god of the rainstorm, but later, for Islam, the name *Quzah* was given to one of the hills at Mecca. The pagan god *Quzah* fired hailstones at demons. Today, Muslims throw stones at Satan as one of the rituals of the Haj.

The *kabba* shrine at Mecca is a cube. Muslims consider it to be the House of God. This is identical to the Jewish Tabernacle. The holiest site in Judaism is a cube-shaped chamber that contained the Ark of the Covenant, which held the stone tablets of the Ten Commandments. The *kabba* is a cube-shaped shrine that holds a stone.

The Jewish Tabernacle was defined by four pillars that held up a cloth veil that covered the cube. A cloth veil covers the *kabba* in Mecca and this cloth is changed once a year during the annual Haj. In Judaism, the cloth is changed once a year, on Yom Kippur. On Yom Kippur there was an animal sacrifice. At the Haj, there is an animal sacrifice.

The Holy of Holies is the inner room of the Tabernacle and the temples that took the Tabernacle's place, starting with Solomon's Temple. Certain branches of Christianity also have the tradition of the Holy of Holies, such as the Eastern Orthodox Church and the Ethiopian Orthodox Church. Inside their churches stands a ciborium, a canopy supported by columns, symbolizing the Holy of Holies. The Tabot, a shrine that holds a replica of the stone tablets of the Ten Commandments is kept inside and is covered with a cloth, just like the *kabba* shrine is covered with a cloth.

The main communities who possessed holy books during early Arab rule were the Jews, the Christians, and the Zoroastrians. When creating the new Islamic religion and holy book, the creators merged beliefs and traditions from these established religions to make the new religion more acceptable. And, by saying certain activities were things Muhammad did, these rituals became Islam-a-cized.

The Quran doesn't give any information on how to be a Muslim. *Hadith* had to be created to detail what Muslims are supposed to do to practice their religion. *Hadith* was created during the Abbasid period. Because the Abbasids originated in Persia, Zoroastrianism greatly influenced the creation of Islam.

The Islamic five prayers were taken directly from the five Zoroastrian prayers.

The Muslim prayer *farg* starts near dawn; the Zoroastrian *havan* starts minutes prior to sunrise. The Muslim prayer *zuhr* starts just after noon; the Zoroastrian *rapithvan* starts at approximately 12:30. The Muslim prayer *asr* starts in the late afternoon; the Zoroastrian *uziren* starts at approximately 3:30. The Muslim prayer *maghrib* starts just after sunset; the Zoroastrian *aevishuthrem* starts minutes after sunset. The Muslim prayer *insha* starts around nightfall with a time limit sometime in the middle of the night; the Zoroastrian *ushan* is from midnight to approximately 35 minutes before sunrise.

Early Islamic literature on laws, purity, and behavior, came directly from Zoroastrian treatises. These include: *The Book of a Thousand Judgments*, which was the legal system of the Sasanians of Persia; *The Book of Duties*, which defined a person's duties from birth to death; and *Laws against the Demons*, which included instructions on dogs, menstruating women, washing and burying a corpse, and other instructions.

The Abbasids were Persian in culture and their administrators and high-ranking leaders were Persian. The above-mentioned Persian treatises were the prototype for Islamic treatises. The Islamic book on jurisprudence, which is titled *Reliance of the Traveler: Tools for the Worshipper*, which is an Islamic Law manual, used Persian laws and commentaries as its prototype. *Reliance of the Traveler* gives instructions on purification, prayer, clothing, menstruating women, washing and burying a corpse, instructions on dogs, burial instructions, and more—exactly as the Persian Zoroastrian treatises do.

Most of the "oldest" mosques we find today were not originally mosques. They were martyriums and churches. Martyriums are memorial structures that enclose the tombs of Christian saints and martyrs.

In the fifth century, round towers came into use in Syria and were attached to martyriums and churches (Gietmann & Thurston 1907). Muslims take credit for the creation of the minaret, but this is false. Martyriums and churches with round towers were converted into mosques, thus giving the false impression that Muslims created mosques with tower-minarets.

Jewish temple-synagogues were also converted into mosques.

Before 200 AD the orientation of the Jewish temple was arbitrary (Binder, Olsson & Runesson 2010; Richardson 2004). The Jewish practice of sacrifice ended after the Second Temple period and the reading of the Torah replaced it. Over time, the Torah shrine developed and it became the focal point of the temple-synagogue. The Torah shrine took the form of a niche or an apse and usually rested at the center of a wall.

When Muslims converted temple-synagogues into mosques, the niches and apses remained, thus causing confusion in later centuries when it was discovered that their orientation was not towards Mecca. These old mosques did not face Mecca because they were originally temple-synagogues.

Many churches included a fountain for baptism or for symbolic foot washing. Jesus washed His disciple's feet at the Last Supper. But temple-synagogues also included water fountains. Although the practice of sacrifice had ended, which was one of the purposes of water fountains at the temple, to purify the sacrifice, Jews continued to have purity concerns. Temple-synagogues included water fountains.

This is why we see the presence of water fountains in early mosques. These "old" mosques were not originally mosques. They were churches and Jewish temple-synagogues converted into mosques.

Floor plans from two mosques in Iraq, allegedly built in the early 700s, one in Wasit and the other near Baghdad, have their *qibla* (Islamic prayer direction) oriented much too far north of Mecca; they face westerly (Creswell 1969; Crone & Cook 1977). Mecca is south of these mosques.

A mosque in Kufa, Iraq, allegedly constructed in 670, also does not have its *qibla* facing Mecca (Creswell 1958, 1969; Crone 1980; Crone & Cook 1977).

According to Muslim sources, Ali married Muhammad's daughter, became like a son to Muhammad, and later left Medina to establish the capital of Islam in Kufa. If this is true, all mosques in Kufa should have faced Mecca.

These three "earliest" mosques in Iraq did not face Mecca not only because there was no Mecca established yet, but because these buildings were originally not mosques.

The floor plan of the Wasit mosque is identical to the floor plan of the Jewish temple. This mosque was a Jewish temple-synagogue converted into a mosque. This means the "mosque" is dated incorrectly.

Historically, Kufa was inhabited by Jews—from 722 B.C. until modern times. Kufa was a thriving Jewish community at the time Muslim sources say the Kufa mosque was built. The mosque in Kufa did not face Mecca because it, too, was most likely a temple-synagogue.

Babylon (Iraq) was the birthplace of the Hebrews and was the birthplace of Abraham. In 722 B.C., the northern tribes of Israel had been defeated by Assyria and Jewish tribes had been taken to Iraq. Jewish scholars produced the Babylonian Talmud between 500-700 AD. Iraq was flourishing with Jews during the period these alleged mosques were built.

By World War I, Jews continued to account for one third of Baghdad's population. Just south of Baghdad, near Wasit mosque, there existed a major Jewish center right up until modern times. In that same area, during Saddam Hussein's presidency, the Iraqi government refurbished the Jewish tombs of Ezekiel the Prophet and Ezra the Scribe. Sunni leadership in the Arab world were very upset with the Iraqi government for doing so.

After the 2003 invasion of Iraq, the tomb of Ezekiel the Prophet was turned into a mosque. In all likelihood, at some future date in time, this mosque will be called one of the oldest mosques in Iraq. Its Jewish history will be erased.

Al-Aqsa mosque in Jerusalem was allegedly built in 709. Its construction is believed to have begun under Abd al-Malik (r.685-705) and completed by his son, al-Walid. But al-Aqsa mosque did not originally have an orientation towards Mecca (see: Gibson 2011).

Abd al-Malik and his sons were Christian, as coins and other evidence attest. Al-Aqsa mosque was not originally a mosque. It was turned into a mosque, as was St. John the Baptist's Basilica in Damascus, now called the Umayyad Mosque (and said to be one of the oldest mosques in the world).

These "oldest" mosques were churches, martyriums and temple-synagogues. Therefore, the dating of the mosques is incorrect.

The Dome of the Rock

We are told the Dome of the Rock was completed in 691-692 and that it is an "Islamic Shrine." But the Dome of the Rock's octagonal design, its interior structure, and its mosaics, were taken directly from the most important churches of early Christendom.

Octagonal and round architecture was first used by Christianity as martyriums, memorial structures that enclose the tombs of saints and martyrs.

These martyriums transitioned into structures that were used for Christian worship and sacraments. History of baptisteries also show a preference to the round and octagonal form because these designs gave maximum interaction between the observer and the sacraments being performed inside at the structure's center.

By the fifth century, domed churches with an octagonal design became a standard architectural form used to mark sacred locations and important Christian memories in the Holy Land (see also: Davies 1962; Jensen 1997). Examples are the Church of the Seat of Mary and the Church of the Holy Sepulcher.

The Church of the Seat of Mary was built around 450 on the road between Jerusalem and Bethlehem. The focal point of the church is a flat, protruding rock where Mary once rested, thus marking an important Christian memory in the Holy Land. An octagonal viewing area was built to surround the center focal point so it could be easily viewed from the outside.

The Church of the Seat of Mary was turned into a mosque around the year 850.

Like the Church of the Seat of Mary, the Dome of the Rock was built as an octagon to have multiple views of its interior, but most interesting is that the Dome of the Rock was constructed using the exact measurements and design as the Church of the Holy Sepulcher (Creswell 1924, 1958).

According to Eusebius (c.339), in his *Church History*, when building the Church of the Holy Sepulcher, the builders were instructed to use an overlay of gold on the domed roof to cause the "building to glitter as if it were with rays of light." The church was also designed to give "passers-by on the outside a view of the interior which could not fail to inspire astonishment." (p.1317-3271 Eusebius)

The Dome of the Rock has this identical gold domed roof and multiple openings to allow passers-by a view of the interior.

The Church of the Holy Sepulcher had been destroyed by the Persians in 614, and at that time, remnants of the tomb of Christ and the True Cross were taken to Ctesiphon, the Persian capitol. In 627, Heraclius destroyed the Persian army in Ctesiphon, recaptured the True Cross, and in 630, he returned it to Jerusalem.

It is possible, since the Dome of the Rock was built using the exact measurements and design as the Church of the Holy Sepulcher, that the Dome of the Rock was originally commissioned to commemorate the return of the True Cross, or to house the True Cross.

When churches were later turned into mosques, their frescoes and mosaics were whitewashed or covered with new construction. Those with the octagonal shape, with their windows and doors placed for optimal viewing of the interior, had their windows and doors sealed over when they were turned into mosques. With their Christian highlights removed, they were then declared to be Islamic structures.

After the Persians destroyed of the Church of the Holy Sepulcher, only the basilica portion was rebuilt. In the year 930, this basilica was converted into a mosque.

The years during which the Dome of the Rock was being built were a period of upheavals in official Christian doctrine. Heraclius had posted a new doctrine in the Hagia Sophia Cathedral in Constantinople in 638, but this doctrine was rejected by Christians in the Levant and the debate over the nature of Christ intensified.

The Byzantine-Persian War had left Byzantium financially devastated and had opened the door to new leadership in the Levant. Persia, too, was in upheaval and was leaderless due to an impotent child King. Local Monophysite Christians began ruling in western Syria while Dyophysites began filling leadership roles in Iraq.

In 680, the Sixth Ecumenical Council met and decreed the doctrine of Christ's "two separate natures." This edict caused Monophysite Christians to be persecuted.

Necipoğlu (2008) points out that the Dome of the Rock began being built under Mu'awiya. Coins and official inscriptions during this period depict crosses and Christian mottos and attest that Mu'awiya was Christian (see: Popp 2011; Popp 2013 "From Ugarit").

But due to the financial burdens that resulted from the Byzantine-Persian War, and leadership upheavals in the war's aftermath, it was Abd al-Malik who completed the Dome of the Rock's construction.

Just as Heraclius had placed his accepted doctrine on the Hagia Sophia, al-Malik placed his accepted doctrine on the Dome of the Rock. Coins and other evidence suggest that al-Malik believed the Second Coming of Christ was about to take place and that he was attempting to unite Christians before End Times (see: Popp 2013 "From Ugarit").

In the Bible, Zechariah received eight visions (Zech 1:1–6:15), four messages (7:1–8:23), and two oracles (9:1–14:21) regarding the future reign of a Messiah. Zechariah spoke of the day when Jerusalem would be plundered by its enemies. This plunder would take place just before the appearance of the Messiah. The Persians had plundered when they captured Jerusalem, thus leaving many to believe the Messiah was coming.

According to Zechariah, after the plunder of Jerusalem, Jesus will descend from heaven and the Lord will go out as "a warrior prepared for battle." A coin minted during al-Malik's rule depicts an apocalyptic Jesus with a flaming sword. As in Zechariah, Jesus is depicted as a warrior on al-Malik's coins (see: pgs. 107-8, Popp 2013 "From Ugarit").

In Zechariah, Jerusalem will become the capital of the world during the millennial reign of Christ and everyone will come to worship Him (14:16).

This is why al-Malik built roads to Jerusalem. Al-Malik anticipated the millennial reign of Christ.

The Dome of the Rock follows the standard floor plan of churches in early Christianity. There is a section for the shrine of the Tabot, which is a replica of the tablets of stone with the Ten Commandments written on them. The middle area is for sacred rites and sacraments. Worshippers stand in the square outside and follow the services through the various open doors.

The Dome of the Rock has this exact design.

The innermost portion of the Dome of the Rock has twelve columns. This was a standard design for early churches. The twelve columns represented the twelve disciples of Jesus.

Necipoglu (2008) notes that the history of the Dome of the Rock was "veiled" by later Islamic myths. These myths were written by Muslim authors centuries later, long after the Dome of the Rock was built.

One of these mythical traditions is Muhammad's flight to heaven, which allegedly took place at the Temple Mount. But this myth was taken directly from Judaic and Christian traditions and the Islamic version was created some 200 years after Muhammad, during the period when Islamic history was being created and elaborated upon.

The Dome collapsed in 1015 and was rebuilt in 1022. Changes were made to it at that time. Then the Dome of the Rock was significantly altered again during the Ottoman period. The Ottoman Empire ruled Jerusalem from 1516-1917.

Never forget, the Hagia Sophia, the most important cathedral in Constantinople, and the seat of the Byzantine patriarch, was turned into a mosque under Ottoman rule. Muslims turned important churches into mosques.

The Dome of the Rock was changed again in 1959. Jordan had annexed the territories it had captured in the 1948 war and the Dome of the Rock has been under full Muslim control since that time. The Waqf (Islamic Trust) has control over the buildings on and around the Temple Mount, including the Dome of the Rock and al-Aqsa mosque.

No archaeological excavations have been allowed on the Temple Mount during modern times.

Al-Aqsa mosque was built on top of Jewish structures. In 1927, al-Aqsa mosque collapsed during an earthquake. During renovations, two photographers went inside the rubble and documented remnants of a Jewish Temple inside and under al-Aqsa mosque. Thankfully, the photos taken in

1927 still exist (see: Ben-David 2015), because today, since Muslims have full control over this site, those discoveries are gone, removed by the Waqf.

Since gaining full control over the Temple Mount area, Palestinians are banned from acknowledging there was ever a Jewish Temple in Jerusalem. It has been removed from their history books.

In 1996, the Waqf acquired a permit to use Solomon's Stables at the Temple Mount as an "alternative" place of worship on "rainy" days. But as soon as they obtained the permit, the Waqf began building a Mega Mosque, the largest mosque in Israel. This mosque has strengthened the Muslim claim over the Temple Mount—which was the real purpose of building the mosque.

In 1999, in the middle of the night, the Waqf brought in bulldozers at the southeastern corner of the Temple Mount and bulldozed the area. They dug a deep, wide pit, destroying whatever was there (see: Shragai 2012).

In 2015, new flooring was constructed inside the Dome of the Rock, ordered by the Waqf. Israeli authorities were outraged that the new construction of flooring may have destroyed something of archeological value. The old flooring had ancient geometric patterns which some researchers believed held clues to where the Ark of the Covenant was buried.

The Dome of the Rock is positioned at the Temple Mount on the site of the First and Second Jewish Temples. The First Jewish Temple is believed to have housed the Ark of the Covenant.

If the flooring of the Dome of the Rock did not offer a clue to where the Ark of the Covenant was buried, the original flooring most probably marked the position of the Tabot.

Most traditional churches in the Levant included at their center a shrine for the Tabot, a replica of the Ten Commandments. In all likelihood, this was what the Waqf destroyed when they reconstructed the flooring of the Dome of the Rock.

The Waqf would not allow Israeli researchers to conduct research on what was under the new flooring before the removal and construction took place. The Waqf did not want the truth about the Dome of the Rock revealed.

The dedication inscription on the Dome of the Rock had given credit to the Abbasid caliph Ma'mum (r. 813-833), but in 1864, it was discovered that *under that inscription*, the name Abd al-Malik was inscribed as the one who completed the Dome of the Rock. Al-Malik was a Christian (see: Popp 2010; Popp 2013 "From Ugarit").

Abd al-Malik minted gold coins depicting the symbol of the founding of Israel through Jacob on one side, and on the other, the depiction of Christ as *Pantocrator* (p.67, Popp 2010; see also: Appendix "The years 633-833).

Christ the *Pantocrator* is Christ holding the book of the Gospels in his left hand and bestowing a blessing with his right.

Al-Malik blended Jewish and Christian symbolism in his coins and inscriptions. Christians considered themselves to be the successors to the Jews. The Israelites had broken the Old Covenant. Jesus established a New Covenant, one that forgives past sins and allows people to renew their relationship with God.

The writings of two theologians, Arius and Origen, were cited in debates during the period of the building of the Dome of the Rock. Arius had argued that it did not seem fitting that God should have a son and Arianism emerged from the debate on the Trinity. Origen wrote roughly 2,000 treatises and argued the Trinity was not an equality.

The inscriptions on the Dome of the Rock talk about the Servant of God, the Praised One, and the Messenger of God. Vast amounts of literature using these identical terms were written before and during the time the Dome of the Rock was being built. Their presence on the Dome of the Rock had nothing to do with Islam.

Abd allah means "Servant of God" and is connected to both Christianity and Judaism. We see this most especially in Isaiah. There are four Servant Songs in Isaiah. They describe the service, suffering, and exaltation of the Servant of the Lord, the Messiah.

Isaiah 40 through 66 talks about the one who is designated as the Servant of God; the one through whom God will accomplish his purposes. This entity, the "one" who is designated as the Servant of God, has been debated for centuries as to whether the Servant is Christ, or whether the Servant is the nation of Israel.

In ancient copies of the bible, whether in Hebrew or Aramaic, the word Messiah is used in the Servant Songs: "Behold, My Servant, Messiah."

Isaiah also refers to this servant as God's "chosen one." The "word" muhammad, long before Islam existed, meant God's "chosen one" and God's "praised one."

Luxenberg (2010) establishes an evolving process of the word muhammad, which included intermediate stages of transition. Luxenberg divides the period that took place before the creation of Muhammad (the man) into three divisions of transition: Muhammad I, Muhammad II and Muhammad III. His "Muhammad I" category is the period before the word muhammad was ever used as a person.

Before and during the construction of the Dome of the Rock, linguistic and other evidence proves that the word muhammad meant "praised be" and was used to describe Jesus: Praised be the Servant of God = muhammad-un abd-allah.

According to Ohlig and Puin (2010) it was not until the 800s that the word muhammad began to depart from its original connection to Jesus (p.10). Up until the 800s, the word muhammad was never used as a name for a person and there had been nothing written about a man named Muhammad, nor an Arab prophet. It is during the 800s that Islamic history began to be created, and with it, a prophet.

In Judaism, the servant in the Servant Songs is identified as the nation of Israel. Isaiah contains an account in which world leaders will cry aloud in the messianic age and Israel's neighbors will be stunned when their age-old judgment of the Jews is proven wrong. In the End Days, the gentiles will discover that the Jews were, all this time, faithful to the one true God. There is no God but God.

Christians in the Levant argued against the Jewish interpretation of Isaiah 53. The Church used Isaiah 53 to demonstrate the authenticity of the Gospels. They argued that this chapter proves that Christ's death was prophesied in the Hebrew Scriptures. Syrian missionaries fervently used Isaiah 53 to proclaim that the Hebrew prophet Isaiah predicted the advent of Christianity centuries before the birth of Christ.

There are 28 biblical passages in the Old and New Testament which teach there is Only One God. In the Servant Songs, there are four specific instances: Isaiah 43:10-11; 44:6-8; 45:21; and 46:9. The Servant Songs focus on the work of God's servant and describe the servant as God's "chosen one."

Elsewhere in the Bible, Abraham and Moses are also called God's servants and the early followers of Jesus connected the servant with Jesus, the Messiah.

These words, including *abd allah*, servant of God, were centuries old Judeo-Christian terminology—long before the creation of Islam. Their presence on the Dome of the Rock had nothing to do with Islam and were not referring to a man named Muhammad.

The *Didache*, the teachings of the apostles about Christian practices, also speaks of the "Servant of God," as does the *Martyrdom of Polycarp*. The *Martyrdom of Polycarp* is a letter written by one of the apostles. Both texts were highly read by people living in the Levant and both speak of the "Servant of God."

The *Martyrdom of Polycarp* used the phrase *"praised servant"* when referring to Jesus.

Long before Islam existed, the word muhammad meant "chosen" and "praised."

"*Praised servant* of God" are words used on the Dome of the Rock, muhammad-un abd allah-i, but these words had nothing to do with a man or prophet named Muhammad, the words were referring to Jesus.

Ohlig (2013) says: "Coins make it clear that for a long time muhammad was not a name, but a motto, which puts the value of the Messiah Jesus, son of Mary—as in the inscription on the Dome of the Rock—right at the center of this both religious and political concept." (p.10)

The Dome of the Rock is considered to be an Islamic shrine, but it was never Islamic.

Why is this so important? Because Muslims use the Dome of the Rock as their claim to Jerusalem.

The original inscriptions were specifically Judeo-Christian and were meant to clarify a stance on Christ's nature and the Trinity. An inscription on the Dome of the Rock states:

Do not introduce anything into your religion and do not say anything about God but the truth. The messiah Jesus the son of Mary is but a messenger of God and His word which He gave to Mary and a spirit of His. And trust God and His messengers and do not say three, desist! It is better for you for God is one God only, how can it be that he has a child? The messiah is not ashamed to be a servant to God.

What later became the Islamic *tawhid* also appears on the Dome of the Rock: "There is no God but God." But at the time the Dome of the Rock was built and completed, this statement had nothing to do with Islam.

Tawahedo (a form of the word *tawhid*) was a Christian statement of the Oneness of God. Moreover, an inscription on the Dome of the Rock that reads *allahu ahad* translates in Hebrew as *adonai echad*, the Lord is One, which is the Jewish declaration of faith.

What Muslims call the *tawhid*, "there is no God but God," was simply a part of the thinking and statements of the time and not an Islamic credo.

Pine (1984) points out that "la ilah illa allah" and "la ilah illa huwa" (versions of 'there is no God but God') were translations of religious slogans that were used in Judeo-Christian debates for many centuries, long before Islam existed.

Yet Muslims believe that the *tawhid*, the declaration of one God, distinguishes Islam from other religions and makes Islam superior.

Muslims raise their index finger, symbolizing one, when they pray. The Islamic State (ISIS) uses the "tawhid finger," the one finger gesture as their symbol of power and exclusivity over other religions.

But the inscription on the Dome of the Rock declaring there being only one God had nothing to do with Islam. Previous to the creation of Islam the phrase "there is no God but God" was frequently used.

During this period, Jesus was referred to as "rasul allah wa abd allah" (messenger and servant of God). This was a religious slogan referring to Jesus.

Luxenberg (2010) points out that mistranslations of the script on the Dome of the Rock were made "because scholars in the Western schools of Arabic and Islamic studies, arriving rather late on the scene, have uncritically put their trust in the traditional Arabic philology, despite the well-known principles of the historical-critical methods. These scholars have been deeply influenced by the strict classical rules of Arabic grammar, which in fact began around the end of the eighth century." (pgs. 131-139)

In other words, translators are mis-translating inscriptions on the Dome of the Rock. They are not reading the inscriptions in the language and style of writing that was used at the time the Dome of the Rock was inscribed. They are placing a system of Arabic into it *that did not exist* at the time the Dome of the Rock was built or inscribed (details on Arabic later).

The Dome of the Rock was completed in 691-692. Consider the following:

Mu'awiya died in 680. The Arab infighting that took place from 680-692 ended with the defeat of two challengers to the Umayyads: Hussein ibn Ali, who was killed in 680, and al-Zubair, who was killed in 692. But the lives of these men seem to be based more on myth than fact. No evidence has been found that supports claims that Ali or Zubair existed in the way described in the Muslim sources. But, "infighting" did indeed take place as the Arabs scrambled for power after Mu'awiya died.

The years 680-692 were also a period of upheavals in official Christian doctrine. Dyophysites were gaining power and Monophysites were being persecuted.

According to Muslim writers of their history, Hussein ibn "Ali" challenged the Umayyad dynasty and Ali's alleged murder in 680 is the Muslim source of the split in Islam: Shi'a vs. Sunni. But it was Mu'awiya who died in 680 and the "split" was within Christianity: Monophysite vs. Dyophysite.

The years just prior to Mu'awiya's death consisted of incredibly intense and hostile debates on the nature of Christ, debates that were supposed to end with the decision of the Sixth Ecumenical Council. But when the Council decided against Monophysitism, the debate intensified in the Levant.

The decision on the nature of Christ made by the Sixth Ecumenical Council fully split Byzantine East from Byzantine West, but it also divided

Christians in the Levant. The "split" in Islam wasn't about Islam, it was the split within Christianity.

Al-Malik completed the Dome of the Rock, and as were the rulers before him, al-Malik held the title of *amir al-mu'minin*, translated as "the religious commander of the faithful." This is how the term *amir* came into being. Byzantine emperors, including Heraclius, were also called *amir al-mu'minin*. This was a Christian principle and not an Islamic one.

Mu'awiya had declared himself protector of the Tomb of John the Baptist and his Basilica. Al-Malik continued this tradition of being the religious commander and when the Dome of the Rock was completed, al-Malik defended the position that Jesus was a messenger and Servant to God and not the son of God.

Popp (2013) concluded from his research that al-Malik was focused on "the anticipation of the end of the world in Jerusalem" and that al-Malik's actions were an attempt to unify Christians before End Times (p.120, Popp 2013 "From Ugarit"; see also: Popp 2010).

Popp (2013) states: "Within the framework of his eschatological ideas he [al-Malik] saw the place at the Rock as the location of the last judgment. Before Judgment Day comes, the unity of all Christians is to be restored...The muhammad (chosen one) is Jesus... [Jesus] is the servant of God (abd allah)" (p.79 "From Ugarit").

Considering the events taking place during the time the Dome of the Rock was constructed, al-Malik, being the religious commander of the faithful, announced a stance on Christian doctrine. The inscriptions on the Dome of the Rock take the position that Jesus was God's messenger and his servant.

The inscriptions also take a stance on the Trinity, and were an attempt to put an end to centuries of debate by using the words: "Do not say three...for God is One."

According to Muslim sources of Islamic history, after al-Malik's death, his two sons followed him as caliphs. Al-Malik's sons were **al-Walid** and **Sulayman**.

Al-Malik completed the Dome of the Rock. He anticipated the Second Coming of Christ. **Al-Walid** means new birth, as in the rebirth of Christ. **Sulayman** means Solomon. Solomon built the First Temple, which was a monument to God and the Covenant with God.

The Old Testament ends with the children of Israel waiting for a Messiah. The News Testament offers a New Covenant.

For al-Malik, the Dome of the Rock represented the New Covenant with God as offered in the New Testament. Al-Malik's inscriptions clarify that there is only one God and Jesus is His messenger.

Van Ess (1992) points out that there was an existing Jewish belief that God rested upon His throne upon the rock at the Temple Mount after the Creation and He left His footprint there.

Jesus was crucified at the Temple Mount and this location was where his ascension took place. Christians believe that Jesus, too, left his footprints there.

Much later, after Islam was created, the beliefs surrounding the Temple Mount were Islam-a-cized. The myth was created that this was the rock in which Muhammad ascended into heaven on a "night journey from Medina to Jerusalem" and that Muhammad left his footprints there.

Words of God? or Man-Made Language?

Muslims are taught that the Quran is the exact words of Allah and therefore divine. And since the Quran is divine, the laws laid out in the Quran must be enforced. This is what Muslims will tell you when they defend Islamic Law.

Imams in mosques around the world teach that the Quran is the exact, unchanging, unaltered words of Allah, and that Allah's words were written down in the classical Arabic you find in the Arabic Qurans that exist today. But this is not possible.

The oldest Qurans in existence show an evolving Quran, one that originated in Aramaic, and one that has changed throughout the centuries. Old Qurans were not written in the "classical" Arabic used in the Qurans of today. Classical Arabic, also called Quranic Arabic, wasn't created until around 150 years after the alleged death of Muhammad.

Muslims will tell you that the Quran was passed down similar to Bedouin poetry, by storytelling and word of mouth, and that this poetry style is the origin of Classical Arabic and the Quran. But since pre-Islamic poetry was never written down until the mid-ninth century, around 200 years after the death of Muhammad, at the exact same time the creators of Islam and the Quran began making the claim that the Quran was similar to Bedouin poetry, how can we possibly consider this claim factual?

There are no references of any kind to pre-Islamic poetry before the mid-ninth century. This sudden appearance of "pre-Islamic" poetry in the mid-ninth century has caused many scholars to believe that pre-Islamic poetry is fake (Warraq 2002, p.38; Husayn 1927; Margoliouth 1925; Mingana 1907, 1920, 1927).

In 1972, a discovery was made in the Great Mosque in Sana, Yemen. Many old Qurans and thousands of Quranic manuscripts were found in the attic while repairs were being made to the mosque. The manuscripts were scientifically dated and authenticated and the dating of these manuscripts started from 671 A.D. The oldest Quranic manuscripts were written in Aramaic.

The "classical" Arabic that was created more than 150 years after the death of Muhammad was never a spoken language. It was a created written language, created specifically for the Quran.

No Muslim, nor any Arabic speaker in the entire world, has ever spoken Classical Arabic as their native language. No one can read or understand Classical Arabic unless they take lessons or study it, just like learning any other second language. Muhammad himself would not understand a word of the Quran if it was read to him.

The "Arabic Quran" was written in a language totally foreign to Muhammad.

Additionally, the Quran has changed, additions have been made, and the Quran has been edited throughout the centuries. Why is this so important? Because Muslims believe they must enforce Islam on the world's population. Barbaric ways of torture and killing are described in the Quran—so Muslims believe Allah sanctions torture and barbaric ways of killing, especially when spreading and enforcing Islam on others.

More than 300 years after the alleged death of Muhammad the concept that the Quran was "divine" was created to give the rulers a tool to control the populations they ruled over. The "Divinity Doctrine" was a turning point in Islam because this is when the fanatical idea of not being able to question anything about the Quran or Islam was put in place. To do so is punishable by death. This Divinity Doctrine has silenced people for many hundreds of years. And now, in our current century, we are beginning to see similar blasphemy laws being put in place in Western countries.

Starting about 1000 B.C., Aramaic began to develop in Syria and became the lingua franca in the Levant, a language that is used as the language between speakers whose native languages are different. Well into the eighth century A.D., Aramaic continued to be the language of the people, the culture, of business and trade, and it was the language of Christian liturgy and missionary work. Aramaic was used for all writings and literature in the region for centuries, even long after the Arab transition to power.

Arab tribes spoke different dialects, often not understood by one another, so Aramaic was also used for communication between tribes who spoke different dialects.

Before the creation of written Arabic, precursor types of Arabic were seen in rock graffiti. These inscriptions were in Dedanite, Lihyanite, Hasaitic, Safaitic and Thamudic dialects and were different from one another. These dialects, when written, consisted mostly of pictograms and were never incorporated into written Arabic.

There was no unification of language among the Arabs, not spoken, nor written.

The missionary work of Christians in the Near East was extremely active and unhindered during the first 100 years of Arab rule. The literature they carried to spread the gospel was in Aramaic.

Later, as Islam began to be created, and written Arabic was being developed, the men trying to read and understand the Quran in Arabic had trouble interpreting the first Qurans. This is because the earliest Qurans were written in Aramaic and as Arabic was being created, and for centuries afterwards, Aramaic words remained in the developing Qurans.

Over time, some of the Aramaic words that remained in the Quran took on new meanings, different from the original Aramaic meanings. They became Arabized, but many other words remained a mystery—unless you read those words as Aramaic.

People who read the first Arabic Qurans immediately began having problems. From 950-1250, hundreds of Muslim "scholars," men who studied Islam and Arabic, and who were trying to make sense of the Quran, wrote about the problems of interpreting the Quran.

Ohlig and Puin (2009) note that the Quran underwent a period of development and changes for about 200 years. Even after written Arabic was created, today's experts in Arabic calligraphy and Quranic paleography estimate that about a fifth of the Quran continued to be incomprehensible because the Quran continued to contain Aramaic words (see: Lester 2002; Luxenberg 2007; Luxenberg 2013; Puin 2002).

Added to the problem of the Quran continuing to be partly in Aramaic, the early Arabic Qurans did not use diacritical marks (markings that distinguish consonants from one another). The early Arabic Qurans also did not have any vowels. Without diacritical markings to distinguish consonants, and no vowels, the Quran was incomprehensible.

The first Qurans written in Arabic did not have vowel markings because a vowel system had not yet been created.

Imagine a word without vowels: bg. Before adding a vowel, this could mean: bag, beg, big, bog or bug. I am simplifying this example, the Arabic vowel system is different, but you can easily see that a word with no vowels can be difficult to interpret.

An Arabic consonant can be changed into a different consonant just by adding one dot, two dots, or three dots. These diacritical markings came to be written and codified at a much later time. Many Arabic consonants have the exact same shape. The only thing that can differentiate one consonant from another is the markings.

An example is that the shape for a "b," "t," "n" and "th" are identical in Arabic. What identifies them is one dot under the shape (making it a "b"); one dot above it (making it an "n"); two dots above it (making it a "t"); or three dots above it (making it a "th"). The first Qurans in Arabic had no dots.

You can see that adding a vowel and consonant markings created many possible variations for just one word. Now imagine an entire Quran written without consonant markings or vowels. That is how the first Arabic Qurans were written.

Grammar, syntax and vocabulary for Quranic Arabic were created and defined in the ninth and tenth centuries. Quranic Arabic was in a constant flux for 150-200 years.

During the first centuries after being written in Arabic, the Quran continued to be *deciphered*. This was because so much of the Aramaic remained. The Aramaic created unfamiliar vocabulary and there were problems with variant interpretations.

A wide range of interpretations and vast amounts of commentaries began to be written on the meaning of the Quran. This caused a major debate to develop. There were those who said the Quran was uncreated and the Eternal Word of Allah, and those who said the Quran had to have been created because they knew about the developments of an evolving Quran and the creation of written Arabic.

Lester (2002) states: "Christians and others latched on to the confusing literary state of the Koran as proof of its human origins. Muslim scholars themselves were fastidiously cataloging the problematic aspects of the Koran—unfamiliar vocabulary, seeming omissions of text, grammatical incongruities, deviant readings, and so on." (p.120)

Under the Caliph Ma'mun, who ruled from 813 to 833, the view that the Quran was "created" became orthodox doctrine. The doctrine that the Quran was created and not the words of God lasted until the end of the 10th century. It was at this time, the late 900s that rulers began to use Islam to control people, and they needed the Quran to be divine in order to do so.

Meanwhile, problems with the Quran continued for many centuries and there were so many different versions of the Quran, that periodically it had to be decided which were acceptable versions. Rulers recognized that without credibility of the Quran, their control was in jeopardy, so Qurans with large variations were destroyed.

Eventually the doctrine that the Quran was the exact words of Allah became the rule and punishable by death if you questioned it. They had to threaten people with death to enforce the Divinity Doctrine, otherwise, too many people over the centuries would have criticized the faults that existed within the Quran.

The Abbasids founded a new, theocratic state. They based "their authority upon legitimacy, exactly as the Sasanians of the Persian Empire had. ...The state became a religious institution." (Goldziher 2013, pgs. 342-3)

The formulation of an established dogma was important to the Abbasid rulers. Then later, this dogma was enforced. A strict intolerance developed towards people with different beliefs and towards people who would not submit to this dogma.

The Yemeni Manuscripts: the oldest Qurans in existence

"...The centrality of the religion under the Abbasids, and its status as a new faith distinct from and opposed to Christianity...meant that the lack of a scripture was a handicap...The more the Arab religion was defined as an incompatible alternative to Christianity, the more pressing became the need for a scripture of its own. ...This scripture had of course to be compiled from the material available." (p.350-1, Nevo & Koren 2003)

A large number of Quranic manuscripts were found in the Great Mosque in Yemen. Carbon dating confirmed the dating and that the manuscripts are not forgeries. Of the more than 40,000 pages of Quranic manuscripts found, 15,000 were restored and 12,000 of these were dated from the 7th and 8th centuries.

The texts differ from copies of today's Quran and show the evolution of the Quran.

Gerd-R. Puin, specialist in Arabic calligraphy and Quranic paleography, and who studied the Yemeni Qurans, concluded that the Quran was an evolving text (see: Puin 2002). Puin says the old Qurans contain Christian biblical stories, but in short form, sort of like a summary. He says the early Qurans were probably written as a tool to be read at a church service (see also: Das 2009).

Puin also pointed out that two tribes mentioned in the Yemeni Qurans, as-Sahab-ar-Rass (Companions of the Well) and as-Sahab-al-Aiqa (Companions of the Thorny Bushes), were not part of Arab pagan tradition. They were Christians. The as-Sahab-ar-Rass lived in pre-Islamic Lebanon and the as-Sahab-al-Aiqa lived in pre-Islamic Egypt (Taher 2000).

Quranic scholars who specialize in Aramaic, Arabic, and Quranic Arabic say that the Quran was originally written in Aramaic and that the word "Quran" is not of Arabic origin. Muslims are taught that the word "quran" is translated from Arabic as "recite." But scholars who specialize in Arabic and Aramaic say the word quran is an Aramaic word that means "a lectionary of scripture," as in, to be read at a Christian service (see: Luxenberg 2007, 2013; Puin 2002; Taher 2000).

The conclusion resulting from non-Muslim scholarship is that the Quran started out as a Christian liturgical book but changed over time as the need for an "Arab" identity emerged. This is also what Christoph Luxenberg, expert in both Aramaic and Arabic, discovered in his research (see: Luxenberg 2007, 2013).

Many Arabs had been Christianized by Syrian Christians who used liturgical books written in Aramaic when they spread the Gospel. Syrian missionaries had gone all the way to China, but also into the Arabian Peninsula (Hackensberger 2004; Luxenberg 2010).

When Syrian missionaries taught Christianity, they used their own writings and copies of the Gospel in Aramaic. Arabic at that time consisted of various dialects but had no written form. The Arabs, too, used Aramaic as their lingua franca.

Luxenberg states, "In its origin, the Koran is a Syro-Aramaic liturgical book, with hymns and extracts from Scriptures... One may see in the Koran the beginning of a preaching directed toward transmitting the belief in the Sacred Scriptures to the pagans ... At its beginning, the Koran was not conceived as the foundation of a new religion." (see: Magister 2004, An interview with Christoph Luxenberg)

Gunter Luling was an expert on the Quran, Islamic origins, Arabic, and the literary texts and written records at the time of Muhammad. Rawandi (2002), who wrote about Luling's research and findings on the Quran, said: "The chief result of Luling's research was that underlying about one-third of the Koran text there are pre-Islamic, anti-trinitarian Christian, strophical hymns, dating from the beginning of the sixth century." (p.654)

Rawandi states: It is "beyond question that the rich Christian Ethiopian hymnody of the early sixth century goes back in the main to a Christian Coptic (Egyptian) original, sometimes word-for-word across hundreds of strophes, the sequence of which is neatly maintained. Frequent misunderstandings ... result from typical misunderstandings of an ambiguous Arabic text minus its diacritical points and vowel strokes." (p.656-7)

By a text "minus its diacritical points and vowel strokes" he is referring to the early Arabic Qurans having no dots to distinguish consonants, and no vowels.

In analyzing the sections of the Quran that describe the creation of Adam and the fall of Satan, Bishai (2002) concludes that Egyptian Christian

(Coptic) texts were the likely source for those sections of the Quran. During the early Christian centuries, Egypt's Copts were well known for their massive production of Apocrypha and writings on the biblical patriarchs. The text of the Apocrypha is believed to be the work of Jewish scholars who assembled in Alexandria, Egypt.

Egyptians had converted to Christianity quickly, and then Egyptian missionaries helped spread Christianity southward into Ethiopia and across to Yemen. Yemen received a double dose of Christianity at the earliest stages of the spread of Christianity, from both Egyptian and Syrian missionaries.

Bishai (2002) states: "Since the early Coptic Church was among the leading churches in early Christendom, it is not surprising to find that many of its apocryphal stories spread throughout the Christian Middle East by way of Abyssinia (Ethiopia). Coptic ideas could have spread...during the Abyssinian occupation of Yemen between 525 and 571 C.E." (p.294)

Das (2009) states: "Islam grew as a political movement... A book like the Quran was required to keep the Muslims united. The Quran is just like a 'status symbol' of Islam, without which Islam would have died...The Quran is purely manmade. Some sort of Divinity was attached to the Quran so that it can command some respect, because it could not stand on its own worth. This way, in acknowledging the claims of the Quran as the direct utterance of the Divinity, the early manipulators had blocked all criticisms, which can otherwise expose it."

The conclusions drawn from reading John Wansbrough's *Quranic Studies* (1977) and *The Sectarian Milieu* (1978) is that the reason why there has never been any Islamic source material from the first 150 to 250 years after Muhammad's alleged death, is that Islam never existed during those centuries.

Ohlig and Puin (2009) noted variations in the Qurans that were found in Yemen's great mosque. Like Luxenberg and many other non-Muslim scholars, they concluded that the Quran was taken from Christian religious writings.

The original version of the Quran, like the word quran itself, which meant a lectionary of scripture, changed over time. As it evolved, archaic behaviors of later rulers were incorporated into it.

A large part of the Quran includes much of the original Christian aspects (though greatly altered to suit Islamic rule). Aaron is mentioned 20 times, Jesus 24 times, Adam 25 times, Noah 33 times, Mary 34 times, and so forth.

The most important people in the Quran are Abraham and Moses. Abraham is mentioned in 245 verses and Moses is mentioned in 502 verses.

The Quran began as a Christian liturgical book written in Aramaic. It was then altered, additions were made, and it evolved into the "Arab" holy book. It became a book that aided rulers in controlling the populations they ruled over.

To Veil or Not to Veil—That is the Question

Mingana (1927) stated: "I am convinced that a thorough study of the text of the Kur'an [Quran] independently of Muslim commentators would yield a great harvest of fresh information. …Syriac [Aramaic] seems to have a much more pronounced influence on the style of the Kur'an… taking the number 100 as a unit of the foreign influences on the style and terminology of the Kur'an, Syriac [represents] about 70 per cent (p.79-80) …There are in the Kur'an many sentences in which the Arabic word used does not fit in with the meaning required by the context, but when compared with its Syriac equivalent its right meaning becomes clear." (p.93)

After the Quran began to be written in Arabic, Aramaic words continued to exist in the Qurans of the 9th through 12th centuries. Islamic "scholars," men who studied the Quran and who tried to interpret its meaning, not realizing that considerable amounts of Aramaic were still included in the Arabic Qurans, attempted to decipher the meanings of the strange words through the context of the sentence or verse.

To this day, interpretations of the Quran continue to be done this way—figuring out the meaning of a word based on the context of the verse.

This leads to many various interpretations. And sometimes, an entire sentence is changed to accommodate an incomprehensible word. This is why many Qurans have "commentaries" explaining what they believe a certain word means, or what a verse means. These translators and people who "interpret" the Quran read Arabic, yet they cannot fully translate or interpret the Quran, hence why they write commentaries. Many commentators of the Qurans in print today use the commentaries and explanations written by Muslim sources from the tenth through twelfth centuries, a period in which there was a flurry of confusion about the Quran and what the verses of the Quran meant.

Hashim Amir-Ali (Ali 1974), who compiled eighteen translations of the Quran dating from 1649 to 1971, found many variations in the most basic of words and sentences, even the *bismallah*, the phrase that prefaces all chapters of the Quran (except one).

To understand more fully, take the word "book." Most every language has a word for book, so there is a word for word exchange when translated. In

French the word for book is libre; in Spanish the word for book is libro, and so forth. With the Quran, about one third of it contains words that do not translate on a word for word replacement basis.

And, some words are incomprehensible.

In Hackensberger (2004), Christoph Luxenberg says: "There is a passage in Sura 24, verse 31, which in Arabic it became, 'That they should beat their *khumurs* against their bags'." Luxenburg points out that the word *khumurs* in Arabic translates as "alcohol." But this creates a sentence that makes no sense. Luxenberg says, "It is an incomprehensible phrase, for which the following interpretation has been sought: That they should extend their kerchiefs from their heads to their breasts."

Luxenberg says: "But if this passage is read in Aramaic, it simply means: They should fasten their belts around their waists." He then relates this to the gospel account of the Last Supper where Christ ties an apron around his waist before washing the Apostle's feet." (see: Hackensberger 2004)

In John 13, Jesus came to the table dressed for the Passover meal. He got up from the supper and laid aside his over cloak and then wrapped a towel around his waist in preparation to wash the feet of his disciples. The act of washing his disciples' feet was to show that he was sent as a servant to man.

Luxenberg's explanation, regarding reading a verse with Aramaic in mind, makes sense because the first Qurans were written in Aramaic and many Aramaic words continue to remain in the Quran.

Some words have slowly, over time, taken on new meaning. The words were Arabized. But other words were not Arabized and remained a mystery; hence, translators and commentators changed the sentence to try to make it work within the context of the verse. Sometimes an entire verse had to be changed or removed to accommodate incomprehensible sentences.

Do not forget, no one speaks the Arabic that is used for the Quran. It is a written language only. Everyone, even native Arabic speakers must learn Quranic Arabic separately from their own native language.

Egyptian Arabic, Moroccan Arabic, Jordanian Arabic, and so forth, are all different and most cannot understand one another's dialect because they are so different from one another. Quranic Arabic is unrelated to any Arabic dialect. Quranic Arabic has a different vocabulary, different grammar system, and a different word formation and structure.

Since the word "alcohol" did not make sense, translators and interpreters chose to change the meaning in a way that worked for them. Different copies of Qurans will have a wide variety of wording for this verse.

This is just one example of many verses that are impossible to translate or interpret. But most troubling about this verse, is that over time, this verse became one of the main verses used to force women to wear the veil and headscarf.

Here are commonly used interpretations of verse 24:31

- M. Ali (1963): And let them wear their head-covering over their bosoms
- A. Ali (1968): That they should draw their veils over their bosoms and not display their beauty
- Sarwar (1982): [Women should] guard their chastity and not show off their beauty except what is permitted by the Law

M. Ali (1963) states in his commentary: "The injunction to wear an over-garment is here given with the object that free women may be distinguished from slaves, so that they may not be annoyed and followed by men inclined to evil."

This explanation is given because during the period in which the first Quran commentaries were written, slaves and prostitutes, most especially prostitutes, would bare their breasts to make it known they were available for hire.

The rationale here is that when Muslims traveled, their women were told to fully cover their breasts and thus show no cleavage, so they would not be mistaken for prostitutes or slaves.

A. Ali (1968) says in his commentary that these were times of constant wars and capture of female slaves. He says Muhammad's wives were asked to wear an outer-garment, an over-cloak, a *jalabiy* or *jilbab*. These are robe-like apparel and most definitely are not a "veil" as we know them today.

Often this robe-like "cloak" was a shawl-like wrap. This shawl, or robe-like cloak, could be pulled around the body, not only to protect them from the elements, but to distinguish themselves as free women, by covering their breasts.

A. Ali (1968) states that, "The need for modesty is the same in both men and women. But on account of the differentiation of the sexes ... a greater amount of privacy is required for women ... especially in the matter of ... the uncovering of the bosom."

Even if we translate this verse as Muslims do today, which often uses the word "veil," it is impossible that the verse is referring to the veil that we see forced upon women today.

A. Ali (1968) says in his commentary to wear what "is most convenient" and refers to the weather conditions and "what you own." If you are poor, or from a lower-class segment of society, you do not own the same type of over-cloak that the wealthy and upper classes owned, so you wear what is "most convenient."

This garment is most definitely not the veil or the burqa that we see forced on women today. Nor is it the headscarf.

Sarwar (1982) translates the verse using the words "what is permitted by the Law." The Quran in Arabic was written sometime between the years 820 to 1000. The Quran developed and changed as written Arabic was being created, adjusted, and formalized.

During that period in which the Quran was being created, and the period when the commentaries on the Quran were being written, prostitutes and slaves exposed their cleavage or dressed scantily so as to be recognizable. Both slaves and prostitutes were available to men for sex. In parts of Iraq and Persia, there were formal written laws prohibiting a female slave to cover herself fully because it would confuse the male population from knowing her "position"—that she was "available" to men for sex.

The Quran does not say a woman must cover her hair. It does not say a woman must cover her head. It does not say she must cover her face. The word for hair in Classical/Quranic Arabic is *shaar*; this word is not used. The word for head is *raas*; this word is not used. The word for face is *wagh*; this word is not used.

If the writers of the Quran wanted the hair, head or the face covered, the writers would have simply used the words for them. There is a word for word exchange for hair, head and for face in Classical/Quranic Arabic. But the words for hair, head and face are not used. Not in Aramaic, and not in Arabic.

So why are veils, *niqab, burqas* and extreme headscarves being forced on women today?

Control. When you control the women, you are controlling about half the population.

The Grand Imam of al-Azhar mosque and university in Cairo, Egypt is a foremost authority in Sunni Islam. Grand Imams of al-Azhar have consistently stated that the headscarf and veil are not a religious requirement. One Grand Imam went as far as banning the *niqab*. Muhammad Tantawi, Grand Imam from 1996-2010 stated in 1996 that: "The *niqab* has no connection with the Islamic religion." He then issued a *fatwa* against wearing the *niqab*.

Al-Azhar has been long considered to be the Oxford or Harvard of Islamic teaching. Muslims from around the world have traditionally gone to al-Azhar to become imams and to study the Quran, *hadith* and Islamic law.

But after the 1960s, Saudi Arabia began using its enormous wealth to promote the Salafi/Wahhabi ideology and began mosque building in many countries throughout the world. Mosques became filled with Salafi preachers in most every country that has mosques. They are the ones preaching the enforcement of veils and headscarves.

Ahmed Muhammad al-Tayib is currently the Grand Imam of al-Azhar. He became Grand Imam after the death of Muhammad Tantawi in 2010.

As the Muslim Brotherhood gained more power, female students were being expelled from universities and women were fired from their jobs if they did not wear the headscarf. They were being removed because of a non-existent religious requirement. In response to this, in May of 2012, al-Tayib endorsed the view that headscarves are not an Islamic requirement.

In the arguments presented, it was stated that the headscarf is not an Islamic requirement or obligation, and that the interpretations and commentaries on the verses in the Quran and the circumstances during which they first appeared had led to the widespread misunderstanding regarding the headscarf and veil. It was pointed out that covering the head, hair or face is not mentioned in the Quran.

Nonetheless, *fatwas* continue to be issued by imams enforcing the veil and headscarf. Even imams in Western countries are issuing *fatwas* enforcing the headscarf and veil.

How Islam is implemented into the modern world

The Saudi system is the system currently being used to spread Islam in the Western world. Their strategy of takeover is based on the *mutawwas* system, proselytizing, starting with the youth, and *ikhwan*, a militant sector used as police. The *mutawwas* and *ikhwan* system was created by Muhammad abd al-Wahhab.

Wahhab was an Islamist preacher in the 1700s. After visiting Medina and Mecca, Wahhab was appalled that the people in those towns were not following what he called "true" Islam. He then travelled to Syria and Iraq and was angered by the notable presence of Shi'a, who he believed do not follow true Islam (see Appendix: "The years 633-833" for more on Shi'a and why they do not follow "Sunni" Islam). Many Bedouin tribes in Arabia were also not practicing Islam, and this, too, enraged Wahhab.

Wahhab was born in the Nejd region of Arabia where Riyadh is located. Medina and Mecca are are in the Hijaz region. In a village just northwest of Riyadh, Wahhab convinced a mob of men to stone a woman for adultery. Before this event, stoning was not a practice, and adultery was never formally punished.

The *amir* of the region ordered Wahhab to be put to death for the murder of the woman, but Wahhab escaped to Dhariyya where he received protection from Muhammad ibn Saud. In 1744, Saud and Wahhab joined forces and Wahhab became the spiritual leader of the Saudi tribe.

Wahhab believed the nomadic Bedouin must be taught to follow Islam. The Bedouin had continued their own traditions and tribal laws, and were not following Islamic laws. Wahhab also believed that the Bedouin's most popular sport, which was raiding and robbing, could be turned into fighting—fighting for Islam. While Wahhab used Islamic puritanism to purify Islam, Saud used puritanical Islam as a system to conquer.

After the death of Muhammad ibn Saud, his son Aziz took his place and in 1773, Aziz took control of Riyadh and made it the Saudi headquarters. Soon after, Aziz and Wahhab dispatched a unit of *ikhwan* (*ikhwan* means brotherhood, as in Muslim Brotherhood). The *ikhwan* went to Iraq and destroyed two Shi'a towns, Najaf and Kerbala, which were important locations of Shi'a pilgrimages.

After Wahhab's death, the *ikhwan* proceeded with Wahhab's goals and took control of Mecca in 1803. While Wahhab's followers captured Mecca, Abdallah, son of Aziz, captured Medina. After much murder and mayhem conducted by the Wahhabis and Saudis, in 1818, units of the Egyptian and Turkish armies entered Arabia. The Saudi and the Wahhabi leaders were captured and taken to Istanbul where they were publicly beheaded.

The Turks then took full control of the Hijaz and the Saudis were restricted to the Nejd. From this point on, there was ongoing massive bloodshed between the Saudi tribe and their rival tribe in the Nejd as they fought to gain power.

The Wahhabis began intensifying the system of *mutawwas*, proselytizing. They taught young boys to read the Quran and learn Muhammad's traditions. The Wahhabis sent *mutawwas* out to teach various clans and Bedouin tribes to behave like Muhammad and to follow the Quran's teachings, but also taught them to be loyal to the Saudi tribe.

Colonies of *ikhwan* were then created and they turned Bedouin nomads into settled people. The Saudis fully supported the *ikhwan* colonies—fanaticism made good fighters against rival tribes.

Wahhabi puritanism was fully enforced under the Saudis: "The prayers that had to be performed five times a day united all the men in the mosques and so kept them well under the control and spiritual discipline of the *mutawwas* ... All the stress was on devotional obedience and it was imposed on them with all the harshness of religious fanaticism. Youth too, came under the control of the *mutawwas*." (p. 64, Van Der Meulen 1957)

In 1912, the *ikhwan* were told to create communes throughout the Nejd. These communes became the prototype for religious militant camps. The Wahhabi leaders filled the *ikhwan* with religious fervor and the Saudis provided the *ikhwan* with weapons and ammunition.

When Mustafa Kamal of Turkey dissolved the Caliphate in the 1920s, Hussein of Trans-Jordan tried to seize the moment; he declared himself Caliph and went to Mecca. In response, ibn Saud mobilized the *ikhwan*. *Ikhwan* units were sent to Trans-Jordan where they massacred a village. Another *ikhwan* unit was sent to Taif, about 50 miles from Mecca, where the *ikhwan* conducted another massacre. This caused great panic in Mecca and Hussein of Trans-Jordan lost control and left. Ibn Saud entered Mecca with an army of *ikhwan* and in January 1926, ibn Saud declared himself King of the Hijaz.

The *mutawwas* system and the *ikhwan* had taken full control of the Nejd, now Wahhabism was introduced into the Hijaz.

"Smoking, music-making, the consumption of alcohol...were strictly forbidden and performance of the five daily ritual prayers in the mosque was made obligatory. When the azan, the call to prayer sounded, police patrols with long canes would stride through the streets shouting: To prayer! To prayer! and beat upon the closed shutters and doors of the shops in the markets to frighten any who might be hiding there. Those who did not walk in the direction of the mosque were helped on their way. Five times a day the town was like a town of the dead... Often on leaving the mosques, the names of the faithful were checked." (p. 110, Van Der Meulen 1957)

After oil was discovered in Saudi Arabia in 1938, oil pipelines were built and water pipelines emerged next to them and then spread to other parts of Arabia. With their massive wealth, the Saudis then began making drastic changes to Mecca and Medina, spending $27 billion dollars in the two cities by 1955, followed by another $70 billion on the areas involved in the Haj.

But oddly, the Saudis bulldozed and destroyed the most important sites in Medina and Mecca that reflected Islamic history.

The mosque that held the tombs of Muhammad and his most famous companions, Abu Bakr and Umar, was demolished. A massive mega mosque complex was built in its place, destroying and covering everything under it, making excavations or future research impossible.

The destroyed mosque had been built by Muhammad and according to Islamic history, was the third mosque ever built. It was built adjacent to Muhammad's house, which the Saudis also demolished. This house and mosque had been a Muslim center and religious school during Muhammad's lifetime, and according to Islamic history, Muhammad lectured there.

Also demolished was the "oldest" sections of the Grand Mosque in Mecca. Why did the Saudis demolish the most important artifacts of Muhammad and the "oldest" sections of the Grand Mosque?

Because Islam is a lie. The Saudis had hired scientists to carbon date and investigate sites at Mecca and Medina. Allowing the truth to be investigated further, and risk exposure, would have meant they'd lose control over the people they ruled over.

Other sites demolished were the graves of those who died at the famous Battle of Uhud, which is the battle between the Muslims and the Quraish tribe of Mecca. Also demolished was the grave of Muhammad's uncle, allegedly one of the first converts to Islam. Fatima's Mosque, the mosque built onto the tomb of Muhammad's daughter Fatima, the wife of Ali, was also destroyed.

Four mosques at the site of the infamous Battle of the Trench were destroyed and massive construction was built to cover the entire location. According to Islamic history, an army of 10,000 and another army of 3,000 fought each other for 30 days at this location. Many allegedly died at this location. There would have been evidence of this battle—if the battle had taken place.

The Saudis also destroyed the oldest cemeteries at Medina and Mecca. According to Islamic history, Muhammad's son-in-law, Ali, and Muhammad's wife, mother, father, grandfather, and other ancestors, were all buried there.

The graveyard of the Quraish tribe was also destroyed. According to Muslim sources, Muhammad descended from the son of Hashim, from a clan of the Quraish tribe. These graveyards would have shed light on Muhammad's ancestry, but were purposefully destroyed.

At least 300 historical sites linked to Muhammad have been destroyed in Mecca and Medina. The Saudis knew if these sites were allowed to be studied or dated, or investigated further, the evidence would have overwhelmingly shown that there was nothing there to confirm Islamic history — only evidence to fully disprove Islamic history.

In May 2015, the Saudis began bombing the old city of Sana, Yemen. They targeted sites that were of no military interest. They targeted the House of Manuscripts, *where the Yemeni Qurans were stored*. Saudi airstrikes destroyed manuscripts that told the history of the Quran's evolution.

The Saudis destroyed more than 80 historical sites—none of which were of any military interest. They targeted the National Museum, which held rare manuscripts, historical records of Christianity in Yemen, and early Islamic artifacts. Most everything in the museum was destroyed.

Chapter 4. The Beginning of the End

Since its creation, Islam has been a system of takeover and control. The Saudis then perfected the system, and as the first Islamic leaders did in the early days of Islam, the Saudis began destroying any historical evidence that contradicted Islam in order to continue their power.

Today, the Saudis implement control into Western countries through *ikhwan*, Muslim "brotherhood," and *mutawwas*, proselytizing.

In America, a large majority of mosques are Saudi funded and run by various branches of the Muslim Brotherhood (see: Berens "Muslim Brotherhood in America"). Islamic Law classes are mandatory in these mosques and Muslim children learn to live by Islamic law and are taught that the behavior of Muhammad is ideal.

Once Islam infiltrates into a Western society, fear tactics and social enforcement are used to enforce Islam, first among the Muslims in their own communities, then Islam is forced upon non-Muslims.

Though Christmas vacation and Easter vacation have been removed from school calendars and replaced with Winter Break and Spring Break, Islamic holidays are slowly being inserted into public school calendars, but without any attempt at making them sound generic as done with Christian holidays.

Congress had adopted a law outlawing female circumcising (female genital mutilation), but a federal judge in Michigan ruled in 2018 that banning this practice is unconstitutional. As a result, female circumcising continues in at least 23 states in America and is on the rise. Honor crimes are also on the rise.

Muslim prayer rooms are being inserted into American schools, yet there is no need for them. Muslims are allowed to skip prayers or combine them at a different prayer time (see: Berens "No need for prayer rooms"). Muslim children are allowed to leave class, while non-Muslim children must remain. This is meant to display Islamic supremacy to our children.

Islam has been inserted into our K-12 curriculum, with no valid evidence that what is being presented is true. Thus, the first stage of the *mutawwas* system is being implemented on our children.

There is a Muslim Brotherhood student association on most every university campus in America—there are more than 800 of them (UTT 2019). Most of these student associations host an annual "Islam Awareness Week," an entire week of Islamic propaganda (Berens "Muslim Brotherhood in America"). Starting in 2003, the daily speeches given during "Islam Awareness Week" were given by prominent, well-known Islamist extremists.

Jihad is a central tenet in standard Islamic ideology as the final step in conquering a land and enforcing Islamic Law. Jihad has been highly promoted throughout the history of the Muslim Brotherhood. The founder of the Muslim Brotherhood defined jihad as: Warfare against non-Muslims in order to establish Islam as dominant. Jihadization is the phase in which Muslims are urged to accept their individual duty to participate in jihad.

The following was taken from my daily journal and describes what happens during the final stage of an Islamic takeover.

Morsi's One Year in Power

July 19, 2012: Today Morsi ordered the release of 572 prisoners who were being held in maximum-security prison—members of the Brotherhood, al-Qaeda and al-Gamaa al-Islamiya.

Note: *One of those released was Muhammad Zawahiri, brother of Ayman Zawahiri, leader of al-Qaeda. Muhammad Zawahiri became the weapons coordinator and directed weapons from Libya to the Sinai and to Syria.*

July 30, 2012: Today Morsi pardoned 26 convicts from death row, most of whom belonged to al-Gamaa al-Islamiya. Some had participated in the Luxor Massacre in which they murdered 62 people, some of whom were children, who were disemboweled while alive.

August 5, 2012: Militants killed 16 Egyptian soldiers at the border of Gaza. Hamas fired rockets at a security station from the Gaza side while approximately 35 militants attacked the security station on Egypt's side.

Note: *This incident marked the beginning of militants flooding into the Sinai. This massacre of soldiers was planned by the Muslim Brotherhood in order to have an excuse to remove military leaders and control the military. Morsi then gave orders to the army, the Egyptian Intelligence Agency, and security police, to stand down to terrorist activity. Terrorists in the Sinai were given full rein to build up their armies. Morsi also used the attack on the security station to criticize the 1979 Treaty with Israel and began attempts to terminate it.*

August 12, 2012: Morsi issued a presidential decree today removing the Head of the Supreme Council of Armed Forces (SCAF), the Defense Minister, and the Army Chief of Staff (the most important leaders in the military).

Morsi has chosen General Abdel Fatteh al-Sisi as his Minister of Defense. Sisi is known for being a very devout Muslim. He has a hard-worn scab on his forehead from praying and he veils his wife.

In the same decree, Morsi amended the Constitution so that it would give full Executive and full Legislative powers to the president—himself.

August 15, 2012: In a news conference, Morsi called Syria's President Assad an apostate and called on Egyptians to go to Syria to help overthrow the Syrian government and replace the government with an Islamic Law State.

Since Morsi was sworn in, he has decreed himself full authority over the armed forces, over all legislation, foreign affairs, political appointments, and military appointments. He also gave himself the power to postpone the next election and will be the sole legislator for an indefinite period.

Morsi has appointed Brotherhood members as chief editors of the largest newspapers. One of these new editors is known for his anti-Christian stance and he has written articles inciting attacks on Christians. These newly appointed editors have begun a censorship campaign.

Morsi met with Hamas leaders and has promised he'll keep the border open.

August 30, 2012: Morsi visited Iran today, the first time an Egyptian president has done so in over 30 years.

Morsi's Brotherhood administration has arrested prominent artists, cinema actors and intellectuals in an attempt to censor all media. Many of these celebrities and intellectuals were arrested on the charge of "Insulting the President."

September 11, 2012: Today, the anniversary of 9/11, the American Embassy in Cairo was bombarded by Islamists.

Essam and I have been going to the Embassy on a regular basis attempting to get Essam a visa to America. There is always a tank and several armed soldiers in front of the gate. There are also tanks placed at both ends of the street so that cars (or car bombs) cannot enter and so that people heading to the embassy on foot can be checked.

Today, the tanks, the soldiers, and the roadblocks on both ends of the street were removed. There was no security. This removal of security was obviously done on purpose. When mobs of violent men attacked the embassy today there was no security of any kind. No police came, nothing.

Note: *In an email from Huma Abedin to Hillary Clinton, Huma gave credit to Hillary for inspiring the 9/11/12 protests in Egypt, Libya, Yemen, Kuwait, Pakistan, Indonesia, Malaysia, Sudan, and India—all countries where the Muslim Brotherhood are well-organized (see: Wikileaks "Hillary Clinton Email Archive"). Hillary participated in creating the lie meant to fool the American public regarding the Benghazi attack.*

September 16, 2012: My brother-in-law lives in Moqattum. A very large number of Christians live in Moqattum and there is an important church there. Large numbers of Salafists have been moving into the area since Morsi became president and the Brotherhood set up a headquarters there.

In the early morning today, the military attacked a compound thought to be an Islamist extremist center. Many residents of Moqattum, including my brother-in-law, saw the military helicopters hovering over the compound and watched as extremists suddenly came out blasting. Turns out, this compound consisted of Sinai al-Salafiya Jihadiya (a Salafi Jihadi movement based in the Sinai). They were so well armed, with anti-aircraft guns, that they were able to chase the military helicopters away.

The Sinai al-Salafiya Jihadiya has made announcements stating they want Islamic Law imposed in Egypt as soon as possible. Six other extremist groups are also demanding that Islamic Law be enforced. Some of these militant groups are setting up headquarters in Cairo.

Note: *The Muslim Brotherhood invited members of the mujahedeen network of mercenary fighters who had fought in Afghanistan and Chechnya to enter the Sinai and form terrorist cells.*

During this period, they created twelve cells, one of which was Ansar Bait al-Maqdis, which means "Supporters of al-Aqsa" (al-Aqsa mosque in Jerusalem). The ultimate goal of Ansar Bait al-Maqdis is to remove the Jewish state.

One of the first missions of the twelve terrorist cells was to remove the military from the Sinai so as to better attack Israel. The Brotherhood fully controlled these cells and would order them to conduct terrorist attacks against the military and security police.

A Brotherhood leader, Mahmoud Ezzet, was responsible for arranging the attacks, at the order of the Muslim Brotherhood Guidance Bureau (the Brotherhood's top leadership). Ezzet was in close contact with Hamas, who would give the orders to the terrorist cells, who would then perform the attacks.

Security had been told to stand down by the Morsi Administration. After the Brotherhood were removed in 2013 and court actions were brought against Brotherhood leadership, security officials testified that Brotherhood leaders frequently went through security checkpoints to meet with the terrorist cells. Some of the Brotherhood's communications at these meetings were recorded, and these came out in the trials.

Also during the trials, it was revealed that Muhammed Zawahiri, the brother of Ayman Zawahiri, leader of al-Qaeda, was one of the men who traveled back and forth to the Sinai from the Presidential Palace in Cairo where he resided. The brother of al-Qaeda's leader was residing at the Presidential Palace with President Morsi and Brotherhood leadership.

The trials also revealed that Safwat Hegazy, another high-ranking al-Qaeda member, made many trips to the Sinai. He had been participating in the transport of weapons from Libya to the Sinai.

An Islamic Constitution

October 4, 2012: The men Morsi chose to write the new constitution all want Islamic Law. The previous constitution had an article safeguarding the freedom of religious practices and beliefs. That article has been removed.

Morsi's Islamists also removed the previous constitutional article that placed the minimum age of marriage at eighteen for girls. One of the Brotherhood's aims is to deprive women of education. They accomplish this by marrying girls very early and this sets the girls up for a life of illiteracy and no ability to gain employment or have any control over their lives.

Article 36 of the new Islamic constitution legalizes female genital mutilation.

October 6, 2012: Activist groups have announced that there were over 150 torture cases during Morsi's first 100 days in office. The 150 torture cases are cases that have been brought to trial and do not count the hundreds more that have been filed that have not made it to trial or were dropped out of fear of repercussions.

October 10, 2012: The wording in some of the articles of the new constitution are either tied explicitly to very strict Islamic law or open to interpretation. Being able to "interpret" and create Islamic Law is frightening.

October 11, 2012: Morsi fired the Prosecutor General (a position similar to the U.S. Attorney General) and appointed a Muslim Brotherhood member in his place. According to Egyptian laws, the President does not legally possess the power to fire the Prosecutor General, nor to choose his own. But Morsi is above the law and now has the power to tell the Prosecutor General who to arrest.

October 16, 2012: The fact that Salafists have surfaced so openly in Cairo is new, but what is even scarier is that their violent behavior is going unchallenged. People had the backup of the police before, now they don't.

There is more than one Salafist political party now, before there were none. They are creating Islamic-based parties, which is outlawed. The Islamists are above the law.

The news articles I read today were from privately owned internet media. Media cannot express the people's views in the hard copy Egyptian daily newspapers. Those are now fully controlled by the Muslim Brotherhood.

One Internet article compared the goals of the Salafist and the Muslim Brotherhood political parties. Both state they want enforcement of Islamic Law and to establish an Islamic Caliphate. Both have stated they want this caliphate to rule Syria, Iraq and Egypt.

There are now Salafist schools and mosques opening throughout all of Egypt. They were outlawed during Mubarak.

Salafists, like the Brotherhood, believe Christians must not be allowed rights.

October 29, 2012: Egyptians just had four days off for the Eid al-Adha holiday. Today's news reported 727 cases of sexual harassment over the four-day holiday.

Sexual harassment took place in public places and in streets and squares throughout Cairo. There were many incidents of men pulling girls along the street by their hair if they weren't wearing a headscarf. But even fully veiled girls were attacked if caught walking with their fiancés.

November 2, 2012: Today there was a large group of Islamists in Tahrir demanding Islamic Law be enforced immediately.

The crowd waved signs saying: "Yes to Islamic Law." The majority were paid and bussed in from the countryside. The buses arrived early in the morning and were lined up in the back streets of Tahrir.

Various Islamist groups announced they are forming a coalition of their political parties stating that this will be done "to ensure that the constitution is designed to enforce Sharia."

Note: *After the Muslim Brotherhood took power there were constant problems that had never occurred before: water was shut off every day for several hours; electricity was shut off for several hours every day; prices of meat rose so high that the average Egyptian had to rely on poultry, but then poultry disappeared when, without any explanation, 80,000 chickens were killed in Mansoura. Egyptians then relied on bread—but then there was an unexplainable bread shortage.*

November 4, 2012: Morsi's Minister of Interior fired the chief of the Sinai Security Police today. Morsi's Minister claims that security in the Sinai "is not properly equipped."

The Brotherhood want more arms funneled into the Sinai for their militant army and the chief of the Sinai Police would have called this out. Morsi is obvious in his desire to stockpile weapons in the Sinai. The weapons streaming into the Sinai are going to the Islamist militias.

Are they are building up to attack Israel?

November 5, 2012: Today in Shobra, a suburb of Cairo, a group of Salafists gathered on land owned by the Christian Church. They hung a sign on the property that said "al-Rahma Mosque" and announced that they will be building a mosque there.

Christians wanted to force the Salafists off the church property, but a local Bishop stopped them. He knew there would be an incident that would result in the Salafists attacking the neighborhood and burning Christian shops and homes.

Al-Gamaa al-Islamiya's political party announced today that it will hold a protest demanding the enforcement of Islamic Law. There was also a statement released by the Salafist party stating that they demand Islamic Law. They stated: "We're going to mobilize the streets. Every Egyptian who cares about their religion will demand that Islamic Law be fully, not gradually, applied."

November 8, 2012: The Ministry of Interior announced that it is allowing the Muslim Brotherhood Supreme Guide to give religious lectures to police officers! The Supreme Guide has already begun lecturing at the police academy twice a week.

Lawyers from the Brotherhood's Freedom and Justice Party asked the Police Academy to allow members of the Brotherhood who are law school graduates to take "a short course" at the Police Academy and then be allowed to be Security Police.

The police administration has already been forced to allow police officers to grow beards. There was a photo in the newspaper of bearded policemen with the prayer scab on their foreheads—a truly scary sight to see!

During Eid, when it was reported that sexual harassment was happening right in front of policemen, I'm thinking these were probably the Brotherhood's police. People have been commenting that they've seen police standing to the side while bearded men are beating someone.

Women's activists have reported that two women have been attacked in a Cairo street and it took a group of civilians to pull the bearded men off the women. They noted that "police" stood nearby watching.

Either the police have been told to stand down when bearded men break the law, or these are the new Islamic Police.

November 9, 2012: Islamist groups gathered today in Tahrir demanding the immediate enforcement of Islamic Law. The buses started arriving early and continued to arrive throughout the day. The people bussed in are paid and given free food. The Brotherhood are convincing the poor that they will continue to get free food if Islam rules Egypt.

November 12, 2012: An Internet news article today had the headline: Amid uneasy calm in Cairo, prime minister says some were paid to protest. "Uneasy calm" is an understatement of how people are feeling. Starting on Friday, not only were people paid and bussed into Cairo, thousands of Salafists and Brotherhood members remained in the streets for three days. And they were very violent.

On local TV, an Islamist was on a program calling for the destruction of the Sphinx and Pyramids. Murgan Salem el-Gohary is known for inciting violence. He was released from prison by Morsi during Morsi's first weeks in office.

El-Gohary said: "All Muslims are instructed with applying the teachings of Islam to remove idols, as we did in Afghanistan when we destroyed the Buddha statues. When I was with the Taliban we destroyed the statue of Buddha, something the government failed to do."

November 21, 2012: This last week, Morsi backed Hamas with arms and fighters against Israel. Israel retaliated with airstrikes against the Palestinian rocket fire.

Oddly, in a live news conference, Morsi was thanked by Obama for Morsi's role in brokering a ceasefire. But Morsi had actually been helping Hamas strike against Israel!

Obama's news conference thanking Morsi made Morsi sound like a peace-maker and a hero, but even worse, Obama made it sound as if Morsi stopped the crisis when Morsi was arming it, providing fighters, and promoting it!

Morsi Declares Himself Dictator

November 22, 2012: Today Morsi issued a decree which puts him beyond the bounds of any type of Judicial supervision. His decree takes away the authority of the Supreme Court Judges. He has overridden the powers of the Supreme Court!

Added to the decrees Morsi made in August, this new decree gives Morsi complete power—absolute dictatorship.

Morsi's takeover of all powers is being condemned by everyone: judges, prosecutors, opposition parties, liberals, and the majority of the Egyptian public. But Morsi and the Brotherhood are defending the move saying it is to "safeguard the Revolution."

It is now clear to all Egyptians what the Brotherhood's plans are. Nationwide protests have already begun. Protesters at the Presidential Palace were immediately attacked by bearded men with guns, clubs and knives.

November 23, 2012: Protest announcements have been made by liberal/secular groups on Facebook. People are being encouraged to protest in all of Egypt's squares against Morsi's decree that gives him total dictatorial power.

It was just announced via Twitter that violent clashes are occurring in Alexandria between anti-Morsi protesters and Morsi supporters. Fifteen have been injured and many cars have been smashed by Brotherhood and Salafists. When Salafist and Brotherhood members arrived at the protest, they began attacking the anti-Morsi protesters with large clubs.

Thousands are beginning to fill Tahrir to protest Morsi's dictatorial decree.

November 24, 2012: It was estimated that tens of thousands of protesters had protested yesterday in Cairo, Alexandria, Port Said and Suez and that over 300 people were injured. None of these anti-Morsi, anti-Brotherhood protesters are "bused in" from somewhere. These are average Egyptians who are outraged at the Brotherhood's goal of making Egypt an Islamic State.

November 25, 2012: This morning there was a program on CNN called "Who is Morsi?" Everything said was totally untrue. It made him out a good guy. Why aren't they reporting Morsi's dictatorial decree? Why aren't they reporting the massive protests against his dictatorship?

Some bold, brave newscasters on Egyptian TV have been expressing their anger at the Brotherhood. So in response, Morsi just declared a law against "live" news broadcasts so that he can prevent their views from being seen by the international media. Live coverage of protests has been banned also. So, everyone is relying on Twitter and Facebook for cell phone video and reports.

There are members of the Western media stationed in Cairo. Why aren't they reporting this censorship? Why do they say that Morsi is "popular" and that he is a "moderate" Muslim when he is not?

November 26, 2012: There were more clashes in Tahrir today. Mostly on the side streets that butt Tahrir, as more protesters headed for Tahrir to protest Morsi's dictatorship. The Brotherhood's police are now attacking these protesters.

Online Egyptian news outlets were shut down by the Brotherhood early today and now the print newspapers and TV news have also been shut down. Hard copy newspapers were not distributed tonight.

November 29, 2012: The Brotherhood announced they will be pushing the Islamic Constitution through quickly so they can declare Islamic Law. The Brotherhood said this rush is meant to "calm people."

Calm people?

News: It was just announced that Morsi's Constitutional Assembly has convened to vote on the final draft of the Islamic Constitution. Some articles passed so far state that "Islam is the religion of the State" and "the principles of sharia are the source of all legislation."

A joint press statement was issued by various anti-Morsi groups calling for another protest to demand Morsi withdraw the constitutional declaration.

November 30, 2012: People are talking about an interview with Morsi in Time Magazine. In the article, Morsi says the majority of the Egyptian people supported his decree.

Why is Western media reporting these lies? Members of the Western media are here! They know what is happening! The people do not support

Morsi's decree of dictatorship! They do not support the enforcement of Islamic Law!

There was another announcement tonight by the Brotherhood telling their followers to "prepare for confrontation." Video clips are circulating on Facebook and Twitter showing Muslim Brotherhood militias prepping for battle and holding clubs, guns and swords.

December 1, 2012: An enormous protest gathered in Tahrir to protest the Islamic Law constitution. Marches arrived from different squares and neighborhoods throughout Cairo.

Morsi Eliminates the Supreme Court and Removes 3,500 Judges

The Supreme Court Judges planned to rule the Islamic constitution illegal, but they were prevented from doing do so by Brotherhood and Salafist mobs. Hundreds of Morsi supporters posted themselves outside the courthouse to prevent the judges from their scheduled hearing on the legality of the Constitutional Assembly and their newly written Islamic constitution. The judges were also meeting to decide the legality of Morsi's decree that expanded his powers to dictatorship.

December 4, 2012: Newspapers, online and hardcopy, and local TV news stations have announced they will close today to protest the Islamic Constitution. Enormous protests against the Islamic Constitution are currently happening in Assuit, Luxor, Port Said, Alexandria, Mahalla, Cairo, Heliopolis, Kafr al-Sheikh, Minya and Damietta.

December 5, 2012: Several Egyptian TV stations have gone on strike. The TV screens are blank! Some stations posted a notice on the screen that says: "In protest to the Muslim Brotherhood and the Islamic Law Constitution."

December 6, 2012: Today, as soon as the anti-Morsi people began organizing protests, the Brotherhood came in and tore down the stages and attacked the protesters. Many protesters were injured.

The attacks on anti-Morsi protesters are being well documented on cell phones. Brotherhood and Salafists arrive with weapons and are beating people in the streets.

Today the Brotherhood also attacked Egyptian TV crews who were trying to report the protests. The Brotherhood didn't want it reported that they were beating people with clubs, but TV crews got the video out anyway.

A Morsi spokesperson said today that the Egyptian people can't do anything once the Islamic constitution is passed and put into action. The spokesman also said if people partake in a protest, they will be considered to be an apostate and killed!

There have been many Internet news reports, complete with video evidence, of bearded Morsi supporters attacking anti-Morsi protesters.

The Brotherhood are very organized. One reporter said that the Brotherhood's cell phones go off simultaneously and then hundreds of Brotherhood members move to their next target. They are receiving text messages giving them the next location to attack.

Six anti-Morsi protesters have been killed and over 600 injured.

Later: TV is back on. On one news station a woman explained what happened to her at the protest at the Presidential Palace. Her face is swollen and bruised, she had been beaten by the Muslim Brotherhood. She said they mobbed her and hit her with clubs. When she fell from being beaten, they stomped on her!

I've seen a lot of video posted on social media and it has been pretty horrifying to watch. The Brotherhood are armed, even with machine guns! Many unarmed protesters are being injured and killed.

One anti-Morsi protester said they wanted their protest peaceful. They had checkpoints at every entrance, even at the metro stops, to make sure no one was carrying weapons. But the Brotherhood have clubs, handguns, machine guns and knives.

She said the Brotherhood cheered when a protester was caught and beaten viciously. I've seen the photos—the beatings were horrific. She said they even hung people. The Brotherhood would cheer and yell "Allahu Akbar!" when they hung people. She also said the Brotherhood always attacked women first.

December 7, 2012: I saw a CNN clip about Syria this morning. The thing that stood out most as I watched was that the alleged "heroes," the "rebels" fighting against Assad, and supposedly for "the Syrian people" all have extremist beards.

Many Syrians who started fleeing Syria over a year ago ended up in my area. Many thousands of Syrians now live in my neighborhood. I meet and talk with many Syrians on a regular basis. They all say the same things. They do not want President Assad to step down. They all say the Syrian Muslim

Brotherhood were behind the whole thing. The "massacre" that started the unrest was done by the Muslim Brotherhood, not the government.

They also say that most of the so-called rebels are not even Syrian. They are mercenary fighters from other countries who came to join the Syrian Muslim Brotherhood in their fight for an Islamic State.

Also, many of these Syrians who have moved to my neighborhood are older; they are grandparents who came with their grandchildren to escape the violence committed by the "rebels." Their sons and daughters stayed behind to join the Syrian Army to fight the Islamic takeover. They say the army is not "government" forces, but an army consisting of all sectors of society, fighting for their country.

December 10, 2012: The vote on the Constitution is on the 15th. This Islamic Law Constitution will change Egypt into an Islamic State with a "Morality Police." All women's rights will be cancelled.

December 11, 2012: The anti-Morsi groups pitched tents in Tahrir and at the Presidential Palace yesterday in preparation for the next protests but they were attacked by the Brotherhood early this morning.

Internet news had this to report: "They showed a military-style precision: Crowds of bearded Islamists proclaiming allegiance to Egypt's President Mohammed Morsi and chanting "God is great" as they descended on tents set up by anti-Morsi protesters outside the presidential palace, swinging clubs and firing rifles. They set up a detention facility, interrogating and beating captured protesters.

"Opponents of Morsi accuse his Brotherhood supporters of unleashing highly trained cadres...Testimonies and videos that have emerged from the nearly 15 hours of street clashes show an organized group of disciplined Islamists, working in units and carrying out military-type exercises ...

"...the Brotherhood...is known for its tight discipline, and it acknowledges that many of its young members undergo organized training.

"During last Wednesday's fighting, nearly 140 anti-Morsi protesters were detained, tortured and interrogated at a makeshift center set up by the Brotherhood along the walls of the presidential palace ...

"The violence came a day after hundreds of thousands marched on the presidential palace ... demanding Morsi withdraw the draft constitution and sweeping powers that he had given himself ... After the giant rally, around 100 protesters set up a tent camp outside the palace. In response, the Brotherhood called a "general mobilization" of its members ... the Islamists then stormed the camp, chanting "God is great" ...

"Buses, shown in videos parked nearby, brought in Brotherhood supporters. By sunset a full-fledged street battle transformed Heliopolis into a war zone. ... Protesters and witnesses put the number of Morsi supporters at up to 12,000 ... bearded men in short robes waved sticks in the air as they chased groups of young men and women..." (see: Egypt Brotherhood)

December 14, 2012: The news is reporting more clashes between Brotherhood and anti-Morsi protestors.

Major clashes happened in Alexandria in front of the main mosque and along the corniche. There are several thousand people in the streets of Alex right now. Many cars along the corniche have been set on fire by Brotherhood mobs.

Someone from the anti-Morsi group said a fight started when four bearded men began attacking people with large knives. An imam at the mosque where protesters had gathered gave a sermon telling people to vote Yes on the Islamic constitution. When the imam did this, some people in the mosque began chanting: "Down with the Rule of the Supreme Brotherhood Guide." Witnesses said that five bearded men then attacked the people who were chanting.

Nine people were killed, and many were severely injured.

Many people are Tweeting photos of groups of bearded men with clubs patrolling the streets.

December 15, 2012: The first round of voting on the new constitution has begun. Christians in southern Egypt were too afraid to vote. For two days, around 50,000 Islamists marched throughout Assiut chanting: "Egypt will be Islamic despite the Christians." Bearded men riding horses and carrying huge swords rode through the streets of Christian neighborhoods. Christians shuttered their stores and shops and stayed inside.

The Brotherhood have total control over cell phones. The Christians of Assuit received simultaneous threatening text messages on their cell phones. In Egypt, you must declare your religion on official documents, so the Brotherhood are tapping into the state's list of Christians, then tapping into the cell phone registry.

Later: The results are coming in for the first round of voting. The results so far are Yes.

An anti-Brotherhood coalition called National Salvation Front announced that the first round was fraudulent and they have filed charges.

They have evidence that the Brotherhood rigged votes and that voting stations had ballots already marked Yes.

There were large groups of Muslim Brotherhood present at most every voting station throughout Egypt, placed there to intimidate voters.

The head of the media committee at the Judge's Club announced that the judges have already received about 340 reports of election violations. Bribes, violence against voters, and preventing Christians and women from voting via violence were the main violations.

At the voting station at the Ibn al-Naffes School, which is for female voters, Christian voters were prevented from entering. Mobs of bearded men stood in front of the voting station and threatened Christians.

Many reported that only fully veiled women were allowed into some voting stations. All others were beaten away.

There were many instances documented of bearded men distributing large sums of money to people to vote Yes.

Reports of voting violations, complete with cell phone video and photo evidence keep rolling in.

December 16, 2012: Several thousand Islamists held a sit-in outside the Supreme Court. The Islamists surrounded all doors to the courthouse to prevent any judge from entering. The chief justice, Maher al-Beheiri, contacted security and notified them that the judges were being prevented from entering the courthouse. Security, now under Muslim Brotherhood control, did nothing.

Note: *It was revealed in the 2013 trials that Muhammad al-Beltagy, a top Brotherhood leader, and Osama Yassin, who was in charge of the Muslim Brotherhood Youth, supervised the activities of the Muslim Brotherhood Youth. Yassin and Beltagy arranged for the Brotherhood Youth and well-trained militants from Hazemoon, a Salafi youth group, to work together.*

Kairat al-Shater, Deputy Supreme Guide of the Muslim Brotherhood, gave the order to encircle the Supreme Court and Yassin and Beltagy used the Muslim Brotherhood Youth and Hazemoon to execute the order.

Khairat al-Shater held a press conference just before the vote on the Islamic Constitution. He said an Islamist coalition of ten groups were working to "protect the legitimacy of the Islamic Constitution." These ten groups consisted mostly of Muslim Brotherhood Youth and Hazemoon. Later, those same ten groups became individual terrorist cells, some of which then joined the Islamic State in the Sinai.

Along with the order to encircle the Supreme Court, Muslim Brotherhood Youth and Hazemoon were ordered to encircle the Media Production Buildings. This media complex is the home of many private Egyptian television stations and media outlets, some of which were trying to get the truth out about what was happening. The Hazemoons and the Brotherhood Youth were used as a militia to attack the media complex and reporters.

Later, the leaders of Hazemoon and the Brotherhood Youth began sending their well-trained youth militias to Syria to fight for an Islamic State.

December 17, 2012: The main coalition against the Brotherhood has demanded a repeat of the first round of voting on the constitution and wants a probe into more than 4,000 well-documented voting violations that took place. The number of documented violations keeps growing as people turn in their video and other evidence.

December 22, 2012: Today is the last day to vote on the constitution.

Power outages have been reported in more than 100 voting stations. The power went out at voting stations in neighborhoods that have large numbers of people who are anti-Brotherhood. The Islamists knew they would lose in those areas so they shut those voting stations down.

Reports of the illiterate being handed ballots already marked with "Yes" are being reported.

Azza Mahfouz, an observer with the National Council for Human Rights, told of various violations at her polling station, including violence towards female voters. She also reported that ballots marked with "Yes" are being distributed to illiterate voters.

The al-Fateh Primary school voting station wrapped up voting three hours early. Many Egyptians vote late after they get off work, so this tactic eliminates hard working Egyptians who probably would vote no.

Muslim Brotherhood and Salafists told their members to go early, vote early, and then stay at voting stations to intimate others. As "No" voters began to arrive in large numbers after work, the voting stations closed.

Though most voting stations are to remain open until 11 p.m., many voting stations closed in the afternoon.

December 26, 2012: An Islamist group in the Sinai is calling itself the "Group for Promotion of Virtue and Prevention of Vice." They've been handing out leaflets warning that anyone caught smoking will have their fingertips cut off.

Note: *When the "Islamic State in Iraq and the Levant" (ISIL) was created in 2013, ISIL posted signs in the territories they ruled over announcing the new laws. Some of these laws were:*

- *All women and girls must wear the burqa.*
- *It is forbidden for women to visit gynecologists.*
- *It is forbidden to smoke cigarettes.*
- *All men's barbershops must close.*
- *It is forbidden to shorten the hair.*
- *All billboards and printed ads for women's stores must be removed.*
- *Whoever uses the term ISIL must be punished with 70 lashes—the correct term is the full words The Islamic State in Iraq and the Levant.*
- *It is forbidden for women to sit on chairs.*

ISIL said women are forbidden to sit on chairs because the chair will stimulate the vagina and make a woman go out of control sexually and thereby will tempt a man to sin. ISIL said controlling women must be done to protect men.

The reasoning for using the Levant in their name is that the Levant includes Israel. They plan to take control of Israel.

December 28, 2012: Islamic Laws made since Morsi took office:

Destroy the Pyramids and Sphinx: Sheik Murjan al-Jawhari made a fatwa calling for the destruction of all idols, relics, and statues in Egypt (this includes museum pieces in the Egyptian Museum). Jawhari said the Sphinx and the Pyramids must be destroyed. Several leading Islamic clerics directed President Morsi to blow up the Pyramids, stating that he "must accomplish what the first Muslim invaders failed to do."

Marrying young girls: A fatwa was announced that girls can be married "at any age" and that they can be married while "in the cradle." Another fatwa was made stating: "a marriage can be consummated when a girl is capable of bearing the weight of her husband."

Ending the Camp David Peace Treaty: Sheikh Hashem Islam, a member of the al-Azhar Fatwa Committee, said that the peace treaty with Israel contradicts the teachings of Sharia and must be ended. He quoted the Quran: "Do not weaken by calling for peace while you are superior." The Islamic logic used was that peace treaties with infidels are legitimate only when Muslims are weak or in need. He said, "Now that Egypt is under Muslim leadership, Allah will help it to defeat Israel."

Murdering those who protest the Islamization of Egypt is allowed: Sheikh Hashem Islam, a member of the al-Azhar committee, declared a fatwa that killing anti-Islamization protesters is permitted and dutiful.

Sheikh Wagdi Ghoneim, also a member of the al-Azhar committee, issued a fatwa that any Muslim who rejects the Islamic Constitution is an apostate and must be killed.

Egyptians must Obey President Morsi: Sheikh Ahmed Mahlawi declared a fatwa that no one is allowed to disobey Morsi. He said the Quran says it is forbidden to disobey the authorities and then quoted the Quran: "Obey Allah, the Prophet, and those in authority among you." He also said that Morsi should be obeyed whether he was elected or not—as long as he enforces Sharia. Mahlawi said that according to Islamic Doctrine, the Islamic ruler must always be obeyed unless he fails to enforce Islamic Law.

It is against the Law to greet Christians: Sheikh Burhami issued a fatwa stating that you must not greet or express good wishes to Christians. Burhami also said that taxi drivers and bus drivers were forbidden to transport Christian priests.

Saluting the Flag is forbidden: Abd al-Akhir Hamad declared a fatwa stating that it is illegal to salute of the flag or national anthem.

Rising Attacks on Journalists, Women and Christians

Muslims attacked a Christian woman on a Cairo train. They chopped off her hair and then threw her off the train. *It was the third exact type of incident in one week*.

January 4, 2013: The editor of the daily newspaper, *Al-Watan,* has been arrested and charged with "Insulting the President."

A reporter from *al-Masry al-Youm* is being charged with "Insulting the President."

Abdel-Halim Qandil, editor of *Sawt al-Umma,* has been charged with "Insulting the President."

TV host Mahmoud Saad is being charged with "Insulting the President."

Five journalists who had covered the protests against the Islamic constitution have been attacked and injured.

Several independent TV stations at the Media Production Complex have been attacked.

Hosseini Abou Deif, reporter for *el-Fagr,* was shot in the head at close range by a Muslim Brotherhood. Deif was filming Muslim Brotherhood members beating up protesters and shooting guns.

Four journalists were severely injured while covering a protest at the presidential palace. They were beaten with clubs.

January 6, 2013: Morsi just placed ten more Brotherhood members in important positions, including Minister of Finance, Minister of Transportation, Minister of Supply, Minister of Telecommunications, Minister of Electricity, Minister of Higher Education, and Minister of Media.

Note: *After placing Brotherhood members in these positions, things worsened. Trains stopped running. There was a gas shortage, causing lines at gas stations to be blocks long and which blocked traffic at cross streets.*

Muslim Brotherhood leaders made daily calls for "stalled car" campaigns. A fake car breakdown would occur in several key locations in Cairo that would cause traffic to stop completely and block the main roads and highways.

There were electricity shortages, water shortages, and shortages of the type of gas people use for their stoves and cooking appliances. These were controlled by the Ministry of Supply and the Ministry of Electricity.

January 7, 2013: The Teachers Union has accused the Ministry of Education of "Brotherhood-izing education" after 22 members of the Brotherhood were placed in senior positions in the Ministry of Education.

Article 48 of the new Islamic constitution allows "the closure or confiscation of media outlets."

Morsi's parliament has just created a "Supreme Council for the Press" to "regulate the industry."

One of Egypt's main independent newspapers, a*l-Masry al-Youm,* just announced that Morsi has accused it of "spreading false news" (the paper was reporting the truth).

Khairy Ramadan, a talk show host, resigned on air for not being allowed to interview a guest of his choosing.

Dream TV has been shut down.

Tawfik Okasha, head of the *Fareen* channel, has been sentenced to four months in jail for "insulting the president."

Popular actor, Adel Imam, and some filmmakers and screenwriters, have been charged with "Blasphemy against Islam" for films they made over a decade ago.

January 9, 2013: Today on TV, extremist preacher Hisham al-Ashry said, "Women must cover up for their own protection…I was once asked, if I came to power, would I let Christian women remain unveiled? And I said, if they want to get raped, then they can…All women must be covered. The promotion of virtue and prevention of vice is within the jurisdiction of the authorities."

In a classroom full of children, a teacher cut off the hair of two Christian girls who were not wearing head scarves—thus setting an example to the other children to intimidate and persecute Christians and other girls who do not wear them.

The Salafists chose a new leader this week, Younis Makhyoun. Makhyoun said the Salafists want "to purify all laws from whatever violates *sharia*. We want to liberate Egypt from slavery and submission while trying to assuage fears of women and Christians by saying *sharia* would liberate even Western women from the West's moral decay."

Ha! Like I really want to be "liberated" by Islamic Law! These people are insane.

January 13, 2013: Several Brotherhood members were arrested in Kuwait and charged with attempt to overthrow the Kuwaiti government.

More that 60 Brotherhood members were arrested in the United Arab Emirates (UAE). They've been accused of plotting to establish an Islamic State in the UAE and of operating an armed militia.

After arresting some Brotherhood members in Dubai, the head of police there made a statement saying that the entire region needs to be prepared to counter the Muslim Brotherhood.

January 19, 2013: Yesterday, members of the real police fired tear gas to stop hundreds of Muslim Brotherhood supporters from torching Christian shops and churches in Qena.

Muslims accused a Christian shop owner of molesting a Muslim girl. There has been no investigation to find out if this is true. And no one has pressed charges. No girl was questioned. In fact, no one is sure that there is a girl! So far it has just been an accusation, resulting in Muslims torching shops and churches and attacking Christians.

January 20, 2013: Today it was reported that Sinai security police (the "real" security police) seized a ton of explosives headed into the Sinai from mainland Egypt.

Explosives and weapons from military aid given to Libyan "rebels," who are Muslim Brotherhood and al-Qaeda, are being transported into Egypt.

Some believe these weapons are intended for Syria. Morsi has given speeches telling Egyptians to go to Syria to fight for Islamic Law. Others believe the weapons are meant for a future attack on Israel.

March 2, 2013: A rumor started in Kom Ombo that a divorced Muslim woman had been kidnapped by Christians and was forced to convert to Christianity (Christians NEVER do this). Muslims said she was being held captive inside a church.

Because of this lie, Kom Ombo's largest church has been under attack for the past three days. Hundreds of Muslims surrounded the church and threw Molotov cocktails at it. After torching the church, the massive mob discovered that the "missing" woman was not in the church.

Christian leaders had visited the church and looked inside to assure the Muslim mob that no woman was being held inside, but the mob continued their violent attacks on Christian homes and businesses. Violence continued against the Christians in Kom Ombo for three days and the church was burned to the ground.

March 7, 2013: The original, real police are protesting against Morsi's Minister of Interior (who heads the police).

In Cairo, the police protest began at the Kasr el-Nil police station. In Tanta, police officers protested what they called "Brotherhood-ization" of police and security. Police protests also occurred in North Sinai, Port Said and in Luxor. In the Sinai and along the Suez Canal, there was a large protest of over 8,000 police officers. Protests were also held in Mansoura in the Delta.

Police in various cities throughout Egypt said they believe the Minister of Interior is trying to Islam-a-cize and Brotherhood-ize the police department as well as force them to put police against the people. They say they have been given two choices by the Muslim Brotherhood government, either attack peaceful protesting civilians, or resign.

March 9, 2013: Al-Gamaa al-Islamiya announced today they have formed "security militias" to replace the security police.

March 11, 2013: Al-Gamaa al-Islamiya and the Muslim Brotherhood made a joint statement today that they have formed "Civilian Police" and that these police will be in cooperation with other Islamist groups to form larger forces.

The announcement said these militiamen "will be allowed to arrest people they believe are breaking laws." These "Civilian Police" have already begun to replace regular police in Assuit and Minya. Assuit and Minya have the largest populations of Christians.

March 16, 2013: More than thirty organizations have called for a protest demanding military intervention against the "Brotherhood-ization of Egypt" and to stop the Islamist militias that are intimidating the people of Egypt.

Petitions are being handed out to authorize General Sisi to arrest Morsi and for the army to take temporary control until a real "free and fair" election can be held for a new president.

April 6, 2013: The Brotherhood announced they want to overthrow the military and bring it under the control of the government.

April 8, 2013: A mob of Muslims attacked Christians at Cairo's main cathedral. Two Christians died and 89 Christians were injured. Witnesses said the Muslim mob threw large rocks at first, then more Muslims arrived and threw firebombs and shot at Christians.

The Christians had been at a church service and were milling around outside afterwards. When the attack began, they ran back inside the church and barricaded themselves inside. But when the Muslim Brotherhood police arrived, they shot tear gas canisters inside the church! They wanted the Christians to run out of the church so that the mob could shoot them.

There were clashes between Christians and Muslim Brotherhood police at a church in Khosoos, too. Twelve Christians were injured.

April 10, 2013: Two Christians were killed today and at least 90 were injured when a mob of bearded men attacked mourners outside St Mark's Cathedral where a funeral service was being held.

Clashes broke out today in Alexandria between supporters and opponents of the Muslim Brotherhood.

Anti-Brotherhood demonstrators planned to march to the military area in the northern part of the city to urge the army to intervene, but as protesters arrived in Victor Emmanuel Square where they were to begin the march, Brotherhood supporters began attacking the anti-Brotherhood protesters and forced them to disperse.

April 11, 2013: Al-Qaeda announced today that al-Qaeda's branch in Iraq has merged with al-Qaeda's branch in Syria. Al-Qaeda's branch in Syria is called Jabhat al-Nusra. Jabhat al-Nusra is one of the "rebel" groups Obama is urging the U.S. to support.

April 22, 2013: The Tamarod Campaign, which has the goal of ousting Morsi and having a new presidential election to replace him, plans to collect 15 million signatures by June 30. They chose this number because 13 million is the number of votes the Brotherhood said voted for Morsi. The Petition Campaign chose 15 million to prove that more people are against Morsi than those who voted for him.

April 23, 2013: A fight between the Judiciary and Morsi's Islamist parliament began today because of Morsi's ongoing attempt to get rid of the Supreme Court judges. Without the Supreme Court, there will be no legal means to prevent Morsi from declaring laws and decrees.

Normally, under the laws in existence for decades, the president's laws and decrees need approval from the judges. Brotherhood supporters are now in the streets demanding the immediate removal of the judiciary.

April 26, 2013: There are no hard copy newspapers left that have not been cleansed by the Brotherhood by replacing the editors or arresting them.

There are a few online newspapers that continued telling the truth, one of them *Egypt Independent*, but this week *Egypt Independent* was shut down and its sister newspaper, *Al-Masry al-Youm,* has been blocked from the Internet.

There was a protest in Alexandria condemning the "Brotherhood-ization" of the Judiciary. Protesters marched to the Alexandria Judges Club where they chanted against the Brotherhood. Then they marched to the military headquarters in Alexandria to let the army know they want the army to remove Morsi.

In Gharbiya, about 70 miles from Cairo, many thousands rallied in the main square to support the judiciary, the army, and the (real) police. The demonstrators chanted pro-army and anti-Brotherhood slogans and begged the army to take to the streets.

While all these protests are going on, Morsi and his Islamist parliament went ahead with a decree that will remove the judicial system.

More than 6,000 judges gathered in Cairo to decide on a strategy to try to stop this elimination of the judicial branch. If the Muslim Brotherhood isn't stopped, there will be no judicial system, no protection for human rights—just Islamic Laws and punishments. And the Islamic Morality Police.

May 15, 2013: Members of Tamarod were attacked today. While Tamarod members were collecting signatures on the petition supporting the removal of

Morsi, mobs of Brotherhood and Salafists began throwing bottles at them, grabbed petitions and tore them up, and threatened the people that were gathering to sign the petition. A female Tamarod volunteer was dragged on the ground by the hair. Many people were injured.

May 21, 2013: Electricity is cut daily, often for several hours. Temperatures are in the 90s and 100s and having no electricity means that food in refrigerators start to spoil. People are losing their meat and poultry, as well as medicines, such as insulin. Continued gas shortages are causing people to wait in line for half a day or longer.

May 23, 2013: The Muslim Brotherhood have completed their takeover of hardcopy media. Today it was announced that Mahmoud Saleh, chief editor of *Ahkbar Il Youm,* was replaced by a Brotherhood member. Saleh reported facts.

May 24, 2013: Trash, which has always been a problem, but there were services set up, has now become a major health hazard. There are enormous mountains of trash throughout neighborhoods that once had a trash pickup. These services have been shut off by the Muslim Brotherhood government. Some government hospitals have shut down because the Brotherhood ended the funding.

An escaped prisoner from Wadi Natroon prison was captured. Wadi Natroon was one of the prisons that were busted into by Hamas during the so-called "revolution." Escaped prisoners are to turn themselves in or face more prison time on top of their original sentence, if caught.

A Supreme Court judge noticed the trial of this escaped prisoner. Judge Khaled Mahgoub, along with lawyers, have been investigating the prison breaks. They have gathered testimonies from prison officials, intelligence, and other evidence.

The current General Prosecutor, hand-picked by Morsi, is trying to remove charges against Morsi as an escapee from prison. Somehow Morsi's name has been removed from the list of prisoners, therefore, says the prosecutor, Morsi can't be considered an escapee!

Security cameras provided video and photo evidence of the fight with the prison guards, the aftermath of destruction, and the opening of the prison cells and release of prisoners.

The evidence and testimony show overwhelming proof that Morsi is an escaped prisoner and a fugitive of the law. And since he has not turned himself in, it is a crime punishable by an additional two years in prison.

There is a record of Morsi's original trial and sentencing. Also, guards and prison employees have testified that Morsi was in prison, yet the prosecutor, since he was hand-picked by Morsi, is throwing the case out— saying there is no evidence that Morsi was in prison!

May 29, 2013: The editor of *al-Ahram* online made a public announcement stating that he has been removed. He called the Muslim Brotherhood the "e-militia" and said the Brotherhood have hired professional Internet hackers to monitor the media online.

Meanwhile, the military police arrested four jihadists in Alexandria. Military police saw four suspicious men and searched their vehicle. They found various weapons, a machine gun, and several hand grenades. During the arrest, one of the suspects threatened to discharge a bomb and chanted "Allahu Akbar." When taken to the police station, one of the jihadists accused the military police of blasphemy.

May 30, 2013: The new Minister of Culture has banned ballet and opera. Members of the Cairo Opera House are protesting outside the Ministry of Culture building and at the Opera House where both the Cairo Ballet and Cairo Opera are based.

The Cairo Opera House opened in 1871 and Aida was written specifically for the Opera House's debut. Aida has been performed as the opening of every season ever since. Ballet dancers, musicians and singers have been sitting outside of the Ministry of Culture building and the Opera House holding banners that say: "No to Brotherhoodization."

June 6, 2013: Morsi announced the demand by Tamarod to have a new election to replace him is "illegitimate." Interesting that he uses the word "illegitimate." He was elected illegally and illegitimately by a rigged and violent election in which Christians, women, and liberal secularists were prevented from voting, and, he is an escaped convict! He is the one who is illegitimate.

June 7, 2013: The Tamarod headquarters was attacked and torched. One of the Tamarod members, Mai Wahba, made an announcement: "We are holding on to our pacifism, we are a peaceful campaign. This event will only strengthen opposition to the Muslim Brotherhood."

The way the petition campaign works is the petition states its purpose, which is to remove Morsi and have a new election, then there is a space for your name, address, and I.D. card number proving that you are legally allowed to vote in an election. When collecting signatures, volunteer Tamarod activists must see and verify the I.D. card before allowing the person to sign a petition. The petitions are taken to a Tamarod headquarters where they are recorded and checked so no one can sign twice.

June 9, 2013: Morsi's Minister of Culture has replaced textbooks with censored textbooks. Egyptian history and various aspects of world history and other information has been removed.

Artists, writers, a movie producer and various entertainers, are joining the sit-in at the Ministry of Culture demanding the resignation of Morsi's Minister of Culture.

A member of the Supreme Council for Islamic Affairs, with well-known Islamist goals, has been appointed president of the National Library and the National Archives. Having an Islamist controlling the historical archives is horrifying. He can order the destruction of anything he wants.

June 10, 2013: When asked about his plans for education, Morsi's Minister of Culture said: "Islamic identity must be enforced in all education curriculum."

June 12, 2013: Last night mobs of Brotherhood and their supporters attacked the protesters at the Ministry of Culture building. Many artists, dancers and others were injured. Hundreds of Islamists came and attacked them with clubs.

Tamarod continues to announce their goal of a massive protest planned for June 30. They want Morsi out by that date and hope to gather millions of people in the streets to show the army the people want Morsi and the Brotherhood removed from power.

June 14, 2013: Tamarod announced that volunteer members will be going to all 29 governorates throughout Egypt. This way all sectors of Egyptian society can participate. Tamarod also announced that "Tamarod Week" will begin June 21 and will be held throughout Egypt. They want to continue spreading awareness about their signature campaign and its goals.

The protest at the Ministry of Culture has been ongoing for nine days. Famous writers, filmmakers, performers of all types, continue to join the protest to demand the removal of the Minister of Culture who they say is Brotherhoodizing the arts.

The protests have been peaceful and have included free performances in the street. Last night during a free performance, a mob of Brotherhood supporters attacked the audience. There were many families watching the performance, including large numbers of children and the elderly.

June 15, 2013: At a conference in Cairo, fully packed with Muslim Brotherhood and Salafists and extremist groups from several countries, Morsi gave a televised speech announcing that he is giving financial support to the Muslim Brotherhood and al-Qaeda groups in Syria so that an Islamic State can be formed.

More than 70 religious organizations from the "Arab world" attended this conference, all Sunni Muslim groups.

Muslim Brotherhood speakers blamed Shi'a for "creating religious strife throughout Islam's history."

One speaker said that Egypt has joined the call for a "Holy War in Syria."

All speakers urged what they called "all forms of Jihad" on Syria. One gave a call to Muslims worldwide to conduct a "jihad with mind, money and weapons against Syria."

Very influential Salafist preachers addressed the crowd, also calling for Jihad in Syria to take down the current elected government and replace it with Islamic Law.

Some imams who took the stage threatened all Shi'a worldwide, calling for a cleansing and a purging of Shi'a everywhere. The audience was told to "offer yourself, your blood and your money to fight them."

This conference was then followed by a sermon at an enormous Cairo mosque in which a Saudi Arabian preacher called on attendees at the mosque to "jihad in the cause of Allah in Syria in every possible way."

Just prior to this Islamist gathering in Cairo, al-Qaeda in Iraq announced that it had merged with Jabhat al-Nusra (al-Qaeda in Syria) to form the "Islamic State of Iraq and Levant." Jabhat al-Nusra (al-Qaeda) fights alongside the Obama-backed "Free Syrian Army." The name "Free Syrian Army" is meant to confuse Westerners. The "Free Syrian Army" was created by the Syrian Muslim Brotherhood in March 2011 and was initially funded by the Egyptian Muslim Brotherhood.

The "Free Syrian Army" started out with two primary brigades. The Khalid ibn Walid Brigade was funded and armed by the Egyptian Muslim Brotherhood and consisted mostly of mercenary fighters. The Farouq brigade consisted of Salafists from Saudi Arabia who were armed and funded by Saudi Arabia and were affiliates of al-Qaeda. The Free Syrian Army's Farouq brigade fights alongside al-Qaeda in Syria.

The Farouq brigade is extremely knowledgeable regarding media. The group has experts who produce videos and dramatized documentaries for the television networks of Qatar (al-Jazeera) and Saudi Arabia (al-Arabiya). The propaganda videos they produce are given to, and used by, Western media.

Note: *Starting in 2012, Obama and John McCain began openly declaring their support for the "Free Syrian Army." The "Free Syrian Army" was lumped into the generic term "Syrian Rebels," though the "rebel" groups consisted primarily of Muslim Brotherhood, al-Qaeda, and foreign mercenary fighters.*

In October 2013, the Free Syrian Army and al-Qaeda in Syria conducted a massacre on Christians in Saddad, a small village about 100 miles north of Damascus. For one week, more than 1,500 Christian families were held hostage by the Obama-backed Free Syrian Army and al-Qaeda.

Women and children were tossed into mass graves and Christians were tortured in the streets.

During that week, the two terror groups killed 45 Christians. Under normal circumstances this would have been called a "terrorist attack." But not one Western media outlet reported this terror attack.

Also in 2013, the Free Syrian Army and al-Qaeda joined forces to attack the Christian village of Maaloula. The Free Syrian Army and al-Qaeda raped, murdered and committed various atrocities on the villagers. Many villagers were massacred by being burned alive.

The Free Syrian Army and al-Qaeda also destroyed 32 ancient churches, convents, monasteries, and most of the historical artifacts in Maaloula. These were the "rebels" that Obama and McCain supported. (For more on Saddad and Maaloula, see "Attacks on Christians")

The following are excerpts from an article that had the headline: "Syrian rebels accept help from US, pledge loyalty to al-Qaida."

"The White House announced that it will supply direct military aid to Syrian rebel forces, notwithstanding the fact that at least one group within those forces swore allegiance to al-Qaida.

"Abou Mohamad al-Joulani, speaking for the Syrian Jabhat al-Nusra, which has joined in the fight to topple the Bashar al-Assad government, promised to support Osama bin Laden's replacement as al-Qaida leader...They [al-Qaida] provided them [al-Nusra] early on with technical, military and financial support, especially when it came to setting up networks of foreign jihadis who were brought into Syria...

"The U.S. recognized al-Nusra as a terrorist group in December. The Economist published a graph on May 17 indicating that of the 9 key rebel groups fighting in Syria, 7 are Islamists with varying degrees of extremism.

Nonetheless, President Obama went ahead with his plans to militarily support the Syrian rebels..." (Dorstewitz 2013; see also: Syrian Opposition Groups Defined; and Berens "US trained and armed")

Morsi replaces governors with terrorists

June 16, 2013: Morsi removed the governor of Luxor and replaced him with a member of al-Gamaa al-Islamiya who was in prison for participating in the Luxor Massacre killing 62 people!

Morsi issued a presidential decree appointing 17 new governors. The changes in governors included the very strategic cities of Alexandria, Port Said, Ismailia, Matrouh, Fayoum, Red Sea, Qena, Luxor and Aswan. Morsi chose the most violent people to be in power in the areas where Tamarod announced it will have the big June 30 protests.

Following Morsi's decree, a coalition of liberal groups issued a statement warning Egyptians of a potential Muslim Brotherhood conspiracy against protests on June 30. The statement said: "The Brotherhood is teaming up with Hamas and other terrorist group leaders to abort the June 30 protests."

Tamarod's main headquarters in downtown Cairo was set on fire again last night. Tamarod's spokesperson, Hassan Shahin, was injured in the fire trying to save petitions. Shahin made a statement saying: "In a new episode of terror, Morsi continues to rule the country through militias."

June 17, 2013: Morsi continues to appoint more Islamic terrorists as governors. Twenty-seven governorates are now under the full control of terrorist governors. These appointments, especially the Luxor appointment, are causing a wave of new protests against Morsi. In Luxor, tourism workers have started protesting outside government offices. They are outraged that a murderer of 62 people is now in charge of Luxor.

June 18, 2013: A large quantity of explosives, missiles and bombs were found by the military in Arish in the Sinai today.

A truck loaded with a half-ton of explosives was seized in Suez.

Military police seized four anti-aircraft missiles and 15 bombs in North Sinai.

In Ber el-Hefn, military police seized anti-tank mines, seven sacks of TNT (each weighing 50kg), and a cannon.

June 19, 2013: Tamarod has reached their goal of gathering over 15 million signatures!

The Brotherhood plans to thwart the June 30 protest by having a protest of their own on June 28. They are calling their protest "No to Violence" (as if they aren't the violent ones!).

The Salafists made an announcement that they are planning a million-man march to support Morsi and the Islamic constitution from June 21 until June 30. They plan to protest at Rabaa al-Adaweya Square and mosque. Their spokesperson said they "will fight Tamarod and our response will be fierce."

June 20, 2013: Another little girl died today from a bad circumcising (there have been several deaths recently). The Brotherhood now offers female circumcising for "free" and these freebies seem to be killing more little girls than ever before.

In Kafr el-Sheik, 25 people were injured when a mob of Brotherhood supporters attacked people protesting against their new terrorist governor.

In Gharbiya, protesters were demanding that the newly appointed governor resign, but they, too were attacked by Brotherhood mobs.

Protests against the newly appointed governor in Faiyoum have been ongoing for days and resulted in injuries when Brotherhood mobs attacked the protesters.

In Mansoura, protesters marching against their newly appointed terrorist governor were attacked by Brotherhood supporters carrying knives and swords and various types of clubs. Six people were injured.

In Mahalla, protesters were peacefully protesting when mobs of Brotherhood and Salafists attacked them. The protesters had been carrying banners that read *ikhwan kazebun*, which translates as "the Brotherhood are Liars." A Salafi arrived with a gun and shot at the protesters. Then militants drove on motorcycles shooting into the crowd.

The U.S. Embassy staff in Cairo have witnessed the extremist takeover, the censorship, the removal of basic human rights, the attacks on women and Christians, the threats, the Islamic Law constitution, Morsi's complete takeover of all powers, and the removal of the Judicial System. So why is Anne Patterson, the U.S. ambassador to Egypt, supporting the Muslim Brotherhood?

Patterson has been criticizing Tamarod daily and said they should not be allowed to protest. Yet she says nothing about the Muslim Brotherhood, al-Gamaa al-Islamiya and the Salafists organizing their huge protests on Friday— even when they have openly stated they will be violent.

The Brotherhood's Arabic Facebook page shows armed Brotherhood, Salafists and al-Gamaa al-Islamiya militias training for fighting. Anne Patterson is well aware of this. Why is she saying the Brotherhood must be allowed to protest this week, but Tamarod must not? Is Obama pushing for an Islamic State in Egypt? It certainly appears so.

June 21, 2013: The Brotherhood have taken over the public bus system. They are using public buses to transport terrorists to their protests.

June 22, 2013: Hundreds of Morsi supporters assembled at Rabaa al-Adaweya Square and mosque for their "protest" which they are now calling "No to violence, Yes to peaceful protests." It's obvious they chose this name for Western media to pick up. But as soon as their protest began, a mob of Morsi supporters assaulted the BBC Arabic team who were covering the protest.

The *OnTV Live* crew was also attacked. They had been broadcasting video of armed Brotherhood militia units doing training practices when the militia turned on them and attacked.

Radical preacher Wagdy Ghoneim said that protests demanding the resignation of Morsi are a war on Islam. Ghoneim said anyone rallying for Morsi's removal is "an infidel and must be killed."

People in Luxor are so upset about a terrorist being made governor they are releasing details about the Luxor Massacre that haven't been shown for years.

Al-Gamaa al-Islamiya cut the noses and ears off the tourists while they were alive, not only to make them suffer, but to see each other being hacked. Even the children's noses and ears were cut off—while they were alive.

A press conference was given today regarding Tamarod's June 30th protest. Marches will start on June 27 and there will be one every day until the big one on June 30. A reporter asked if the Brotherhood should be thought of as an enemy and the answer was: "A government that has killed its people, that is corrupt at all levels, and is unresponsive to its people, is an enemy."

The objective for June 30 is to organize small protests in all of Egypt's streets, which will then march to main streets, and then march to various squares. They want all Egyptians to not only witness the protest, but to participate in it. A Tamarod member at the news conference said: "We will roll like snowballs, dropping from everywhere, and then stage sit-ins."

Meanwhile, the Brotherhood posted a YouTube video. I have to laugh, on their "English" page they said they are "No to Violence," yet they posted this violent, extremely threatening YouTube video on their Arabic pages. In the video, a Brotherhood member says, "This is a message for liberals, if Morsi is taken down, there will be bloodshed, blowing up cars everywhere, and remote-control explosions everywhere."

Just announced: Morsi's prison escape case is now being referred to Egyptian prosecutors and Morsi is being charged. Senior members of the Muslim Brotherhood who broke out of prison during the January 2011 protests are to be charged as well.

The court has dispatched a message to Interpol to arrest Samy Shehab (a leader of Hezbollah), Ayman Nofal and Muhammed al-Hady (leaders of Hamas), and Ramzy Mowafy of al-Qaeda. They are currently in the Sinai. These terrorists took part in the prison breaks.

Also, 34 senior Brotherhood members are now under investigation for "espionage and the demise of Egypt."

The judge who spoke at the hearing said the prison break resulted in the escape of 11,161 terrorists and top members of militant groups.

Muslim Brotherhood members in various villages are passing out flyers that say if anyone participates in the June 30 protest, they will be considered infidels, and anyone who opposes Morsi will be charged with "Insulting the Prophet," "Insulting the Call to Prayer," and "Opposing Islam." The Brotherhood are also telling their supporters to hit Tamarod protesters with stones or homemade petrol bombs.

June 23, 2013: When Morsi spoke at that conference of Islamists against Syria's president Assad, Morsi and other speakers called for jihad against all Shi'a. Salafists took this as an order to kill Shi'a in Egypt. There are large numbers of Shi'a families in Giza.

The murders of Shi'a in Giza were recorded on cell phones. These videos have gone viral. I've seen the entire attack from several different sources and angles. It was brutally vicious. The neighbors became a giant crowd of spectators and actually cheered the murderers on and yelled Allahu Akbar. These were their next-door neighbors being massacred!

I am sickened. No one tried to stop the murders and it went on for many hours.

After the Shi'a were dragged out of their homes and brutally murdered, around 3,000 locals went on a rampage attacking Shi'a houses and destroying them.

June 25, 2013: Throughout the Brotherhood's "No to Violence" protest they've been holding banners showing guns, people being hung, and worse. Now the Brotherhood are attacking the press, who are trying to record the violence at the "No to Violence" protest.

Brotherhood have been videotaped carrying guns and other weapons.

Several journalists were attacked and TV crews belonging to at least three stations have been attacked.

A host on a popular TV show received a death threat live on air during a call-in talk show. The caller said, "We will come to you and kill all of you with machine guns."

At a pro-Morsi rally in Qena, al-Gamaa al-Islamiya announced they plan to kill all Christians and liberal secularists on June 30. They asked for the people of Qena to "Jihad for the protection of Islamic Law."

Sheik Saber Hamza, a leader of al-Gamaa al-Islamiya said, "June 30 will be the day of Jihad in the way of Allah and the protection of Islamic law." He told the crowd, "We will defeat the Christians on June 30."

Chants were led by speakers on stage, including:

"Oh Christians, on June 30, the Army of Muhammad will protect religion."

"Islamic, Islamic, in spite of the Crusaders."

"Islam is coming, the Quran is coming, Jihad is coming."

5. The End

June 28, 2013: Today, security forces stopped and checked a large bus and three micro-buses heading into Cairo and found more than 100 clubs, several boxes of Molotov cocktails and many gasoline cans.

Muslim Brotherhood have been sniping from rooftops in various squares throughout Cairo.

Clashes have erupted in towns in northern Egypt after people tried to stop bearded men from shooting from rooftops.

A woman filmed a frightening event from her apartment window. A group of bearded men, one waving an al-Qaeda flag, were on a rooftop across from her apartment. Two of them were sniper firing at people in the street below. Two teenagers had gone to the rooftop to watch people rallying below in the street, unaware that militants were on their rooftop sniper firing. The bearded men saw the teenagers, grabbed them and threw them off the roof of the high-rise apartment building. Both boys died.

Villagers in the Delta are reporting armed Muslim Brotherhood gathering at squares.

Villagers in Alexandria are reporting armed Muslim Brotherhood arriving in buses.

Villagers throughout Egypt are documenting sniper firing from buildings and armed Brotherhood and Salafists walking the streets. They are posting it on social media as evidence that the Brotherhood and their supporters are the violent ones.

As I watch all these things coming in from friends all over Egypt and from people on social media sharing their photos and video, it is clear the Brotherhood are planning to kill anyone who opposes them.

The Brotherhood are claiming on social media that "former regime groups" are trying to cause problems and that they, the Brotherhood, are standing up to the "old regime." This is a lie meant for Western media to pick up. It is them, the Muslim Brotherhood, who are violent.

The Brotherhood and Salafists are gathering at Rabaa al-Adeweya Square and mosque (aka Rabaa).

In Kafr Shokr, minivans were stopped that were carrying armed bearded men. When security forces stopped the vans, the militants attacked the security police. When local residents tried to help the security police, the militants shot some of the residents.

All parts of northern Egypt are having major clashes.

People in the Delta have been sending Tweets about armed militants being everywhere in most every street. Villagers throughout the Delta and near Alexandria say busloads of armed militants are entering the villages in droves.

And still, though Western media is here, no news of any of this is being reported on Western news.

The following is part of an email I just received from a friend in America:

Cheri,
You know this isn't going to be a peaceful Sunday. Historically these events never end well. Diplomacy always yields to violence, especially when religion is involved. Unfortunately, I had to turn my back on organized religion many years ago. The amount of war, death and grief that religions have caused is astonishing. Most of us want to just live in peace yet once religion is added to the recipe of life it erodes any ability to tolerate others.

Religion and our quest for infinite knowledge of who we are and how we got here is the cause for such tales to be told throughout time. Religion also causes hatred. So, I suspect some will die and nothing will change. I wish I could add some hope, but religion spoils everything.

In a second email, the same friend wrote in part:

Today, none of the people I know who call themselves Christians are really Christians. Would Jesus Christ have invaded Iraq? Would Jesus Christ support the death penalty? Would Jesus rig the system to make the rich become filthy rich?

I have given my friend's emails much thought. Religion was not promoted in my home, but interestingly, I searched for religion throughout my childhood and into my adult life. For most of my life, I searched.

Starting from about age twelve, I'd go to the library and read about various forms of Christianity, but also about Buddhism and Judaism. Any chance I could, I'd go to church with girlfriends. I took religious classes at various times of my life. I learned things I could take with me in life, but none of my reading or classes had any real answers.

I look back and now wonder, what exactly was I looking for?

Then I became interested in Islam, but more because of my interest in Egyptian culture, and Islam was an integral part of the culture.

During my first year living in Egypt, I contemplated converting to Islam. It "appeared" so harmless on the surface. But I had gone to Egypt knowing only the good things about Islam, which were lies. In America, I had been told that Islam means peace and that Muslims promote peace.

But while living in Egypt I learned that Muslims are taught a different meaning for the word peace. Muslims are taught that peace is only achieved when Islam takes over the entire population and Islamic Law is implemented on all people.

In Egypt, Muslims continuously told me Islam was the only way to gain entrance to paradise. But I came to learn the paradise of Islam is a drastically different notion, with a vastly different set of beliefs attached to it, than Christianity's concept of heaven.

I began to see the bad things about Islam immediately. I couldn't help but see them—those bad things were in my face on a daily basis.

When Coptic girls are kidnapped by Muslims, these girls do not convert, even when tortured in the most horrifying ways. I'd think, "Just convert! Why go through days and weeks of hideous, excruciating pain and mutilation?" But I fully understand it now. I would never, even upon hideous torture, convert to Islam.

In regards to going to heaven or hell, an American friend once said to me, "If you don't hurt people and have basic ethics, what is there to fear?" And this is what lies at the heart of the differences between Muslims and people of other faiths.

Islam's core ideology is violent conquest and the enforcement of Islam on all people. There is no Ten Commandments type of teaching as in Christianity and Judaism. Buddhism, too, instructs people not to kill, steal or lie and has a reciprocity rule of treating people equally and instructs you to treat others as you desire to be treated.

But the Quran is explicit that people are not to be treated equally. The Quran teaches that non-Muslims are not equal to Muslims and that non-Muslims must not be given the same rights as Muslims. The Quran teaches that Muslim women have half the rights of Muslim men. Non-Muslim women and slaves have no rights.

Because Muhammad tortured people, and maimed and harmed people in a wide variety of ways in order to spread Islam and force Islam on others, and because Muslims are taught to emulate Muhammad, Muslims see nothing wrong with harming people of other faiths. In fact, they are instructed to do so in the Quran and *hadith*.

Now some people will say the Bible has hideous behavior, but the difference is, the Bible describes archaic behavior from the past. The Quran on the other hand commands Muslims to participate in violence and hatred towards non-Muslims. The Bible is *descriptive* whereas the Quran is *instructive*.

Islam is a system of control. It's a system that sends its *ikhwan* out to do the dirty deeds of those in power, so that those in power can remain in power.

But even in the midst of all this terrorizing, and believe me, it is all around them on a daily basis, the Christians of Egypt remain strong in faith and do not waver. It is an amazing thing to witness.

As far as my friend's questions: "Would Jesus have invaded Iraq? Would Jesus support the death penalty? Would Jesus rig the system to make the rich become filthy rich?"

Jesus asked us to turn away from wrongdoing, showed compassion for all people, and taught numerable other compassionate and civilized principles to live by. Jesus was a good example for all to follow.

My friend said, "None of the people I know who call themselves Christians are really Christians."

Well, I am blessed, because the people I know who call themselves Christians, really are Christians. And they set a great example for me. Their actions and their faith alter my life positively every single day.

June 29, 2013: This morning all of Cairo woke up to the water and electricity shut off. And the violence continues.

Brotherhood supporters are in the streets threatening Christians.

Signs carried by Brotherhood supporters at Rabaa Square say: "Join the June 30 protest and we will burn your shops and churches."

Western Media Collusion

June 30, 2013: While the Tamarod, anti-Morsi, anti-Brotherhood people, gather in Tahrir and elsewhere throughout Egypt, the main Muslim Brotherhood protest is at Rabaa Square.

There are many photos circulating on Twitter showing police holding signs that say: "No to Morsi." Police are also seen on top of police stations cheering the June 30 protesters as they walk by.

As people walk towards Tahrir and other squares they are singing national songs!

Throughout the night of June 29, several security stops discovered more buses and carloads of Islamists with machine guns and other weapons heading into Cairo.

Tamarod numbers are enormous, millions, and not only in Tahrir and at the Presidential Palace. Tamarod protests are happening in every square throughout Cairo and in all major cities throughout Egypt.

The elderly and the very young, who aren't going to a square, are coming out of their homes and are standing in the streets waving red cards, which mean "out." These red cards can be seen everywhere! Other signs say, "Morsi Must Go" and "Leave." Judging by the enormous amount of people in the streets and holding these red cards and signs, most all of Egypt is asking Morsi to resign.

Meanwhile various Brotherhood leaders are making speeches at Rabaa Square and the crowd is repeatedly chanting: "Kill them, Kill them!" One Brotherhood member on stage told supporters: "The liberals have put their neck under the guillotine and we must act now."

A video on social media shows Brotherhood leaders at Rabaa telling the crowd that they "will restore the Islamic Caliphate and Jerusalem will be the capital." One speaker told the crowd they "must strike Jews and Christians now."

Morsi just made a statement threatening TV stations with closure if they "contradict societal values" (meaning if they report the truth). Right after Morsi's statement, Muslim Brotherhood in Rabaa Square began chanting, "Oh Morsi give us the go ahead and we'll bring your enemies in body bags."

Morsi just made another statement saying he will not step down, that he is the "legitimate" president and that the protesters are "thugs from the old regime."

Everyone now is saying it is too late for dialogue. Throughout 2011 and 2012, Obama, Western media, and "think tank" experts who constantly appeared on Western media, relentlessly said Egyptians must have "dialogue" with the Brotherhood and let them be part of the "new democracy." But Egyptians now recognize that this was a ruse purposefully used to help pave the way for the Muslim Brotherhood takeover.

Tamarod members on stage in Tahrir are saying they must get rid of Morsi first so they can organize without fear of jail or torture and so they can have fair elections this time.

Photos continue to be posted of police smiling, laughing, and holding "No to Morsi" signs, or the red soccer sign for "Out."

The official Muslim Brotherhood website just posted a statement saying there were some cars that went around the city playing "revolutionary" music to "create the illusion" that something was going to happen. Ha! They are calling the national anthem "revolutionary" music!

Still nothing from the U.S. media about this event. Nor about the Brotherhood snipers and other Brotherhood violence. What little news my American friends are passing on to me via Facebook is slanted in favor of the Muslim Brotherhood.

Note: In 2014 and 2015, members of the U.S. Congress attempted to designate the Muslim Brotherhood a terrorist group, but so-called "experts" from "think tanks" testified at Congressional hearings and persuaded Congress to vote no. The "experts" and the organizations they are affiliated with are Islamist propagandists who receive funding from Muslim Brotherhood members in Qatar and the International Muslim Brotherhood (see: Berens, "Who are the Experts").

July 1, 2013: I look at what the Muslim Brotherhood's English spokesperson, Gehad Haddad, is saying and it is outright lies.

Egyptians are giving Gehad Haddad hell on Twitter about his lies, yet he continues rattling off lie after lie. Western media is picking up his "official" statements and reporting them in Western news as truth.

Western media are here. They can just look out their window and see what is happening, or step out onto any street.

Western journalism is dead.

The army spokesperson just made an official statement:

"Egypt and the whole world have witnessed demonstrations by the great people of Egypt to express their opinion and their will, peacefully and in a civilized and unprecedented manner. Everyone saw the movement of the Egyptian people and heard their voice with the utmost respect and attention...The Egyptian armed forces, as a party in the equation of the future, and based on historical and national responsibility in protecting the safety and security of this nation, emphasize the following:

1. The armed forces refuse to be a party in politics or go against the democratic thoughts that emanate from the people of Egypt of their own free will.
2. The national security of the state is at risk from the developments taking place in the country, which makes it imperative for us to prevent these risks.
3. The armed forces have sensed the seriousness of the present situation and carries with it the demands of the great Egyptian people. A time frame of one week had already been set for the demands of the people to be met, and with no avail, which has led to the great people of Egypt to take to the streets and voice their dissent.

4. The loss of more time will only bring more division and wrestle.

5. The good people of Egypt have suffered and have not found any response to their woes and trouble, and this casts a moral obligation on the armed forces to answer the demands of the people. The armed forces call for the demands of the great people of Egypt to be met, and we give all political parties 48 hours to resolve all conflicts and issue.

Right after the army made this statement, the U.S. made an official statement that the army must keep Morsi. Obama is so creepy!

Meanwhile, armed Brotherhood gangs are shooting in Arish and Port Said.

In Faiyoum, gangs of Brotherhood supporters are attacking people.

Bombs have been found in the Brotherhood's main headquarters.

July 2, 2013: Finally, an article by Western media that speaks some truth. Here are some excerpts: "Will Obama and US stand with or against Egypt's people? In a rare historic moment for humanity, the BBC reported on June 30, 2013, that 'the number of anti-Muslim Brotherhood protesters today in Egypt is the largest number in a political event in the history of mankind.'

"... [Tamarod] called for protests on Sunday, June 30, and the Egyptian people responded with an historic display of solidarity. Americans should be ecstatic at the widespread yearning for liberty expressed in the Tamarod protests. Yet to the Egyptian public, the U.S. government appears to be on the wrong side of the fence: it's backing the Morsi regime.

"... Today, the American people find their government supporting a regime that is antithetical to their values. It's time for President Obama to unmistakably call on Morsi to heed the voice of his people and call for early elections. This is the only move that can repair the damage done by the current failed U.S. foreign policy and the only way to begin to undo the damage already done by U.S. Ambassador Patterson." (Meunier 2013)

In response to outlandish statements made by the Obama administration, stating that the army was attempting a coup, the army has replied with a statement saying they desire no coup, and that they want to help the Egyptian people move forward without fear of violent attacks.

19:30 Cairo time: General Sisi has officially asked Morsi to step down to save lives. There are about 30 million people in the street, waiting for Morsi to remove himself.

Morsi just gave a live televised speech. Here are the main sentences of Morsi's speech, some of which he said more than once:

No force on earth will impose its power on me.
I insist on legitimacy.
I will safeguard legitimacy with my life.
There is no substitution for legitimacy.
The existing constitution cannot be replaced because it is legitimate.
Violence is orchestrated by the old regime.
I stand before you to defend my legitimacy.
Holding onto legitimacy will protect us from traps and narrow tunnels.
Legitimacy is our only safeguard.
It is forbidden, forbidden, forbidden to do anything against my legitimacy.
Don't let anyone fool you, I'm just a guard of legitimacy.
I will walk with you until the end, on the path of legitimacy.

Note his constant use of the word legitimate. The Abbasids set up a system (Islam) in which "legitimate" power is based on the implementation and enforcement of the Quran and *hadith*.

The Army has just closed Egypt's borders with Libya, Sudan and Gaza. Banks just announced their closure for fear of robbery and violence.

Some of the state television stations that were censored by Morsi and which were filled with Brotherhood "managers" have evacuated. Other TV stations, that are reporting live broadcasts of what is really happening in Tahrir, in Rabaa, and other parts of Egypt, are being protected by army tanks to protect freedom of the press. Everything is live on air.

Police are handing out water as protesters continue to arrive into Tahrir.

Inside Tahrir, police are being put on the shoulders of the people. The people are thanking them for being on their side.

The crowds at Tahrir and the Presidential Palace are growing larger while they wait for the next army announcement.

Western media is still avoiding the truth and ignoring the background of what is happening. If you don't have the "backstory" how could you possibly understand what is taking place? They aren't reporting anything truthful, nor the background.

American reporters are not reporting the Rabaa protest where the Muslim Brotherhood are repeatedly chanting, "Kill them, Kill them." Nor are they reporting on the number of buses filled with weapons that continue to be confiscated at security points heading into Cairo. Nor are they mentioning that more than 30 million Egyptians are singing national songs almost non-stop in squares and streets throughout Egypt!

Morsi is Arrested: The Bloodshed Begins

July 3, 2013: Morsi has been placed under house arrest. Muhammad Beltagy, a Brotherhood leader, is on stage at the Rabaa sit-in telling supporters: "Say goodbye to your mother, father, and wife, because you will sacrifice your soul to defend Morsi's legitimacy."

The Western news I've seen so far has slanted things in favor of the Brotherhood using the same rhetoric, that Morsi was a "freely elected" president and that the military is enacting a coup—a lie.

Mobs of Islamists have attacked the cathedral in Qena. The mobs then ran throughout the town looting Christian homes and businesses at gunpoint. Muslim mobs also attacked and damaged the Holy Virgin Church in Marsa Matruh.

July 5, 2013: The army just made a statement. Here's the main part: "Ethics and Morals of the armed forces do not allow it to adopt the mentality of military coups. The army has previously been deployed in the streets on several historic events and did not instigate a military coup, but only stood firmly by the side of the Egyptian people and their will and desire for change. We also stress the fact that our action was merely a reaction that goes hand in hand with the will of the Egyptian people."

Meanwhile, the Muslim Brotherhood's Supreme Guide, Muhammad Badie, just got on stage at the sit-in at Rabaa and told the crowd of Morsi supporters to rise up against the Christians in jihad.

July 7, 2013: The Brotherhood's Supreme Guide just announced that Brotherhood supporters will remain at the sit-in at Rabaa until Morsi is reinstated.

Meanwhile, a group that calls themselves Ansar al-Sharia (Supporters of Islamic Law) has announced they will use violence to impose Islamic Law on all Egyptians. The announcement said the military is against Islam and therefore they, Ansar al-Sharia, will fight jihad against the Egyptian military. The announcement also said they have declared war on all Christians.

It was just reported that a Christian priest was shot in Arish.

Several Christian houses and shops were set on fire in Luxor.

In Minya, St. George's church was torched, and another church was shot at in the Delga area. Also in Minya, a Muslim mob looted and destroyed many Christian homes.

July 8, 2013: U.S. media continues to say it was a "coup" and that the military chose the new interim president. This is a lie. Tamarod leaders have been overseeing the transition in coordination with leaders of groups that represent various sectors of society. They chose Supreme Court Judge Adly Mansour as interim president.

The day after Morsi was arrested, the water, electric and gas shortages ended. Water is back on full force and the daily hours of power shut-offs have ended. All gas stations have received gas and there is no more gas shortage.

July 9, 2013: Today, 27 Christian homes were torched in Luxor.

The Muslim Brotherhood and other Islamist groups made an official statement today that they have united and declare a Jihad against Christians. Immediately following the statement, Muslim mobs went on a rampage burning Christian homes, shops and churches quoting this Quran verse:

"For those who resist Allah, the punishment is Fire" (Quran 8:14)

Morsi supporters at the Rabaa sit-in were filmed vowing suicide bombings against civilians who back democracy and they also vowed to attack all Christians.

I saw a video today that was filmed at the Rabaa sit-in. A veiled woman shouted: "I am a religious lady. I tell the Christians *we will set you on fire! We will set you on fire!*"

She was so hateful as she shouted those words. Her idea of being "religious" is frightening.

The Muslim mobs in Luxor who burned 27 Christian homes killed four Christians and injured at least 32. They even attacked a Christian nursery school! Who in their right minds attacks children?

Christians ran to the local police station for protection. The Christians barricaded themselves inside the police station while the Muslim mob outside chanted, "We sacrifice our blood and souls to protect Islam!"

Muslim Brotherhood have opened fire on the Mar Mina Church in Port Said. Many Christians have barricaded themselves inside.

A flyer from the Muslim Brotherhood to Christians is being handed out in Christian areas throughout Egypt. The flyers say: "Your businesses, cars, homes, schools, and churches will be torched." Two Quran verses are written on these flyers:

"Kill the disbelievers wherever you find them, capture them, and lie in wait for them at every ambush." (9:5)

"Fight the disbelievers until there is no more disbelief and until all religion is for Allah alone." (8:39)

July 12, 2013: Morsi and ten senior Brotherhood members have been charged with inciting violence. Muhammad Badie, the Supreme Guide, showed up at the Rabaa sit-in last night and instructed supporters to conduct more violence. Afterwards, thousands of Brotherhood supporters ran amuck in downtown Cairo and attacked people in the streets killing at least 30 people. More than 200 people were injured.

July 14, 2013: More charges are being filed against Morsi. Besides inciting the killings that took place at the presidential palace after his announcement of dictatorship, in which many people were grabbed by Brotherhood members and tortured to death, he is now being charged with crimes against Egypt, such as giving top secret military documents to Qatar, giving top secret intel to Hamas, and creating a foreign militia against the state of Egypt.

Militant groups in the Sinai have attacked military and security forces every day since Morsi's arrest. They have made announcements via YouTube saying they have pledged to drive the Egyptian military out of the Sinai and that they are going to establish an Islamic State in the Sinai.

July 15, 2013: Police and military were attacked again at Arish and other northern Sinai villages. The number killed has not been officially released, but there were many deaths. The jihadists also attacked the Israeli resort of Eilat. A military spokesperson said that different militant groups are spread throughout the Sinai and that weapons had been coming in primarily from Libya.

Additionally, three people were killed and 17 were wounded in an attack on a bus in northern Sinai. Militants used rocket-propelled grenades to attack the bus, which was carrying workers from a cement factory.

July 17, 2013: Muslim Brotherhood inside Rabaa Square are randomly shooting people on the outskirts of the sit-in.

Militants are using anti-aircraft rockets and machine guns to attack an army camp near the border of Gaza.

Four Brotherhood members who were attending the sit-in at Rabaa, grabbed a civilian who lived in the area who was trying to go home after work. They accused him of stealing then cut off his thumbs. Egyptian police found the victim chained to a car bleeding. The victim said he did not steal anything and was just walking home from work.

Brotherhood and their supporters have been camped out in Rabaa Square since June 28. The square is heavily guarded by Brotherhood members who stand behind barricades. Locals living in the nearby apartments say they've seen Brotherhood members carrying guns and other weapons.

Residents in the area around Rabaa Square have been reporting being threatened by Brotherhood members and their supporters. People say they are afraid to leave their apartment because, to get out, they must exit into the square where the Brotherhood are camping out.

July 19, 2013: In the last two weeks, 39 terrorist attacks have taken place in northern Sinai.

July 24, 2013: General Sisi gave a speech today. Here are excerpts:

"On three different occasions, we provided former president Morsi with strategic assessments of the situation and relevant developments and recommendations on how to overcome the current crises. This is documented.

"As part of my job, I have talked with various political and religious leaders. I have always stressed the idea of the state and the nation and that the president had to be a president for all Egyptians.

"I told Morsi to invite all political parties to the Air Defense Base and assured him that I would not be a part of that matter, and that the only reason for this meeting was to create the opportunity for all parties to meet together and to start the political process, so as to mend the disputes. The next day at noon, after sending the invitations, while I was talking to former President Morsi to see about the arrangements for the meeting, he told me to call this meeting off.

"I told the former president to take care; the project he was up to could not be implemented. I asked him to terminate this project [the Islamic Project]. The size of the rejection is greater than you imagine. In addition, in several meetings, we proposed solutions out of the crisis.

"The 48-hour ultimatum was not a sudden decision. We did not take such action and move tanks into streets while everything was normal. We aired a statement via the media. We read the statement to the President before we aired it to the media. We told him that we had time to find a way out of the crisis.

"Today I am saying to all Egyptians that during the past two weeks, I have heard many rumors... I learned that civilians were obtaining stolen military uniforms, and that many countries are smuggling weapons into Egypt. The conspiracy became clear. In the coming period, there will be stories that the Egyptian army is fighting each other. This is untrue.

"The Egyptian army is as united as one. The Egyptian army is one of a kind, and such division can never happen.

"I am calling for you to ponder: Is it right to say, 'We [the Brotherhood] either rule, or we destroy the nation.' Does this make any sense? Does your ideology call for that?

"Let me tell you something which really happened before the speech that was delivered at the Cairo Conference Center. I told two of their leaders that the situation was really dangerous and there had to be a genuine reconciliation. We reached an agreement concerning reconciliation. The next day, I stayed with the former President for two hours from 11:00 to 1:00 trying to tell him points that might help achieve these goals, and he assured me that he would address these points in his speech. I went to the Cairo Conference and I was surprised that what he said was a totally different speech.

"What I want to tell you is that during the two-hour meeting with two of their leaders, one hour was taken up in them telling me that if a big problem occurred, there would be a lot of violence because they had armed militias.

"Now I request that all Egyptians mass in the streets this Friday. Why should people mass in the streets? To give me an order to confront potential violence and terrorism, and to show the world your will as you did before. I'd like you to confirm to the world that you have your own free will and decision. The police and the army will secure the demonstrations, not only in Cairo and Alexandria, but also in all the governorates all over the country."

July 26, 2013: Today, thousands of weapons were confiscated in the Sinai, but not before militants killed 16 security police and 11 civilians.

The Brotherhood continue to cause violence and destruction around their two sit-ins at Rabaa and Giza Squares.

Security forces just seized 809 shotguns in transit to Rabaa Square.

The U.S. news is continuously talking about the Muslim Brotherhood's right to "peacefully" protest. The problem is, our media never reports that the Brotherhood's sit-ins are not peaceful.

U.S. ambassador to Egypt, Anne Patterson, has been working hard to return the Brotherhood back to power. In response, Tamarod has called for the expulsion of Patterson. Muhammad Abdel Aziz, leader of Tamarod, said at a press conference: "Patterson is not welcome in Egypt. The U.S. ambassador plays a U.S. intelligence role in support of terrorism in Egypt."

Egyptians are beginning to rally to show full support for the police to end the Muslim Brotherhood sit-ins. A giant banner has been placed in Tahrir that says: "The people, the source of all power, mandate the army and police to purge terrorism."

Tanks are guarding streets leading into Tahrir Square and helicopters hover overhead. Police are stationed at various entrances to Tahrir to protect people.

OMG! The Brotherhood have taken orphans from Egypt's orphanages and have placed these children in Rabaa Square on the front lines, so that the children will be shot first if there is a confrontation. The children have been forced to wear the white shrouds that are worn for burial. On the children's backs, the Brotherhood have written: Future Martyrs.

Why doesn't the world give a damn about what is happening? Video clips of these poor children being led around the outskirts of the Brotherhood's sit-in are going viral on Twitter and Facebook, yet Western media is not picking up the story.

Some Egyptian TV news stations have made a call out to international media, begging the international community to help end this kidnapping and abuse of children. Video of these children being paraded around in death shrouds is being aired continuously. But not one Western media outlet is reporting on this. Western media has sold out to the Muslim Brotherhood.

Note: *Estimations put the total number of people who took to the streets across Egypt in response to Sisi's call to fight terrorism at more than 33 million people. The Egyptian people clearly sent the message to go ahead and disperse the Brotherhood sit-ins.*

July 27, 2013: Seventy-four people have died around the Muslim Brotherhood's Rabaa sit-in. They were attacked when they tried to come or go from their apartments.

The Brotherhood announced they are conducting a "Jihad for Allah" and that their supporters will receive martyrdom and go to paradise if they die in attacks on civilians, Christians, military and the police.

July 28, 2013: Muslim mobs stormed three churches in Minya and set them on fire. Two of the churches held priceless artifacts--destroyed. The mob also vandalized and looted Christian shops.

Four Christians were killed in Luxor.

A Christian business owner was decapitated in Port Said.

Christian shops were trashed and looted in Marsa Matrouh.

Residents living near and around the Brotherhood sit-ins have been making formal complaints to the police regarding the violence on them when they try to go in or out of their apartment buildings.

The sit-in at Rabaa Square and mosque has grown very large. They have been busing in people from the countryside.

In one incident, Morsi supporters at Rabaa attacked local residents and some of the locals got angry that they can't come and go. Arguments started and the Brotherhood began beating people. The Brotherhood were armed, hence shooting started. The death toll is now over 100 civilians killed and hundreds more injured at Rabaa Square.

Local residents in the area of the two sit-ins have been talking to reporters and have said they just want the people participating in the sit-ins to be peaceful. But now, after these horrific killings of local residents living in the apartments at Rabaa Square, residents are asking the police to disperse the sit-ins immediately.

Egyptian Security is charging Muslim Brotherhood members and Hamas of arming men at the sit-ins and also placing armed snipers on the rooftops of buildings surrounding the squares where the sit-ins are taking place.

When they arrested one Brotherhood leader, they found 1.2 million Egyptian pounds in cash in his possession. Investigators say millions of pounds have already been used to purchase weapons and to pay their supporters to carry out their violent plan.

Brotherhood supporters who have been arrested said Brotherhood leaders told them to "Jihad for the victory of Islam."

Today the army dropped flyers via helicopters on the two sit-ins. They did this a few times throughout the day. The flyers ask the people at the sit-ins to stop the violence.

Meanwhile, the Obama administration is bitching that Egypt is not allowing "peaceful protests." Obama's position on this is excruciating for Egyptians, who can't fathom why the U.S. is lying about events and keeping the truth from the American people.

July 29, 2013: I made this Facebook post:
Our media continues to spread inaccurate and very misleading info about what's happening in Egypt. Imagine if terrorists were in Central Park armed and shooting at the public. And while they held part of Central Park hostage, the terrorist leaders announced on TV and YouTube that Christians and police must be killed. Then, after these announcements, the terrorists went out and

began killing Christians, burned their homes and businesses and burned churches.

If this were to happen in Central Park or any other public place in the U.S., SWAT teams or National Guard would go in and break it up.

The problem with the U.S. media is that they don't tell you what has been happening, that the Muslim Brotherhood have done what I just described. Since Americans never heard about any of the atrocities that led up to this situation, Western media then leads you to believe that the Brotherhood are being abused and prevented from "peacefully" protesting.

These Muslim Brotherhood terrorists are waving al-Qaeda flags and they state on live TV that they will be happy if they are killed fighting for an Islamic takeover.

Why is our media promoting the Muslim Brotherhood and supporting their terrorist activities by continuously stating that they are "peaceful protesters?"

July 31, 2013: Thirty police officers have been killed in the last 29 days and many have been injured.

August 2, 2013: The orphans have been taken to where the Brotherhood have killed local residents. Brotherhood members purposefully set fires in several strategic parts of an apartment building. As residents began fleeing the burning building, the Brotherhood shot them. After murdering these innocent people, Brotherhood members then took the orphans over to the dead bodies and made the children smell the blood and told them, "This is the smell of paradise."

And Obama wants Americans to believe the Muslim Brotherhood are peaceful?

Eleven bodies have been found near the Rabaa sit-in. All bodies had been tortured.

Several people were attacked by a group of Morsi supporters near Rabaa on July 5. Members of the mob that attacked them were armed with knives and machine guns. The following is part of a report and interview with survivors:

"They grabbed me...They called us infidels...I was beaten with bars and given electric shocks...[I] heard a woman detainee being sexually assaulted and beaten... I could hear the girl screaming when she was given electric shocks. I then saw two bearded men go into the room and heard the girl screaming more..."

"One of the Brotherhood's captives...was abducted and his body was found by his mother at the morgue. His body was covered in bruises and had burn marks on the chest, back, arms and both legs. He had also been stabbed in the chest and had a fractured skull. A neighbor who was with him during his abduction said that armed Muslim Brotherhood supporters were shooting live rounds at the residents.

"Another witness said he and his friends were captured and dragged to the sit-in and were beaten. He saw a Muslim Brotherhood slit the throat of another captured victim. He also saw the Muslim Brotherhood stab someone to death." (Amnesty 2013)

August 3, 2013: Today I saw a hideous video of terrorists in Syria (called "rebels" or "opposition" by Western media) killing and then cutting the liver and heart out of a Syrian army member "in the name of Allah" and then the terrorist declared that this is what his group will do to all the enemies of Allah.

Seven of the nine "rebel" groups fighting in Syria against the Syrian government are listed as terrorist groups. These terrorist groups, called "rebels" by Western media are trying to establish an Islamic State and impose Islamic Law.

The Syrian public has been repeatedly saying that the "rebel" groups are not fighting for a free Syria as Western media declares, but for an Islamic State.

As they are doing in Egypt, our media ignores the pleas from the Syrian people.

August 4, 2013: More Christian houses were torched in Minya yesterday. Seventeen people were injured. Seven Christian homes were totally destroyed, five cars owned by Christians were destroyed, a kiosk owned by a Christian was destroyed, two markets and a pharmacy destroyed, all of which were owned by Christians. The Muslim mob also attacked a church.

Police arrested people today who had gathered 42 young children from extremely poor neighborhoods and had bussed them to the outskirts of the sit-in at Rabaa.

The children had been told they were going somewhere to receive new clothes. These 42 children were going to be placed on the frontlines, just like the children from the orphanages.

Four police officers were wounded and police vehicles were set ablaze when security held off a Muslim Brotherhood attack on a military facility. Wounded security police officers told investigators they engaged only after the Brotherhood began using firearms.

Police are terrified of being accused of wrongdoing and hold off defending themselves until the last minute.

The interim government posted an official statement on its Facebook page about the attack and included photos of U.S. weapons that were used in the attack on the military facility. The photos included an exploded missile that hit the third floor of the facility and which resulted in injuring three officers. Also, back in January, the Egyptian military had discovered a stockpile of U.S.-made weapons in the Sinai.

The following is a summary of part of a speech made by General Sisi today:

"Morsi and the Muslim Brotherhood's concept of the state was an ideology that they have for building a country based on restoring the Islamic Caliphate.

"The Muslim Brotherhood has an international presence in more than sixty countries around the world. The ideology of the Muslim Brotherhood has nothing to do with statehood, nor nationalism, nor patriotism. There is no goal of a state or a country. The Muslim Brotherhood is totally related to an ideology of a religious Caliphate.

"We Egyptians wondered during this last year of struggle: Where is the United States and the European Union and International organizations supposedly interested in security and well-being of countries aspiring for freedom and democracy? Does Egypt not have the right to democracy and freedom? You abandoned the Egyptians. And the Egyptians will never forget."

August 6, 2013: Today authorities at Cairo International Airport prevented an attempt to smuggle in a large number of weapons and also hundreds of Egyptian army uniforms and army identification cards—faked of course. The smugglers also had black flags with "No God but Allah" printed on them.

The faked Egyptian Army uniforms were obviously going to be used by the Muslim Brotherhood to fool the public.

Tamarod, the National Salvation Front, and the June 30th Front made a joint statement today. They asked security police to confront terrorism and those who are inciting violence. They stated that the Egyptian people are in full support of police and security and that the people of Egypt have the right to live without terror. They also said they reject international efforts supporting terrorism (this was aimed mostly at Obama).

August 7, 2013: A video of a bearded man placing an al-Qaeda flag on top of St. George's church in Sohag went viral today.

Morsi supporters gathered at the church, then one of them climbed to the rooftop and placed the flag of al-Qaeda on the church. The mob then began chanting: "Islamic State, Islamic State." People who were inside the church when the mob arrived, quickly locked themselves in. Police arrived shortly afterwards and dispersed the mob.

Just a few hours after the Sohag event, hundreds of Morsi supporters surrounded a church in Girga and did the same thing.

August 8, 2013: Obama just pledged $195 million additional "aid" to Syrian "rebels." This means the U.S. will have given more than $1 billion aid to terrorists.

Note: *The Obama administration used false photos of a chemical attack to create a pretense for supporting the terrorists. Chemicals had been used by the Muslim Brotherhood and al-Qaeda, not the Syrian army or government (see: Berens "Irrefutable evidence that the Syrian government did not conduct chemical attacks on its people").*

August 11, 2013: Police will be patrolling the surroundings of the two Brotherhood sit-ins repeatedly for the next few days announcing via loudspeakers that the people inside are to disperse immediately. This is what's being said by loudspeaker:

"We ask that you leave the sit-in from the designated safe exits. Do not resist police with arms or weapons. Possession of weapons will be considered life threatening to police. We ask that you leave now and no one will be prosecuted."

Meanwhile, Muhammad Beltagy, a Brotherhood leader, told supporters inside Rabaa Square to remain. He said: "Your brothers in Algeria gave the greatest example when they offered a million martyrs. We, for the sake of religious freedom, are capable of offering more than that."

He refers to the civil war the Algerian Muslim Brotherhood started in the 1990s that lasted almost ten years—ten years of murder and mayhem at the hands of the Brotherhood who wanted Algeria to be an Islamic State.

I shook my head at his use of the words "religious freedom." According to Islamic Doctrine, only Islamic Law can lead to "freedom."

Intensified attacks on Christians

August 14, 2013: The dispersal of the Muslim Brotherhood sit-ins took place today.

Everything was videotaped and from every angle imaginable. It has been aired on TV, Facebook and Twitter for all to see. The authorities did this extra amount of documentation because they didn't want the international community to accuse them of wrongdoing.

At the Giza sit-in, they made announcements to disperse and told Morsi supporters to use the safe pathways out that had been created for them. There were no major problems dispersing the sit-in at Giza.

But the Brotherhood leadership has been residing inside the Rabaa sit-in. They used Rabaa as their base camp to incite violence and had stockpiled weapons there.

Police began dispersing the Rabaa sit-in just before dawn. They had already done three days of non-stop announcements to disperse and they directed people to the safe exits out, complete with police escorts and protection. Many people at Rabaa took advantage of leaving during that time.

Wearing gas masks, police entered, firing enormous amounts of tear gas as they penetrated the camp. They then escorted any remaining people out who suddenly decided to evacuate.

Army helicopters were above the sit-in photographing everything. The video showed the police (SWAT-like teams) entering, helping anyone out who wanted out, then suddenly the Brotherhood began shooting.

There were many hundreds of armed Brotherhood who rushed from the center of the sit-in and from the mosque that is situated at Rabaa Square. The Brotherhood were heavily armed and prepared for battle.

At 9:40 a.m. all trains were stopped to prevent militants from entering Cairo.

By 10:30 a.m. more than 200 Muslim Brotherhood and Hamas members were arrested, including some top leaders.

At 10:45 a.m. a Muslim Brotherhood spokesperson made an announcement stating all Muslim Brotherhood and Morsi supporters must go out and destroy churches and begin the Jihad.

At 11:00 a.m. it was announced that the bridges have been closed that connect to Cairo to further prevent terrorists from entering the city. A police van on one of the bridges, filled with police, was pushed off the bridge by a mob of Muslim Brotherhood. This was all caught on video and is being aired on TV.

Units of Brotherhood militias have shut down several locations of the Ring Road, a highway that circles Cairo. This had obviously been well planned in advanced.

11:35 a.m.: It was announced that at least five police have been killed in attacks on police stations, many more police have been injured. Christians and churches are now beginning to be attacked throughout all of Egypt: in Faiyoum, Beni Suef, Suez, Tanta, Minya and Assuit.

12:00 p.m.: TV announcements are saying to stay inside your homes, so police can tell who is who. Everyone is obeying. Those who have friends or family out and about are told to call or text and tell them to come home or go inside some safe place and stay there.

12:20 p.m.: Photos and videos are coming in from media and civilians, showing that the Muslim Brotherhood are extremely well-armed, similar to a military, and that they are arriving in large units. All have machine guns and military rifles.

1:15 p.m.: Police in combat with some of these Brotherhood militia units have had to retreat to re-organize. The Brotherhood are coming out in large, extremely well-armed groups at strategic locations.

1:30 p.m.: The military just released an aerial view with a very clear video of what is happening. The Brotherhood are well-armed and attacking like an army.

1:45 p.m.: At least 12 police stations have been attacked.

2:30 p.m.: Muslim Brotherhood are targeting Christians in Luxor. They have torched Christian shops and also the historical Horus Hotel (owned by a Christian). The Horus has been burned to the ground—totally destroyed in a well-executed arson attack.

3:00 p.m.: Muslim Brotherhood snipers continue to shoot from strategic rooftops throughout Cairo. Churches throughout Egypt continue to be attacked and burned. The Virgin Mary church in Minya dated in the 300s AD has been totally destroyed.

3:45 p.m.: A human shield formed in an attempt to protect the Mar Girgis Church in Tanta (a historical church). Clashes are now taking place there. A police station was overtaken by Brotherhood units in Beni Suef.

4:15 p.m.: Christians and churches are being attacked throughout Minya governorate.

4:30 p.m.: Tora Prison (housing Morsi) has been attacked. The famous library in Alexandria has been attacked.

4:32 p.m.: The army announced it has been officially deployed to help police. The army was filming via helicopters and monitoring everything, but had not participated in any of the operations up until this point. It has become obvious the police cannot handle all of these attacks by themselves, especially since police stations are being simultaneously attacked.

4:40 p.m.: Nuns in Assiut barely escaped death at the hands of Muslim Brotherhood. The nuns somehow made it to the roof of a church while it was burning and in complete flames. Local Christians then rescued the nuns from the rooftop.

Arrested so far: Safwat Hegazy (extremist preacher who has been inciting violence in his sermons and on YouTube); Muhammad el-Beltagy (senior Brotherhood leader who incites violence in speeches and on YouTube); Ahmed Aref (a Brotherhood spokesman); and Essam el-Erian (a senior Brotherhood leader).

The Ministry of Interior was on live TV reading an official statement, but then stopped and said: "Don't tell me the protests were peaceful sit-ins. These were armed terrorists. The world media has been given live video from the air for all to see."

One of the reasons why they filmed everything was to be able to show proof that police gave people plenty of time to leave the sit-in. And, even after the dispersal began, police put themselves in the line of fire to help people escape when the Brotherhood began shooting.

The Brotherhood were in the center where they were protected by people who were placed on the outskirts. People on the outskirts were placed there to die. These were people who had been bussed in from the countryside and were given free food and money to attend the sit-in. They were brought in to create a buffer zone around the Brotherhood and their armory in the center. The Brotherhood started shooting from within, and the people placed on the outskirts were directly in the line of fire.

There were about 15,000 people at the sit-in; 149 Brotherhood and supporters died during the dispersal. Separate from that number, 55 policemen were killed during the Rabaa dispersal.

There were large numbers of arrests of Brotherhood and Hamas members at the Rabaa dispersal. They were not killed. The police never tried to kill anyone unless in self-defense.

The videos show the Brotherhood blasting away from the center of the square and from the mosque. Nonetheless, police continued to try to arrest them, not kill them; hence, many top Brotherhood leaders were arrested from inside the Rabaa sit-in.

Police statements said that after the shooting began by the Brotherhood, they tried hard to get people out who suddenly changed their minds, but by the time Brotherhood and Hamas started firing, it became difficult to get out of the line of fire. Many of those people who were killed were shot by the Brotherhood and Hamas.

Later: A White House statement was just given saying, "The U.S. condemns the violence against peaceful protesters."

After the White House statement, the spokesperson for the Ministry of Interior appeared in a press conference very angry. He noted the large number of arrests, not deaths. He said they did their utmost to save lives.

He also noted that according to international standards, that 10 percent of protesters in a non-peaceful sit-in is an expected death toll. The death toll was less than that and was due to police making every attempt to disperse the sit-in with the least number of casualties.

I notice our media is using the words, "the army" or the "military state" when describing the dispersal of "peaceful" protesters. The dispersal was done by the police, not the military. The military wasn't called in until long after the dispersal, and then, not until more than 12 hours of non-stop Brotherhood attacks throughout all of Egypt. The police could not handle the enormity of the number of terror attacks.

U.S. media is making it out like the dispersal was a military move, part of a coup, and that the military is killing civilians. Our media is portraying the Muslim Brotherhood as heroes who were "defending democracy." Not one Western media outlet is reporting what really took place.

August 15, 2013: Observers in different cities report that 29 churches were torched by Muslim Brotherhood and their supporters yesterday and at least 58 more churches have been torched and ransacked today.

There was a horrible attack on a police station in Kerdassa, where Brotherhood stormed the police station and killed 11 policemen. Some of the policemen were disemboweled while alive. Some of the bodies were mutilated and body parts removed.

Yesterday, 24 police stations were attacked, and 146 policemen died in those attacks.

Sixty-five people were killed in Minya today. Twenty of the dead were police and security personnel.

The cleanup crews at Rabaa have found a large mass grave inside the mosque where the Brotherhood had their final shoot out before torching the mosque. There was a torture chamber set up inside the mosque. After people died from torture, the Brotherhood tossed the dead bodies in a pit they had dug inside the mosque. The Brotherhood tried to hide the evidence of their torture chamber by torching the mosque.

The Brotherhood have announced that tomorrow they are holding a protest titled "Day of Anger" in retaliation for what they say was a "massacre of peaceful, non-violent demonstrators" at Rabaa. They plan to rally their supporters after dawn at 28 locations and then head through Cairo to meet up in Ramses Square for noon prayer.

Note: *The final autopsies of the 23 bodies found tossed in the pit inside the Rabaa mosque reported that all 23 bodies had been severely tortured. The tortures resulted in various traumatic injuries to the back, chest and head. Every one of the bodies had all of their toenails removed. Residents living in apartment buildings at Rabaa square had reported missing family members. Some of the bodies found in the pit inside Rabaa mosque were innocent people that just happened to live near the sit-in and had been captured by the Brotherhood while they were on their way to or from work.*

August 16, 2013: The Brotherhood has made a press release stating, "We will continue to gather in the streets without violence or vandalism."

Good God, it's so obvious they make these statements for Western media, who indeed use their statements. It is no longer a matter of fact checking or an innocent mistake. Western journalists are here and they know the truth, but they report the lies anyway.

The Brotherhood and their supporters are running rampant all over Cairo causing much destruction and terrifying the public today. I was on Facebook when someone began a chat session with me. This Facebook friend's home is just around the corner from my apartment:

Him: They fired at my home 15 minutes ago, are they peaceful people like your Obama said. They have machine guns!
Me: OH that's horrible! Are the people in your building protecting themselves?
Him: Yes, but people are very upset. My children are crying. They are terrorists.
Me: I know, that is why I do Facebook to try to tell Americans this.
Him: What are their rights that Obama is talking about?
Me: Obama is hated by many Americans now.
Him: I think if it would happen in USA what will be his reaction?
Me: Cities would respond with the national guard or special police teams.
Him: These people, muslim brotherhood have a bad and killing history.
Me: I know.
Him: Your Obama should read history. We are not like palestine people.
Me: I know, I really do know.

We then got disconnected. He left due to machine gun fire on his building.

Meanwhile, I am keeping up with friends in various places in Cairo and also following Egyptian Twitter and Facebook. The attacks in my neighborhood were pretty serious. Two pickup trucks full of Brotherhood members carrying machine guns drove back and forth along the main road less than a quarter mile from my apartment and shot at shops, apartments, and at people.

The Brotherhood and their supporters are now breaking up a main road in downtown Cairo. The entire road is being destroyed. They do this everywhere they go. Egyptian TV is showing live footage of at least four locations where the Brotherhood are causing trouble. Many are heavily armed, some with machine guns.

If this protest is supposed to be "peaceful" why are so many of them armed with machine guns and military rifles?

This is their game. They announce to Western media they are peacefully demonstrating, then when they begin shooting, and the police respond, they say, "We are being attacked!"

TV news is showing people jumping off a bridge to escape Brotherhood who are shooting machine guns.

Media is reporting that 64 police have been killed so far today.

The Ministry of Interior is announcing to avoid the streets of central Cairo to allow police to confront the terrorists.

Machine gun fire has started up again near my apartment as Brotherhood units drive along 26th of July Street shooting at shops and people. Friends are filming this from their balconies.

Friends living in Maadi are reporting that the Virgin Mary Church in Maadi has been torched.

August 17, 2013: Churches, convents and Christians continue to be targeted. Police stations continue to be attacked and when police try to defend themselves, they are outnumbered and killed.

CNN creeps me out. I can't imagine why they purposefully choose to ignore what is happening. They are reporting the Muslim Brotherhood lies. It is very upsetting to watch.

American friends keep sending me articles for my opinion as to whether they are truthful. *The New York Times, Washington Post* and *Wall Street Journal* all quoted the Muslim Brotherhood's statements verbatim.

The Brotherhood had released a statement that "more than 2,200 peaceful protesters were massacred by military forces." Everything about that statement was a lie, the number killed, that the protesters were peaceful, that it was a massacre, and that the military was involved when they were not.

Yet even though Western media is here and has witnessed the truth, they used the Muslim Brotherhood's lies in their reports.

Egypt's State Information Service (SIS) just released a statement. Here are parts:

"At a time when the SIS expresses its respect for the freedom of opinion and expression, it noticed that some media coverage has steered away from objectivity and neutrality … [and are] conveying a distorted image that is very much far from the facts. This raises many questions about the neutrality of this media coverage and its goals …

"Some Western media coverage…is biased to the Muslim Brotherhood and ignores shedding light on the violent terror acts that are perpetrated by this group… the terrorizing of citizens [and] killing of innocent people, setting churches and public and private property on fire along with storming police stations, blocking roads and all other forms of thuggery and sabotage.

"The danger of the al-Qaeda organization and the fact that the Muslim Brotherhood has sought its support is completely ignored. …[On Friday] more than five vehicles entered Ramses square in downtown Cairo carrying the black flag of al-Qaeda and automatic weapons ...

"Several international media sources have ignored making reference to the huge numbers of victims from the Armed Forces and the police in face of the Muslim Brotherhood's violence.

"The acts of violence by the Muslim Brotherhood attest to the fact that they have exceeded all red lines regarding common humanitarian rules. The Brotherhood is sheltering inside mosques and are using mosques in their confrontations with police forces.

"While the SIS reiterates its keenness on maintaining all channels of contact open to all foreign correspondents and media people and its respect for the freedom of opinion and the other's opinion, it urges all media outlets to be accurate in their coverage and not to rely on false information."

August 18, 2013: A museum in Minya was destroyed. Ancient artifacts were smashed and destroyed. History is being eliminated.

A church in Mallawi was also destroyed. This church marked where Mary, Joseph and baby Jesus crossed the Nile and is where annual Christian ceremonies depicting the crossing have taken place every year for centuries.

A church and its school in Beni Suef were attacked by a mob of Muslims. The mob broke off the crosses on top of the buildings and put up an al-Qaeda flag. The attackers then destroyed the ancient church.

In Minya, a Catholic school was burned to the ground and a Christian orphanage was also destroyed. Sixty-five Christians were killed. On one of the main streets that has many shops and stores of all kinds, the Brotherhood painted black X's on Christian shops. Every one of those Christian shops were then destroyed.

Many cities throughout Egypt had this happen, Christian shops and homes were marked with black X's to depict which ones to destroy.

In Faiyoum, Muslim mobs looted and then torched five churches.

The Egyptian Council of Churches made an official statement today. In it they said they are disturbed and in a quandary regarding the deliberate misinformation campaigns by the West.

More than 80 churches have been torched. Around 40 of them have been damaged beyond repair, and many of those destroyed were ancient and historical. So far, I have not seen anything in Western media on this massive number of attacks on churches and Christians these last four days. Reporters are here. They show up for the press conferences. They know exactly what is going on. Why are they not reporting the truth?

Mostafa Hegazy, political adviser to interim President Adly Mansour, made a televised announcement today. He said in part: "Egyptians today know who has let them down and who stands by them as well as who provides financial and moral cover to those who exercise violence."

In the announcement he mentioned the inaccurate reports by Western media. Hegazy said, "Where are the stories about the burning of churches. Is this not news? Where are the stories of the Kerdassa policemen who were killed and their bodies mutilated? Where is the news about the Mallawi Museum? Where is the news about the burning of entire cities?"

Hegazy questioned media outlets that continue to describe the protesters as peaceful. He said: "I do not see any peaceful protesters. We saw machine guns and snipers. Where are the stories about the use of women and children as human shields?"

A Press Package was given to all members of the international press today. Each page of the PowerPoint part of the package showed a photo made from a video, with the link to the full video. I watched each video. The videos are documentation and evidence that the Muslim Brotherhood were armed and threatening at all times.

Not one Western media outlet has relayed any of the information in the Press Package.

Note: *The autopsy reports on the bodies of those killed at Rabaa exposed the bullet types in the majority of the bodies were not the types used by police. Additionally, the bullets found in the majority of the bodies at Rabaa were the same bullet type used in the Muhammad Mahmoud Street shootings that took place November 19-25, 2011 in which 42 people were killed.*

August 19, 2013: Two police vans were ambushed in northern Sinai and 25 policemen were killed execution-style.

August 25, 2013: The latest count of churches torched during the Muslim Brotherhood rampage this last 10 days is over 90.

August 27, 2013: We get Libyan news since its right next door. Here is what's coming out about Libya from their own news outlets: Armed militias are blocking large sectors of Libyans from having any participation in a new government. A constitution is being written, but it does not represent the diversity of Libya's people and is leaning towards Islamic Law. There is an enormous amount of killing and torture to terrorize the people into silence.

The current government's ruling party is the Justice and Construction Party, which is the Libyan Muslim Brotherhood's party. There is no army, no police. Armed militias are in control. There has been a wave of assassinations that have killed dozens of politicians, activists, judges and members of security agencies.

Armed groups held the Justices of the Judicial Branch captive so as to push through the Political Isolation Law. There are detention centers run by armed Muslim Brotherhood militias.

Al-Qaeda has made southern Libya its new base of operations. Al-Qaeda members from Mali and other African countries are gathering in Libya, thus making Libya the headquarters and capital of al-Qaeda in the Islamic Maghreb.

September 5, 2013: A bomb was set off at the Ministry of Interior Building today. Ten policemen and nine civilians were injured.

September 13, 2013: Egyptian TV today reported that Hamas has been teaching Egyptian militants how to plant car bombs and that Hamas gave 400 landmines to Muslim Brotherhood Youth Groups.

Right now the Brotherhood are attacking the police station in Mahalla.

September 16, 2013: Attacks on Christians in Minya governorate continue. At least ten Christian towns are being terrorized. More than 100 Christian families have had their homes and shops destroyed.

On August 14, when the police dispersed the Brotherhood's sit-in at Rabaa, Brotherhood leaders in Minya began making announcements from loudspeakers at mosques calling for jihad against Christians. Immediately following these announcements, Islamists began running through the towns with machetes and guns and slaughtered as many Christians as they could.

The Brotherhood and their supporters have looted the 1600-year old monastery of the Virgin Mary and also St. Abrahams. They took everything, the pews, icons, even the gates. Then the buildings were torched and destroyed.

The looting lasted for days because there was so much to take—all that beautiful history, art, and icons.

September 20, 2013: Explosives experts defused two bombs that had been planted on a Cairo subway.

October 6, 2013: The Brotherhood held "protests" today. Though each individual rally was not very large, Brotherhood members were armed at the rallies and filmed themselves flashing their rifles and other weapons.

Explosives have been found throughout Cairo today. Bomb squads have been called and are disposing them.

Border guards confiscated ten explosive devices and five rockets in Rafah, on the border with Israel.

Twenty-five Brotherhood members were arrested for possessing explosives. They were planting bombs in subway stations.

October 7, 2013: At Ramses Square, the "protesters" went on a rampage smashing parked cars and setting them on fire. This morning there were three separate terror attacks in greater Cairo.

October 11, 2013: The Brotherhood protested again today. They call their protests "Day of Rage" just as they did throughout 2011-2012. In Alexandria, police used teargas to disperse them when they began to destroy public and private property. Their protests in Cairo and Giza also turned violent.

~~~~~~~

I continued to keep a daily journal. It is filled with reports of continuous attacks on Christians.

In 2014, most of the Brotherhood's militias pledged their allegiance to ISIS. Christians were beheaded. Throats were slit. The number of kidnappings of Christian girls rose dramatically. There were major church attacks and bombings and other ongoing violence against Christians.

Yet the majority of Egypt's Muslims did not speak out against these attacks on Christians.

In some villages in the Sinai, Christians were forced to evacuate and leave their homes and businesses—permanently. Yet the Muslims of Egypt were silent about this also.

In many Christian villages throughout Egypt, when Muslims go on a rampage targeting Christian shops and homes, the police do nothing. They've been told to stand down by the local Muslim leadership.

And even when Christians have all the right permits to build or repair a church, the Muslims fight it, and the Christians are left in despair, often secretly meeting in each other's homes to hold services—which is against the law—and therefore opens the door for more attacks.

Most Muslims in Egypt did not want Islamic Law forced on them, but ultimately, the majority had no desire to fight for equality or social justice for Christians, or for women. Islamic doctrine is clear that Christians do not have equal rights, and neither do women.

Sexual harassment of women not wearing the headscarf has risen, yet there are no attempts to discourage it. And as more women put on the headscarf in an attempt to prevent attacks, this only promotes harassment towards those women who don't.

Studies and surveys have shown (see: Stats about Muslims):

- More than 60 million Muslims have a favorable view of ISIS
- The world's most violent cities in the world are those dominated by Islam
- 81% of Muslims support ISIS ideology
- 700 million Muslims want Islamic Law
- 266 million Muslims want Islamic Law forced on everyone in the world

Sharia is rapidly being forced into the U.S. workplace. Though Muslims only represent a small percentage of the American population, Muslims file 40% of workplace discrimination complaints. These lawsuits are forcing American workplaces to be *sharia* compliant (see: More Muslim Stats).

There has been an influx of 42.4 million immigrants into America in recent years; the majority are from Muslim countries. The result of this influx is the implementation of *sharia* compliancy in our schools (see: Stats about Muslims).

Additionally, 91.4% of these Muslim immigrants are on food stamps and 68.3% are on Cash Welfare (see: More Muslim Stats).

The State Department under Hillary Clinton and Gehad Haddad

Gehad Haddad was City Director of the Clinton Foundation's New York office from August 2007 until August 2012. While at the Clinton Foundation, Gehad set up the foundation's office in Egypt.

Gehad was a key advisor to Hillary and had direct involvement with the State Department during Hillary's tenure as Secretary of State.

Gehad became Senior Adviser on Foreign Affairs for the Egyptian Muslim Brotherhood in May 2011.

In 2012, Gehad became Media Spokesperson for the Egyptian Muslim Brotherhood and served as Chief of Staff to the Muslim Brotherhood's top leader, Khairat el-Shater.

Gehad was also designated the Official English Spokesperson for the Muslim Brotherhood and became the Brotherhood's Media Strategist.

Gehad was a middleman between Hillary and the Muslim Brotherhood, and as Media Spokesperson and Media Strategist for the Muslim Brotherhood, he also dictated what was printed in the Western press.

Gehad's wife is the daughter of Mahmoud Abu Zeid, a member of the Muslim Brotherhood *Guidance Bureau.*

Gehad is the nephew of Muhammad Ibrahim, a leader in the Muslim Brotherhood *Guidance Bureau.*

Gehad's father, Essam Haddad, is a member of the Muslim Brotherhood *Guidance Bureau.*

The *Guidance Bureau* is the top of the Muslim Brotherhood hierarchy and leadership and directs and manages the *International Muslim Brotherhood.*

While working for the Clinton Foundation, and as an advisor to Hillary while she was Secretary of State, Gehad Haddad was related to top Brotherhood leadership of the *International Muslim Brotherhood.*

The *International Shura Council* consists of 90 members from inside Egypt and 40 outside Egypt. The *International Shura Council* creates strategies and makes decisions on how to enforce Islam on the world.

Other members who have participated in running the *International Muslim Brotherhood* include the leader of the Syrian Muslim Brotherhood, Hassan Huwaidi, and Tunisian Muslim Brotherhood leader, Rashid al-Ghannushi.

In 2006, after the consolidation of the Muslim Brotherhood's control of Turkey under Prime Minister Erdogan (who later became president), Istanbul became the center for Muslim Brotherhood leadership. From 2006-

2010, Turkey hosted ten *International Conferences of the Muslim Brotherhood* where they plotted strategies of takeover in Egypt, Syria and Tunisia.

An Egyptian Muslim Brotherhood leader exiled in Qatar, Youssef Qaradawi, participated in these conferences in Turkey. Qaradawi coordinated funding for the *International Muslim Brotherhood* through the "Union of Good," which is a coalition of 57 Islamic charities in 21 different countries. The 57 charities can make financial transfers between coalition members between the 21 different countries. This is partly how the Muslim Brotherhood is funded internationally.

Gehad Haddad was Director of the Clinton Foundation from 2007-2012 and participated in the conferences in Turkey and was involved in financial transmissions. The Clinton Foundation received donations in return for Hillary's support for the Muslim Brotherhood.

In 2011, when the Muslim Brotherhood wanted the Syrian government taken out and replaced with an Islamic State, they called on Muslim Brotherhood members worldwide. By 2015, Muslims from at least 80 different countries had gone to Syria to fight for Islamic takeover (see: Berens "Who are the refugees").

Though many eventually joined ISIS, which was the merger of al-Qaeda in Iraq and al-Qaeda in Syria, the call to jihad in Syria was originally made by members of the *International Muslim Brotherhood*, which is led by the Egyptian *Guidance Bureau*.

The doors had previously been shut to the Muslim Brotherhood in Egypt and Syria, where they had been banned because of their terrorist activities. Many other countries banned them from forming political parties because of their past attempts at violent overthrow of governments.

But with the help of people like Hillary Clinton, who accepted donations in return for promoting propaganda in favor of the Brotherhood, those doors were re-opened and once again the Muslim Brotherhood began the violent takeover of governments.

In August 2012, Gehad Haddad's father, Essam Haddad, was appointed as an assistant to Egypt's President Morsi for "foreign relations and international cooperation." Essam was a member of the Muslim Brotherhood *Guidance Bureau* and was also Chairman of the *Islamic Relief*, which is headquartered in the UK.

Islamic Relief is a fake Islamic "charity" tied to the *International Muslim Brotherhood* and is controlled by Hamas leadership.

The *International Muslim Brotherhood* has stated they have operations that influence the U.S. government and the U.S. media. The Brotherhood reported that Hillary Clinton provided support for these operations and that the key person managing these operations was Gehad Haddad.

Via the Clinton Foundation, and then the State Department under Hillary, Gehad Haddad became involved with various NGOs. Those NGOs were used, under Gehad Haddad's management, to help fund and control the 2011 Arab Spring "revolutions."

The State Department under Hillary also doled out money to fake human rights groups like those belonging to or affiliated with George Soros (see: Propaganda Organizations).

The main agenda of these fake human rights groups was to spread pro-Muslim Brotherhood propaganda and propaganda against the governments of Egypt and Syria.

The Broadcasting Board of Governors, of which Hillary was a member of, was in charge of Voice of America, Radio Free Europe, Radio Free Asia, Radio Sawa and Alhurra, all of which the Muslim Brotherhood used to further spread anti-government propaganda to further the goals of removing governments.

Resistance?

After the successful removal of the Serbian government, the State Department's regime change system was broadened. George Soros donated enormous sums of money to front groups partnered with coup training organizations such as *Resistance!* and CANVAS, but also funded propaganda campaigns that demonize governments.

Through the Broadcasting Board of Governors, propaganda to support militant movements and the removal of governments was spread via Voice of America (VOA) and Radio Free Europe (RFE).

VOA and RFE are U.S. government-funded international broadcast sources that produce TV and radio content specifically developed to influence public opinion. Funding originally came from CIA funding, but is now appropriated annually by Congress. VOA and RFE broadcast their reports throughout the world via affiliate outlets. The U.S. uses these media propaganda outlets to interfere with and to promote the removal of governments.

VOA and RFE participated in the propaganda campaign for the 1979 Iranian Revolution, a revolution that removed the government and replaced it with an Islamic State. VOA and RFE also played a significant role in the 1989 Revolution in Czechoslovakia.

Violent protests prompted a crackdown by Czechoslovak riot police. VOA and RFE reported that a student, Martin Smid, had been killed during the clashes. This report was false, Smid was alive and well, but VOA and RFE never corrected their story. The false news story spread and gave cause for a larger protest that continued until the government was brought down.

In 2008, VOA began to broadcast more thoroughly to the Muslim world. Also in 2008, the State Department created the Alliance of Youth Movements and began recruiting and training militants from Muslim majority countries.

Additional funding for anti-government propaganda was funneled through the U.S. think tank, the International Crisis Group, of which George Soros and Zbigniew Brzezinski were trustees.

Brzezinski was the architect of the CIA program "Operation Cyclone" which trained and funded the Afghan rebels known as mujahedin. Members of the mujahedin went on to form the Taliban and al-Qaeda. CIA funding then armed and trained Islamists from Albania, Kosovo and Bosnia to fight Serbs (primarily Eastern Orthodox Christian) and Croats (predominantly Catholic).

In 2008, Brzezinski became Obama's foreign policy advisor on the Middle East. Brzezinski is the father of MSNBC's Mika Brzezinski. MSNBC was a corporate sponsor of Movements, the recruitment and coordination center for the State Department's Youth Movements Summit and for CANVAS. The Movements website was used to recruit militants and send them to the Summit and to coup training centers.

"Civil Society" groups were created, which were presented as "humanitarian" groups, but all were front groups for propaganda against governments and funded by George Soros' International Crisis Group (ICG).

These front groups included the Arabic Network for Human Rights, Egyptian Organization for Human Rights, Human Rights Watch, and the Syrian White Helmets (for White Helmets, see: Berens "White Helmets"; Berens "Propaganda organizations").

ICG and all of George Soros' "human rights" front groups sought the removal of non-Islamic governments in Muslim-majority countries. These non-Islamic governments were to be replaced with Islamic ones

Brzezinski, a trustee of ICG, was national security advisor under Jimmy Carter. Brzezinski had orchestrated the fall of the Shah of Iran in 1979—which resulted in the implementation of an Islamic State.

The Shah had run the country through a combination of a strong military and support from the United States. When the U.S. withdrew support, allegedly for "human rights" violations, Islamists took control, Iran became an Islamic State, and the military was replaced with the Islamic Revolutionary

Guard. The Islamic Revolutionary Guard consisted only of pious Islamists who would defend the Islamic takeover.

During the years Mahmoud Ahmadinehad was president of Iran (2005-2013), Muhammad Baradei, an Egyptian living in Austria, was a trustee of George Soros' ICG. Baradei was also the Director of the International Atomic Energy Agency. During his position as Director, Baradei lied about Iran's nuclear program, saying that Iran's President Ahmadinehad was not pursuing nuclear weapons. But the truth was, Ahmadinehad was indeed pursuing nuclear weapons.

Just days after the start of "Arab Spring" protests in Egypt, Muhammad Ghanem, a leader of the Muslim Brotherhood, called for war with Israel. In an interview on Iranian TV, Ghanem said the Egyptian army would not be able to stop the Muslim Brotherhood (Elam 2011).

A war with Israel was why a flood of Iranian officials began entering Egypt right after the Brotherhood took control of Tahrir Square and this is why they were holding talks with Brotherhood leadership.

Calls for war with Israel were being made, and similar to the 1979 Iranian Revolution, there was a plot to disable the Egyptian army in order to succeed with this plot. If U.S. military aid to Egypt was removed, it would implement the downfall of Egypt's army.

U.S. embassy officials in Cairo were in regular contact with militant youth leaders from the Muslim Brotherhood throughout 2008 and 2009. A leader of the April 6th Youth Movement who was also a member of the Muslim Brotherhood Youth had met with House of Representative staff members, two Senate staffers, and several think tank members (see also: WikiLeaks: "Egypt Protests").

By 2010, the Brotherhood knew they had the full support of the Obama administration and knew Obama would threaten to remove aid to Egypt's military once the protest and false flag event was implemented.

More than half of Egypt's military aircraft and two-thirds of its tanks are American made. The Egyptian military relied on America for spare parts and maintenance on its equipment. Egypt's military received 1.3 billion dollars annually in military aid from America. This aid covered 80 percent of Egypt's arms purchases. Additionally, the Egyptian military was allowed to purchase big items on credit and pay over a long period of time.

Via threats to shut off all military aid, Obama was able to influence Egypt's military leadership, first during the Arab Spring "protest" and then during Egypt's presidential election.

As soon as the protests and violence began, Obama demanded that Mubarak step down immediately. Mubarak had provided a stabilizing influence in the Middle East, was a friend to Israel, and had helped Israel secure its borders, yet Obama was not open to any discussion of any kind. Obama wanted Mubarak gone. And, Obama was not only supporting the Muslim Brotherhood, he was supporting Iran's plans for nuclear weapons (see: Hall 2015).

The Obama administration supported the Muslim Brotherhood and al-Qaeda in Syria and Iraq (2012 Intelligence doc; Dept. of Defense; see also: Berens "U.S. trained and armed"). In April 2011, weapons worth several millions of dollars began to be smuggled to Muslim Brotherhood and al-Qaeda in Syria and Iraq (Berens "U.S. trained and armed").

By early 2012, Obama authorized the CIA to train the terrorist armies that were invading Syria. To help with funding, the CIA made a deal with Saudi Arabia, Qatar and Turkey (Berens "U.S. trained and armed").

In late 2012, David Petraeus, CIA director at the time, held a meeting in Jordan with intelligence officers from several Muslim countries. A system was set up to arm terrorists in Syria, but coordinated with CIA officers in Jordan and Turkey. Immediately after this meeting, the CIA began training terrorist armies at bases in Jordan and Qatar (Berens "U.S. trained and armed").

With Islamist armies set up in Syria, Iraq and Jordan, and the Muslim Brotherhood armies in Egypt's Sinai, Israel would be surrounded by Islamist armies who openly called for Israel's demise. The Obama administration's support for these terrorist armies demonstrates that the Obama administration may have been covertly supporting a plot against Israel.

The Obama administration also supported the Libyan "rebels," whose leadership were members of Muslim Brotherhood and al-Qaeda. A goal of al-Qaeda and the Muslim Brotherhood was for the countries of North Africa to become Islamic States which would then unite under a Caliphate. Under a Caliphate, a united Islamic Army would be created. This army would have been a massive threat to the rest of Africa, but also to Europe.

In 2015 alone, at least 300,000 Islamists went to Syria to fight with terrorist armies. The largest numbers came from Tunisia, Morocco and Algeria, and there were well-established Islamist militia training camps in Libya, Nigeria and Somalia (Berens "Who Are the Refugees"). The goals of the Muslim Brotherhood and al-Qaeda were rapidly being achieved: Islam was taking over North Africa, Syria and Iraq.

In September 2012, immediately following the various U.S. embassy attacks that took place on the anniversary of 9/11, Huma Abedin sent an email to Hillary Clinton crediting Hillary for the 9/11/2012 protests in Egypt, Libya, Yemen, Kuwait, Pakistan, Indonesia, Malaysia and Sudan (WikiLeaks: Hillary

Clinton Email Archive). Hillary had been an accomplice in setting up fake "protests." The protests had been coordinated with the Muslim Brotherhood in those counties.

The only Arab Spring country that remained unscathed from the U.S. backed Arab Spring "protests" of 2011 was Algeria. During the 1990s, al-Qaeda and the Algerian Muslim Brotherhood worked together to implement an Islamic State. After experiencing a decade of violence from the Brotherhood and al-Qaeda, which almost destroyed Algeria, when the 2011 Arab Spring protests broke out in Algeria, the Algerian government recognized the protest for what it was.

The Algerian protests were led by Ali Yahia Abdennour and Mustafa Boshashi, who were heads of the Algerian League of Human Rights, which was partnered with the National Endowment for Democracy (NED) and Freedom House, two of the NGOs which fund CANVAS and that organized through Movements and the State Department's Youth Movements Summit. The Algerian League of Human Rights is one of the façade human rights groups funded by George Soros.

The Algerian government, aware of these deceptions, immediately sent in a massive police presence that purposefully outnumbered the protesters 20 to 1. Squashing the "protest" was the only way to prevent a false flag event and an Islamic takeover.

Just days after Egypt's protest began, the National Democratic Institute (NDI) opened offices in Alexandria and Assuit, cities with the largest numbers of Muslim Brotherhood.

Immediately following, the NDI offices received $14 million dollars from USAID (Seed 2013). These millions were used to pay protesters to keep the protests going for months and were meant to throw Egypt into chaos while the Brotherhood implemented full control. This NGO funding also went for the acquisition of weapons for the Brotherhood's militias so they could fight the Egyptian Army.

In July 2008, Obama gave a speech promising he would create a "Civilian National Security Force" that would be "just as powerful, just as strong, and just as well funded as the US Military." Was Obama planning to fund this army through the various NGOs set up by the State Department? Or by George Soros and his affiliate organizations? Or possibly through the Muslim Brotherhood's diverse means of funding, just as Hillary accepted many millions from Muslim countries through her foundation?

Is this army already in training, similar to how the Muslim Brotherhood militias secretly trained in Egypt? Are they just lying in waiting?

Groups inside America have taken the same *Resistance!* and CANVAS training courses which became the CIA's strategies to remove governments. They have been trained to conduct false flag events to blame police and to promote hatred for the U.S. government. They have been taught how to mobilize quickly using social media and how to create a massive presence when needed—to give the "impression" that they represent the majority.

In May 2017, Hillary Clinton announced her new political organization that she said will serve the purpose of funding "resistance groups" who will resist President Trump and the Republican party. Her organization is a 501(c)(4), which means donors will not be disclosed (see: Resist 2017).

Immediately after forming this organization, the organization spent millions of dollars financing candidates in the mid-term elections. With limitless funding, it's no surprise that several of these candidates won.

These new members of Congress want open borders, are pushing to defund Homeland Security and want to abolish Immigration and Customs Enforcement (ICE).

Many illegals crossing into the U.S. via Mexico have been smuggled into the U.S. via networks specializing in individuals from the Afghanistan-Pakistan region and the Middle East. More than 30,000 illegals from countries listed as having *high terrorist concerns* have crossed into the U.S. from Mexico since 2015. One border patrol agent said, "There is a clear pipeline from the Middle East through Mexico" (see Berens: 30,000).

Conclusion: What can we do?

Muslim sources of Islamic history want you to believe that after converting to Islam, Arab tribes supplied many thousands of warriors for the Islamic conquest of the Levant and Persia. You are told that the decision to invade these lands was taken in Arabia, from an isolated, uninhabitable location.

You are told many thousands of stories of what Muhammad said and did and are told these stories must be taken as fact, even though there is no evidence of any kind to verify these stories as factual.

You are told that many of the things Muhammad said and did some 1400 years ago must be made into laws and that Muhammad's behavior is ideal and must be emulated—even though Muhammad was a robber, rapist, murderer, torturer and pedophile.

This propaganda about Islam and Muhammad has been placed into our K-12 school curriculum. The life of Muhammad and the Islamic conquest are being taught as fact in our universities without any avenue to question it.

The Islamic takeover is in its final stage in many parts of the world. Central Asia, North and Central Africa, Malaysia and Indonesia have become Muslim majority and Islam is being enforced in these countries.

Islam has become a serious threat in Northern and Western Europe and India is experiencing a hideous and violent transition to Islam. Islamophobia Laws (blasphemy laws) are being implemented in Australia and Canada.

To combat the rapid growth of Islam in our own country, we need to immediately stop debating Muslims *on their terms*. Currently our debates wholly consist of re-hashing unreliable Muslim sources from the ninth and tenth centuries. Instead we must introduce and discuss modern research and facts that contradict the Muslim sources.

Yes, it's extremely important to know what Muslims are taught and what they believe, but we must begin introducing the facts that will disable Islam at its core so that we are better able to fight the subversive takeover taking place in our own country.

We must begin making demands that our university programs balance the Muslim version of Islamic history with research that presents the facts that question it. And most importantly, we must encourage a new wave of research to replace this absurd reliance on Muslim sources from the ninth and tenth centuries.

Thanks to eight years of Obama we saw an influx of Muslim immigrants in astronomical numbers. The majority of these immigrants have no intention of assimilating. They are forming their own communities and are enforcing Islamic Law in those communities.

The Egyptian Muslim Brotherhood entered America in 1962 and began their system of changing American youth by infiltrating universities. The Pakistani branch entered America in 1971 and created jihadi camps.

Thousands of mosques in America are used by the Muslim Brotherhood to radicalize and promote jihad (Berens "Jihad in American mosques"; Guandolo 2019).

Evidence from a 15-year FBI investigation (UTT 2019) revealed:

- There is a massive jihadi network in the United States primarily controlled by the U.S. Muslim Brotherhood
- The objective of the network is to replace America's Constitutional Republic with an Islamic State under Islamic Law
- The most prominent Islamic organizations in the United States are a part of this jihadi network

A violent sector of anti-American society has been radicalized and has mobilized inside America. Gun control is promoted by all Muslim Brotherhood organizations in America. It's a no-brainer why they want to take away our guns. Become aware of gun laws your state is proposing and fight back. The NRA website offers great information and is a good place to start.

In 1981, the Palestinian Muslim Brotherhood entered America and an aggressive political agenda began at that time. Today, decades later, it has become blatant that many of our politicians have been co-opted by this agenda. Follow Muslim Brotherhood organizations on social media. They have state and local affiliates on Facebook and Twitter. Follow them and you will begin to see how enormous this threat is and you will be more able to fight them (see: Berens "What is the Muslim Brotherhood Doing in Your State?").

The Muslim Brotherhood created student organizations on American university campuses. Whether you have children or not, follow these organizations on social media. You will learn the strategies that are being used on the youth of America and you will be better prepared to fight their propaganda. Awareness of their activities and strategies is paramount.

In the 1990s, American media began to be co-opted. Via control of university bureaucracy placed decades earlier, fact-based journalism in university programs has been removed. This was done to more easily insert mass media propaganda. Watch and promote alternative media sites that do not report propaganda and fake news. Experiment with different conservative talk radio shows that discuss factual political news and events.

We have been witnessing massive censorship on Facebook and Twitter. Join alternative social media sites in preparation for further censorship, but also to have a place where you can network and rally. Sign up for LibertyRush, Codias, MeWe, GAB and others in preparation for intensification of Facebook and Twitter censorship.

In 1996, the Somali branch of the Muslim Brotherhood arrived in America and intensified the Islamification process. Since their arrival, radical Islam has become visible in every state.

If you have a large *sharia* adherent population in your city or state, you must get involved in state and local government immediately. What are the visible signs of *sharia* adherence and what does it mean? See: Berens "Jihad in American Mosques" for descriptions and case studies.

In Chapter Three, I purposefully chose and cited research from specialists in the fields of Aramaic, Arabic, Quranic Studies, Islamic Studies and so forth. Use Chapter Three as a Handbook to fight the Islamic takeover in America. Focus on the discrepancies in the Muslim version of Islamic History and spread the word.

Make sure you read: "The Islamification of Biblical History" in the Appendix to fully understand the fabricated Islamic version of biblical history—which is warping the minds of American youth. Even if you are not religious, read information from websites that give archeological evidence of events in the Bible (one example is: www.biblicalarchaeology.org). Unlike Islam, which has absolutely no archeological evidence of its early existence, there is an enormous amount of evidence that backs the Bible.

Muslims around the world are taught that Jerusalem belongs to Islam. Learn the facts and fight with facts.

Fight your employer and local schools and prevent them from creating Islamic prayer rooms. Fight them with facts, see: Berens "No Need for Prayer Rooms at Schools or Workplace: Muslims are allowed to miss prayers."

During the Abbasid period, as Islam was being created, around 90% of the books in the larger cities were destroyed. Though done differently, the same strategy is taking place today. Books that challenge Islamic history are being removed from bookshelves. Muslim Brotherhood organizations are currently targeting libraries.

Google searches for truth, will only result in lies. Google has removed factual non-Muslim research articles on Islam. I know because I have witnessed their disappearance. Even if you use alternative search engines, the database of information is established by Google. Never trust the Internet if the information given re-hashes Muslim sources. Become savvy as to how corrupt the Internet has become in regards to Islam.

Make requests at your local library to purchase books that counter Islam or that question Islam. Fight to get these books on the bookshelves. The future of America depends on being able to combat Islam with facts. If you belong to a book club, get these books added to the reading list.

Many states in America have made "foreign" laws illegal, making some Americans feel a false sense of security. While it is excellent that some states are doing this, don't feel safe. Every Muslim who goes to mosque is told that he or she must live by Islamic Law. Every mosque in America teaches Islamic Law to its congregation. See: "The Primary Role of the Mosque is the Seat of the Islamic Government" (Guandolo 2019).

Most every university campus in America that has a Muslim Brotherhood student organization (there are more than 800 of them) has an Islamic "council" on campus where advice is given as to how to live by Islamic Law.

Young males attend mandatory *sharia* classes held at mosque. These young men will be enforcing *sharia* on their future wives and children.

Massive numbers of Muslims are already living by Islamic Law.

Muslims in America have their own Islamic Law courtrooms, called Shura Councils. Several of these exist throughout America. Muslims go to mosque or to Shura Councils when they need a judge or a courtroom. Islamic Laws are being created at many of these centers (see also: Islamic Sharia Tribunal Begins Operating in Texas).

Soon the Muslim Brotherhood in America will try to enforce Islamic Laws on Americans. It will begin with Islamophobia Laws, which are blasphemy laws and censorship laws in disguise. Once these censorship laws are put into place, we will become impotent.

Follow activity taking place in your state and local government. The Muslim Brotherhood organizes frequent visits to state capitols and local council meetings to push their agenda on your state and local representatives. Become aware of laws being proposed. Awareness is key so you can prevent these laws from being enacted.

Turkey and Saudi Arabia have been working for decades at converting Central Americans to Islam and there has been an intensified program of mosque building in South America. There is a direct pipeline for terrorists from the Middle East to South and Central America. Our borders are vulnerable, see: Berens "Terrorists from the Middle East are traveling through Mexico," and, Berens "al-Qaeda has intensified its operations".

It is more important than ever before that you support the building of a border wall and promote the enforcement of immigration laws.

The Muslim Brotherhood has more than 70 well-established organizations inside America. The Muslim Brotherhood has been organizing in America since the 1960s. The Brotherhood has altered our youth, altered our police forces, and altered our government. Two examples should move you to action:

1) Before the Las Vegas massacre, the Las Vegas Police Department participated in a massive "Muslim Outreach" program. Part of the program was that Las Vegas police officers had to attend mosques regularly. The LVPD's officers participated in Islamic customs, female officers wore hijabs during Friday prayers, and officers met with mosque leaders to help reduce "red tape" when mosque members were arrested.

2) In Broward county, Florida, where the school shooting took place, and which implemented another movement to take away gun rights, a Broward county deputy visited 16 mosques and trained Muslims to arm themselves. As in Las Vegas, those mosques were Muslim Brotherhood mosques.

Most smaller police departments have not yet become infected by Islamification, and most police departments have a Facebook page or website. Go to those webpages and get to know your local police department. Most have public events. Go to their events and meet members of your police. Then, ask your local police department to invite *Understanding the Threat* to give a training session (www.understandingthethreat.com).

Demonizing police is a strategy meant to disable police or remove the police. In America, the Muslim Brotherhood demonize police by promoting the falsity that police target African Americans. They used Black Lives Matter to spread and promote this propaganda. For truthful statistics, see Bandler (2016) and Hosko (2018).

Become informed before you jump on the cop hating bandwagon. If massive protests occur, causing chaos and mayhem, you do not want your police demonized to the point where they are afraid to act or told to stand down. And, make sure you elect local politicians who are pro-police.

Join Act for America (ACT). ACT educates citizens about Islam and helps pass security-related bills.

If you are a parent, start home schooling, or become much more involved in your local schools. Islam is being heavily proselytized in public schools. Never forget, the *mutawwas* system starts by brainwashing children.

If you belong to a religious community, start inviting *Understanding the Threat* to advise and educate. The Muslim Brotherhood are arming themselves in American mosques. Make your church, synagogue or other community aware.

This book details the horrors of what happens to a country once Islam has infiltrated, but also demonstrates what happens when people become complacent and do nothing to stop it.

Do not be complacent.

APPENDIX

The years 633-833

"To complete the picture and legitimize their own rule in religious terms, the Abbasids used the story that the grandson of Muhammad...being the inheritor of the religious authority of the [Ali] line, had transferred it to the Abbasids. ...[This] connected the Abbasid Arab state with the history of Islam...The repeated promise of equality in everything to everyone who joined the Muslims... this was the main political claim of the Abbasid traditions, because in it rested the legitimacy of any non-Arab ruler to reign" (p.349-350, Nevo & Koren 2003).

During the creation of Islam, the issue of religious leadership was solved partly with the creation of Ali. The story was created that Muhammad's daughter, Fatima, married Ali and their offspring were the rightful successors of Muhammad.

In its origins, the word *ali* was a Christological term that meant "exalted one." Ali, the exalted one, was placed as Muhammad's son-in-law in order to be acceptable as successor to leadership. The "chosen one," which originally referred to Jesus, became Muhammad and Ali became his "exalted" associate.

Jesus had twelve disciples. The majority of Shi'a are known as "Twelvers." Twelvers are the followers of the twelve imams considered to be the rightful successors of Muhammad.

According to Shi'a, Ali was persecuted and then martyred (as was Christ). The "twelve" imams (similar to Christ's "twelve" disciples) were also persecuted.

The Muslim explanation of the split in Islam is that after Muhammad's death, the Muslims split into two camps. Some (who became Sunni) believed that Muhammad did not have a successor because he had no son, so they elected Abu Bakr to be the leader of the Muslims. Others (who became Shi'a) did not accept this because they held that Muhammad had a daughter. This daughter married Ali, who became like a son to Muhammad. Their descendants were the rightful successors to religious leadership.

Twelvers do not accept *hadith* transmitted by their enemies, such as those stories about Muhammad passed down by Aisha (Muhammad's child bride) and others who they consider the enemies of the twelve imams.

In other words, many laws created from Sunni *hadith* are not accepted by Shi'a. Therefore, Sunnis believe Shi'a do not follow "true" Islam and this is one reason why Sunnis "purify" Islam by committing genocide on Shi'a.

According to Shi'a, the split in Islam began with Ali and ended with Muhammad ibn al-Hasan, the twelfth, or 'hidden' imam. This 'hidden' imam lives in occultation and will reappear at End Times. This imam will reappear simultaneously with the Second Coming of Christ. Shi'a Twelvers believe Christ will assist the twelfth imam in establishing peace in the world.

In 617, the Persians had plundered Jerusalem and expulsed the Jews. From these events, the Jews concluded that the King Messiah was about to arise and he would build a new Temple. The Christian interpretation was that the Temple built by this Messiah would coincide with the Second Coming of Christ.

The Arabs had existed in the Negev region of Israel since Old Testament times, and centuries later, had fought with the Jews in Jerusalem. Many Arab tribes were highly influenced by both Judaism and Christianity.

In the Old Testament, the twelve tribes that descended from Jacob were called Israel. Jacob and his family went to Egypt where the Israelites multiplied and became the Israelite people. God made Himself known to Moses and rescued the Israelites from Egypt. The Israelites were given the Torah and a Covenant with God.

Eventually the Israelites sought leadership and Saul was chosen. Following a civil war with Saul, David forged a unified Israelite monarchy and established Jerusalem as the capital. After David's death, his successor was his son, Solomon. Solomon built the first Jewish Temple in Jerusalem.

Coins bear the legend "Zion" during the rule of Mu'awiya (r.661-680). According to Popp (2010), this was part of the Arab Christian concept. The Arab Christians saw themselves as the "heirs of the tradition of Israel…The conception of a 'new Zion' was anchored in the Syrian church traditions of the 'true Israel'." (p.45)

The Levant had previously minted coins in copper, showing their secondary status to leadership in Constantinople, but during Abd al-Malik's rule, he began minting coins in gold. This signified an attempt to split from Byzantine leadership.

Abd al-Malik's gold coins differed from traditional Byzantine coins; the depictions on al-Malik's coins symbolized the founding of Israel through Jacob (father of the twelve tribes of Israel). Al-Malik also had coins minted with the image of the seven-branched Jewish lamp (see: Popp 2010, pg. 73).

Ohlig (2009) states: "Because of the Syrian mentality's relationship to Jewish ways of thinking, and also because of the use of the same language, namely Aramaic, there was a growing convergence between Jews and Christians around the year 700" (p.371, "Syrian and Arabian Christianity").

According to Popp (2010), starting in 693-694, "Abd al-Malik's gold coins…set his relationship with the 'true Israel' against the Christological relations indicated by the image on the Byzantine coins: on the one hand, the depiction of the symbol of the founding of Israel through Jacob, the "Stone" in the form of the biblical *Yegar Sahaduta*; and on the other, the depiction of Christ as *Pantocrator*." (p.67)

The image of the Beth-el (i.e. the "House of God" from Genesis 28:15-10) is represented by the *Yegar Sahaduta,* which is a pile of stones.

Beth-el was about 10 miles north of Jerusalem. It was there that Jacob had a vision and at this place God talked with him. There he built an altar and called the place Beth-el. Here the Ark of the Covenant was kept for a while under the care of the grandson of Aaron (Judges 20:26-28).

Popp (2010) states: "The disappearance of the sign of the cross…did not, therefore, result from an Islamic rejection …The replacement of the sign of the cross with the image of the *Beth-El* in the form of the *Yegar Sahaduta* [pile of stones] was a part of the ideological controversy" (p.60, Popp 2010).

When al-Malik's son, al-Walid, took power (r.705-715), he chose to be the protector of St. John's Tomb and Basilica in Damascus. Up until this time there is still no mention of Mecca in Arabia, an Arab prophet, or anything related to the Arabs having a religion of their own.

"In the place of a Messiah with a flame-sword, which indicated the end of the world was nigh, there was now a preacher, in the form of St. John the Baptist, who already centuries before had called for change" (p.98, Popp 2013, "From Ugarit").

St. John the Baptist's Basilica was chosen because according to the Gospels, John's mission was to pave the way for change so as to be able to hear and receive the message of Christ. Baptism, immersion in water, symbolized repentance and preparation for change.

Al-Malik believed the Second Coming of Christ was about to take place. His son was named al-Walid. Al-Walid means "new birth," as in the new birth of Christ and preparing for Christ. Al-Walid chose St. John the Baptist's Basilica because it represented cleansing of sins in preparation of Christ.

After al-Walid, Abd al-Malik's other son, Sulayman took power.

Sulayman means Solomon. Solomon built the First Temple, which was a tribute to God and reaffirmed the Israelites' Covenant with God.

The Old Testament ends with the children of Israel waiting for a Messiah. The New Testament introduces John the Baptist who offers a ritual cleansing which will erase past mistakes in order to begin a new relationship with God.

The Old Covenant expected perfect obedience, but being human, people were unable to keep the Old Covenant (they broke some of the 'Thou Shalt Nots'). The New Testament offers a New Covenant and teaches that God will forgive.

In 617, Jews began anticipating the arrival of a "King Messiah" who would bring in the Messianic Age. Abd al-Malik means "Servant of the King." His sons were named al-Walid (new birth) and Sulayman (Solomon).

The rule of Abd al-Malik and his sons lasted until 717.

Starting in 695, iconoclasm was on the rise. Iconoclasm is the belief in the destruction of religious icons and images and also churches if religious images were inscribed into their walls. The Israelites had broken the Covenant with God when they worshipped idols. Christians did not want to repeat this mistake by worshipping images and icons.

Government-led iconoclasm began in 695. By 717, icons and images were banned and Emperor Leo III ordered the widespread destruction of religious images and monuments. By 754, Constantine V declared image worship blasphemy. The destruction conducted by Christian iconoclasts from 695-754 had nothing to do with Islam.

The Monophysites used icons and images. As the transition took place from Monophysite to Dyophysite rulership in the Levant, the Monophysites were persecuted and their churches were defaced, and sometimes, destroyed. Monophysite leaders in the Levant were forced to go underground to hide from persecution (hidden imams).

During the transition period, and before Islam was created and fully codified, rock inscriptions in the Negev of Israel state: You are the Lord of the world, the Lord of Moses and Aaron" (*amin rabb al alamin rabb Musa wa Harun*). Harun means Aaron.

Aaron ranks as one of the three most important high priests in the Bible. He was the founder and head of the Israelite priesthood and together with his brother Moses, led the Israelites out of Egypt. But Aaron has also appeared in different roles in Christianity. The first Christian communities in Israel believed the sons of Aaron were of the highest priesthood.

In the Qumrān sect, a Jewish community that flourished during the birth of Christianity, Aaron was the symbol of a strong priesthood. In the Dead Sea Scrolls, two messiahs were expected, one from the sons of Aaron, and one of Israel. Once again, we see this belief in the arrival of two Messiahs.

A gold coin dated at 793 reads: abd allah harun (Servant of God, Aaron). Other inscriptions on coins used the word rasid/rashid = guided one (see: p.159, Popp 2013, "From Ugarit").

Coins during this period did not mention the name of a ruler.

Though a ruler is not mentioned, and the words harun (Aaron) and rasid/rashid (guided one) were never combined, when Islamic history was later created, the creators chose to create a ruler named Harun al-Rashid who they say ruled from 786 to 809.

Aaron had strong ties to both Judaism and to Christianity. How better to remove Christian and Judaic ties than to make Harun/Aaron the Abbasid "hero" Harun al-Rashid who waged jihad against the infidels.

When the capital was moved to Baghdad in 762, the first Abbasid administration consisted primarily of Christians and Buddhists. Buddhist temple leaders held high authority as viziers (see Popp 2010, pgs. 91-93).

The first Abbasids were not Muslims.

After Islam was more fully codified in the mid-ninth century, Harun al-Rashid was inserted into Islam's history. The creators of Islamic history say Harun al-Rashid executed the chief Buddhist leaders and their clan for failure to submit.

This was the birth of "jihad" against those who do not submit to the new rulers. Those who submit will be treated with equality. Those who do not submit must either be killed or pay high taxes (jeezya) and be treated with inequality.

As Nevo and Koren (2003) point out, this emphasis on equality to all who submit "was the main political claim of the Abbasid[s]..." (p.349-350, Nevo & Koren 2003).

By giving equality to the Arabs in return for submission to Abbasid authority and rule, Arab mercenary armies became armies for the Abbasids. Well-known for their ruthless fighting practices, they conquered and took territory for the new rulers.

The Islamification of biblical history

According to Muslim sources, Muhammad al-Ṭabari was a collector and commentator of *hadith*, wrote commentaries on the Quran, and wrote a massive volume on Islamic history. Current Islamic "scholars" rely heavily on al-Tabari for historical Islam. According to al-Tabari, Adam, Eve, Noah, Moses and Abraham were all Muslims.

Allegedly, al-Tabari lived from 839-923 and was a Muslim historian whose annals are the most important source for the early history of Islam.

According to Muslim sources, al-Tabari mostly used "oral transmissions" for his collection of *hadith* and for his histories.

As outlined in Chapter Three, "oral transmissions" should never be taken as factual.

Al-Tabari is translated as "the one from Tabaristan." Tabaristan was an area in northern Persia, what is currently Turkmanistan. But if one analyzes the works of al-Tabari, it becomes evident his writings were not written by one man; they were written by a team of writers who were chosen to create a history that would help enforce political Islam (see: Popp 2013 "From Ugarit"; Popp 2013 "The Influence").

According to al-Tabari, Adam and Eve were banished from Paradise and reunited near Mecca. Thus, Adam and Eve were Islamacized (see also: Khoury 2001; Kister 1993; Schock 2001).

Adam landed on the hill of Safa and Eve landed on the hill of Marwa (see also: al-Masudi 1998, p.18). They were reunited in Muzdalifa, the area between the two hills, and thus, the hills and Muzdalifa were blended into the background for Haj pilgrimage in Saudi Arabia.

In this way Mecca was placed into Islamic history and became the area where Allah made a covenant with the future descendants of Adam (see also: Bowering 2001). Adam brought the 'black stone' of the *kabba* from heaven and also 'the rod of Moses' (al-Tabari, p.126-7).

These stories make Adam and Eve the first pilgrims to Mecca and establish Moses as Muslim.

Allah sent the *kabba* down to Adam to provide him with a place of worship (al-Tabari, p. 122-123). According to al-Tabari, the *kabba* was built with a pile of stones. Remember, the Beth-el, the "House of God" from Genesis, is represented by a pile of stones. According to Muslim sources, the stones used for the *kabba* were taken from Mt. Sinai in Egypt, Mt. Olive in Jerusalem, Mt. Lebanon, which is mentioned in the Bible as part of the Promised Land, Mt. Ararat, which according to Genesis, is where Noah's Ark lies, and Mt. Hira, where Muhammad allegedly received revelations from Allah (p.123-124).

Abraham's son Ishmael is associated with various sites near Mecca, which were eventually written into Muslim traditions and are now stations in the Haj in Saudi Arabia.

Ishmael's insertion into Arabia came from a re-writing of a passage from Genesis in which Hagar and Ishmael wander in the wilderness of Beer Sheba. When Ishmael is about to die, an angel appears and reveals a well of water.

Muslims re-wrote this story and changed the location to the Hijaz region of Arabia where Mecca lies. According to Muslim sources, this well of water is the sacred well next to the *kabba* (see also: Hawting 1980; Torrey 1967).

According to Islamic history, when Hagar and Ishmael were looking for water, Hagar called out to her son in Hebrew, but Ishmael answered in Arabic. This establishes Arabic as the new holy language (see: al-Masudi, p.44).

Another change in biblical history, originally altered by ibn Ishaq, but picked up by al-Tabari and other Muslim "historians," is the addition of the name of the mother of Ishmael's sons. Muslim sources named her Sayyida bint Mudad and say she was a member of a tribe near Mecca (al-Tabari, p.351-52).

This change in biblical history places Ishamel's sons in the Hijaz region of Arabia.

Ishamael's first sons were turned into ancestors of Muhammad, beginning with Abdallah (abd allah), Muhammad's father (see also: ibn Hisham 1971).

Further evidence that the Quran was originally a Christian liturgical book

In Christoph Luxenberg's, *The Syro-Aramaic Reading of the Koran*, Luxenberg analyzes samples of the Quran which he believes have been misread and misinterpreted due to the Quran's Aramaic origins. Samples include one of the most misunderstood texts in the Quran: the Virgins of Paradise.

Luxenberg notes that verses 44:54 and 52:20 are usually translated something like: "We have paired them with dark, wide-eyed maidens." But in Aramaic, Luxenberg says this sentence means: "We will make you comfortable under white, crystal clear grapes." (p.251)

Luxenberg points out that the "virgin" segments were in all likelihood taken from the fourth century Aramaic hymn of Ephraem called *On Paradise*. Ephraem's hymn gives a vivid description of the grapes and grapevines of Paradise.

Luxenberg states, "The Koran is doing nothing more with this metaphor than describing this fruit of Paradise par excellence in a totally special way and emphasizing it over the other fruits of Paradise." (p.259)

Quran verses 2:25, 3:15 and 4:57 are usually translated and interpreted using the words "companions pure and holy" (i.e. virgins). If read as Aramaic, Luxenberg says this phrase means "all manner of species of pure fruits." (p.266)

Quran verse 37:48-49 is usually interpreted something like: With them are damsels restrained in glance, wide-eyed, as they were eggs (or pearls) well-guarded (Bell 1958); or, And besides them will be chaste women, restraining their glances, with big eyes of wonder and beauty. (Ali 1968)

But Luxenberg says, when this verse is read as Aramaic, the verse means: "They will have hanging fruits (grapes), jewel-like, as were they pearls yet enclosed in the shell." (p.267)

Quran verse 38:52 is usually interpreted something like: And beside them will be chaste women restraining their glances, companions of equal age. (Ali 1968)

In Aramaic, Luxenberg says the verse should be read: "Among them will be juicy fruits hanging down (i.e. grapes)." (p.271)

Verse 76:19 usually reads something like: Round amongst them go boys of perpetual youth. (Bell 1958)

Luxenberg says, in Aramaic, the 'boys of perpetual youth' refers to parts of the New Testament (Mt. 26:29; Mk. 14:25, Lk. 22:18), which refer to the Last Supper. (p.285)

In the New Testament, Christ raises his chalice, gives thanks and passes it round to his disciples, saying, "I will not drink henceforth from this child of the vine, since I will drink it new with you in my Father's kingdom. (Mt. 26:28-29)

Luxenberg says this drink, the 'child of the vine,' is the Aramaic reading of Quran verse 76:19. It is not "boys of perpetual youth," but wine.

Luxenberg states: "The Christian symbolism of the wine of Paradise can probably be traced to these well-known words from the Last Supper. Also, based on this are the Christian notions of Ephraem the Syrian concerning the grapevines of Paradise. Finally, traceable to this are the falsely understood huris [the word usually thought to mean virgins] and the correctly understood white grapes." (p. 285-286)

The fruits of paradise are described by Ephraem the Syrian as being fruits that are choice picks, i.e. pure, white, jewel-like, and often compared to pearls. These verses are Christian symbolism of the grapes and wine in Paradise and are not referring to virgins, nor boys of perpetual youth.

Mosaics inside Syrian churches also depict the vines and grapes of paradise.

The Syrian Christian concept of paradise, which was a state of happiness and peace, was removed during the evolution of the Quran and the

Persian Zoroastrian concept of paradise was inserted in its place. The earliest commentaries made on Qurans were made by Persians.

The Syrian Christians were "content if their souls were safe in the bosom of the patriarchs... [and they were refreshed] with cool, white grapes from the vines of Paradise" (p.362, Popp 2013 "The Influence").

The Abbasids inserted the concept of Persian temple slaves into the Islamic idea of paradise. The Persians believed that virgins guide the souls of the dead to paradise. (see: Popp 2013, "The Influence")

The commentaries made by "scholars" during the early development of the Quran inserted their idea of paradise into the incoherent text of the Arabic Quran.

Important facts that took place during Mu'awiya

In 648, Constans II, the Byzantine emperor at the time, tried to separate himself from the conflict within Christianity. He removed the declaration made by Heraclius in the Hagia Sophia Cathedral and forbade discussions about whether Christ possessed one or two wills or one or two energies.

Nonetheless, the debate continued and Monophysite Christians in the Levant and in Egypt continued to be persecuted.

Before the Arab conquest, Egypt had been governed by a Roman civil service and military, who also made up the ruling class. The native Coptic Egyptians were excluded. The Romans ruled from Alexandria but had a fortress built in Babylon (on the outskirts of what is now Cairo). They built a chain of fortresses, each with a small army attached, southward toward Sudan so as to keep their rule and to collect taxes.

The Arab conquest of Egypt was achieved with a very small army of around 40 Arab mercenary fighters. Egyptians hated the Romans and the Byzantine leadership that took their place and conducted constant rebellions against them. The native Egyptians joined this Arab army to oust Byzantine leadership in Egypt.

The Copts paid taxes to the new leadership and provided food for their army. The new rulers lived in Damascus and military leaders in Egypt kept isolated and lived on the outskirts of the city of Cairo separated from native Egyptians.

The Arab military leaders inside Egypt created a small tent city called Fustat and the Arab mercenary fighters remained inside it. Throughout this period there is no evidence of any kind regarding conversions to Islam or that the Arabs were Muslims. The Arabs were described as pagans from desert regions.

After the death of Heraclius in 641, the emperors who followed were weakened due to financial problems and also the conflict on doctrine.

Mu'awiya tried to take advantage of the situation growing in Constantinople while Byzantium was weak. In North Africa, protests had erupted over Constantinople's stance on Monotheletism and Monoenergism. Christians in Egypt and North Africa were on Mu'awiya's side because Mu'awiya was a Monophysite.

Maximus the Confessor, known for his religious treatises, was drawn into the controversy on doctrine. In a debate held with many North African bishops, Maximus took the position that Jesus possessed both a human and a divine will.

In 649, Constans II had Maximus the Confessor brought to trial for his position on Jesus. Maximus was convicted and his tongue and right hand were mutilated.

In 649, Mu'awiya set up a navy manned by Monophysite Syrian Christians, Egyptian Copts (Monophysites), Jacobite Syrian Christians (Monophysites) and Arab mercenary units. Mu'awiya's navy defeated the Byzantine navy in 655 (Lewis 1951; Lewis & Runyan 1990).

Debates and protests on doctrine continued, and in 662, fed up with doctrine disputes, Constans left Constantinople for Rome. Mu'awiya took advantage and formed an alliance with Syrian and Egyptian Monophysites (see: p.53, Popp 2013, "From Ugarit"). With Constans II in Rome, Mu'awiya decided he had an opportunity to take Constantinople.

Mu'awiya's troops made it to Chalcedon, about four miles from Constantinople. The Byzantines had always been able to hold off the Persians at this location because the Byzantines were superior at sea combat. Mu'awiya used the Egyptian fleet, who were masters at sea.

But, Constans II was killed in 668 and his son Constantine IV took his place at the palace in Constantinople. Constantinople was no longer abandoned. Mu'awiya's attack on Constantinople failed and then a horrible storm caused much of his army to be destroyed. After the double catastrophe, Mu'awiya withdrew (see: Popp 2013 "From Ugarit" p.55).

Iconoclasm: it was the Christians who destroyed icons, images and monuments

In the early 700s, the great iconoclastic controversy hit. In the Near East, paganism became more visible as Arab mercenary fighters filtered into the urban centers. Religious art and icons began to be compared to paganism and condemned by those who adopted a literal interpretation of the Ten Commandments, which forbids the making and worshipping of images.

There were also economic motives. After the Byzantine-Persian war, Byzantium was financially devastated. Emperors used iconoclastic reasoning to confiscate valuable art in churches and used it for their own endeavors.

Iconoclasm also arose because Byzantine emperors were losing their authority due to the popularity of icons and the various religious leaders who promoted them. Byzantine leaders tried to reclaim their authority via iconoclasm.

In 695, Justinian II added a full-face image of Christ on his imperial gold coins. This caused outrage by those who adopted the literal interpretation of the Ten Commandments. The destruction of images and icons began to intensify at this time.

The intensification of iconoclasm after 695 led to government-led iconoclasm. In 717, Emperor Leo III banned icons and images and he ordered the widespread destruction of religious images and monuments. People who continued to use icons and images were heavily persecuted. In the Nestorian church of Persia, opposition to religious images became the norm and churches removed icons.

In 754, Constantine V condemned the use of icons and declared image worship to be blasphemy. During the 760s, iconophiles were vigorously persecuted.

In 787, Constantine's son and his widow Irene revoked the iconoclast policies, but iconoclasm was reinstated shortly afterwards under Leo V. By 814, iconoclasm was established as imperial policy and icons were forbidden. Churches with icons and images decorating their walls were defaced and some were destroyed.

Leo V's successors, Michael II (820-829) and Theophilos (829-842) continued the policies of iconoclasm.

From 717-843, religious art, icons and images were forbidden and icons, images, churches and monuments were destroyed—by Christians.

*sources for Iconoclasm: Kazhdan 1991; Meyendorff 1996; North 1991; Rodley 1994)

SOURCES

2012 Intel doc: *The West will facilitate the Islamic State*. http://www.cheriberens.net/2012-intel-document-west-will-facilitate-rise-of-islamic-state-in-order-to-isolate-the-syrian-government.html

Ali, Abdullah Yusuf. *The Holy Qur'an: Text, Translation and Commentary*. Dar al-Arabia Publishing. Beirut, Lebanon: 1968.

Ali, Gawad. *Detailed History of the Arabs before Islam*. Beirut: 1980.

Ali, Hashim Amir. *The Message of the Qur'an*. Charles E. Tuttle Company. Tokyo, Japan: 1974.

Ali, Maulana Muhammad. *The Holy Qur'an: Arabic text, English translation and commentary*. Ahmadiyyah Anjuman Isha'at Islam. Lahore, India: 1963.

Alisfahani, abu al-Farag. *Kitab al-Agani*. Cairo, Egypt: 1928.

Al-Masudi, Ali ibn al-Husayn. *Ithbat al-wasiyya lil-imam Ali ibn abi Talib*. Beirut, Lebanon: Dar al-adwa, 1998.

Al-Qaeda has intensified its operations worldwide. http://www.cheriberens.net/al-qaeda-has-intensified-its-operations-worldwide.html

Al-Qaeda: Many faces of an Islamist threat. http://www.cheriberens.net/al-qaeda-the-many-faces-of-an-islamist-threat.html

Al-Razzaq, Abd. *Tafsīr al-Qur'ān*. Ed. Muṣṭafā Muslim Muḥammad. Maktabat al-Rushd. Riyad, Saudi Arabia: 1989.

Al-Shami, Khalid. *Statements by Muslim Brotherhood Leaders on Succession to Murshid General*. Al-Quds al-Arabi. London: 2009.

Al-Tabari, abu Gafar Muhammad. *Collection of Quran Suras and Commentaries*. Cairo, Egypt: 1968.

Al-Tabari, Muhammad ibn Jarir. *Ta'rikh al-rusul wa-l-muluk*. Edited by M. Ibrahim. Cairo, Egypt: Dar al-ma'arif, 1987.

Amnesty International. Egypt: Evidence points to torture carried out by Morsi supporters. August 2, 2013. https://www.amnesty.org/en/press-releases/2013/08/egypt-evidence-points-torture-carried-out-morsi-supporters/

Attacks on Christians. Sadad: http://www.cheriberens.net/massacres-at-sadad-syria.html
Maaloula: http://www.cheriberens.net/syrian-army-fights-for-maaloula.html

Avni, Gideon. *The Persian Conquest of Jerusalem (614 CE): An archaeological assessment*. Excavations and Surveys Department, Israel Antiquities Authority. Israel: 2010.

Avni, Gideon. "The Urban Area of Jerusalem in the Roman and Byzantine Periods: A View from the Necropolis." *Journal of Roman Archaeology* 18: 373-396, 2005.

Avni, Gideon, and J. Seligman. "New Excavations at the Church of the Holy Sepulchre Compound." In, *One Land, Many Cultures: Archaeological Studies in Honor of Stanislao Loffreda*. Eds. G. C. Bottini, L. Di Segni and L. D. Chrupcala. Studium Biblicum Franciscanum. Jerusalem: 2003.

Balhag, Salih, and Salwa al-Ayub. *Arab Christianity and its Development from its origin to the tenth Christian century*. Beirut: 1995.

Bandler, Aaron. "5 Stats you need to know about cops killing black." *Daily Wire*: July 7, 2016. https://www.dailywire.com/news/7264/5-statistics-you-need-know-about-cops-killing-aaron-bandler

Barnavi, Eli, editor. *A Historical Atlas of the Jewish People.* Schocken Books. New York: 1994.

Bashear, Suliman. *Arabs and Others in Early Islam.* Darwin Press. London: 1998.

Bashear, Suliman. "Arabs and Others in Early Islam." *Studies in Late Antiquity and Early Islam* 8, Feb. 1998.

Bashear, Suliman. "Qur'an 2:114 and Jerusalem." *Bulletin of the School of Oriental and African Studies,* vol. 52, no. 2, pp. 215-238. University of London: 1989.

Bashear, Suliman. *Studies in Early Islamic Tradition.* Max Schloessinger Memorial Foundation. Jerusalem: 2004.

Bell, Richard. *Introduction to the Quran.* Edinburgh: 1958.

Ben-David, Lenny. "Secrets under the Al-Aqsa Mosque." *Jerusalem Center for Public Affairs.* October 27, 2015.

Bensaada, Ahmed. *Arabesque Americaine.* Michel Brule: May 2, 2011.

Berens, Cheri. *30,000 illegals from countries listed as having high terrorist concerns crossed the Mexican border.* http://www.cheriberens.net/30000-illegals-from-countries-listed-as-having-high-terrorist-concerns-have-crossed-the-mexican-border-into-the-us.html

Berens, Cheri. *Al-Qaeda has intensified its operations http://www.cheriberens.net/al-qaeda-has-intensified-its-operations-worldwide.html worldwide.* http://www.cheriberens.net/al-qaeda-has-intensified-its-operations-worldwide.html

Berens, Cheri. *Global Muslim Brotherhood.* http://www.cheriberens.net/the-global-muslim-brotherhood.html

Berens, Cheri. *Inside the Quran: Hatred and Violence.* http://www.cheriberens.net/inside-the-quran-hatred-and-violence.html

Berens, Cheri. *Irrefutable Evidence that the Syrian government did not conduct chemical attacks on its people.* http://www.cheriberens.net/irrefutable-evidence-that-the-syrian-government-did-not-conduct-chemical-attacks-on-its-people.html

Berens, Cheri. *Jihad in American Mosques.* http://www.cheriberens.net/jihad-in-american-mosques.html

Berens, Cheri. *Muslim Brotherhood in America.* http://www.cheriberens.net/the-muslim-brotherhood-in-america.html

Berens, Cheri. *No Need for Prayer Rooms at Schools or the Workplace: Muslims are allowed to miss prayers.* http://www.cheriberens.net/no-need-for-prayer-rooms-at-schools-or-workplace-muslims-are-allowed-to-miss-prayers.html

Berens, Cheri. *Propaganda organizations disguised as humanitarian groups.* http://www.cheriberens.net/these-groups-are-propaganda-organizations-disguised-as-humanitarian-groups.html

Berens, Cheri. *Saudi Arabia and the destruction of Islamic history: Sources.* https://www.independent.co.uk/news/world/middle-east/medina-saudis-take-a-bulldozer-to-islams-history-8228795.html https://en.wikipedia.org/wiki/Destruction_of_early_Islamic_heritage_sites_in_Saudi_Arabia https://www.islamicpluralism.org/764/islamic-heritage-lost-as-makkah-modernises

Berens, Cheri. *Terrorists from the Middle East are traveling through Mexico.* http://www.cheriberens.net/terrorists-from-the-middle-east-are-in-the-caravan-traveling-through-mexico.html

Berens, Cheri. *U.S. Intel report describes how the Muslim Brotherhood began controlling western media.* http://www.cheriberens.net/us-intel-report-describes-how-the-muslim-brotherhood-began-controlling-western-media.html

Berens, Cheri. *U.S. trained and armed terrorists in Syria: A $500 million dollar program.* http://www.cheriberens.net/us-participated-in-a-500-million-dollar-program-to-train-and-arm-terrorists-in-syria.html

Berens, Cheri. *What is the Muslim Brotherhood doing in Your State?* http://www.cheriberens.net/what-is-the-muslim-brotherhood-doing-in-your-state.html

Berens, Cheri. *White Helmets: an Islamist propaganda group and funded arm of the U.S. government.* http://www.cheriberens.net/white-helmetsnbspan-islamist-propagandist-group-and-funded-arm-of-us-government.html

Berens, Cheri. *Who are the experts who testify against designating the Muslim Brotherhood a terrorist group?* http://www.cheriberens.net/who-are-the-ldquoexpertsrdquo-who-testify-against-designating-the-muslim-brotherhood-a-terrorist-group.html

Berens, Cheri. *Who are the refugees that are coming to America?* http://www.cheriberens.net/who-are-the-refugees-that-are-coming-to-america.html

Berens, Cheri. *Women's march towards Islam?* http://www.cheriberens.net/womenrsquos-march-towards-islam.html

Berens, Cheri. *Yemen Sources.* https://geopolitics.co/2016/09/22/beyond-the-bloodletting-in-yemen/ https://www.economist.com/erasmus/2015/09/09/the-religious-and-cultural-heritage-being-ruined-by-yemens-war and http://www.unesco.org/new/ar/culture/theme/single-view/news/unesco_director_general_calls_on_all_parties_to_protect_yemeni_heritage/#.VtKmnPkrLIU

Berg, Herbert. "The Implications of, and Opposition to, the Methods and Theories of John Wansbrough." In, *The Quest for the Historical Muhammad.* Edited with Translations by Ibn Warraq. Prometheus Books. New York: 2000.

Berg, Herbert. *The development of exegesis in early Islam: the authenticity of Muslim literature from the formative period.* Routledge. UK: 2000.

Beyer, Rudolph. "The Strophic Structure of the Koran." In, *What the Koran Really Says.* Edited by Ibn Warraq. Prometheus Books. New York: 2002.

Binder, Donald, Birger Olsson and Anders Runesson. *The Ancient Synagogue from its Origins to 200 C.E.* Brill: 2010.

Bishai, Wilson B. "A Possible Coptic Source of a Qur'anic Text." In, *What the Koran Really Says.* Edited by Ibn Warraq. New York: Prometheus Books, 2002.

Bitton-Ashkelony, B. "Encountering the Sacred: The Debate on Christian Pilgrimage in Late Antiquity." *The Transformation of the Classical Heritage Series* 38: 22-24, 78. The University of California Press. Berkeley, 2005.

Bloom, Jonathan M. "The Minaret." *Saudi Aramco World.* Aramco Services Company: Houston, Texas. March/April 2002.

Bowering, G. "Covenant", *Encyclopedia of the Quran*, vol 1: 464-67, 2001.

Brock, Sebastian. "Syriac Sources for Seventh Century History." *Byzantine and Modern Greek Studies* 2: 17-36, 1976.

Brock, Sebastian. "Syriac Views of Emergent Islam." In, *Studies on the First Century of Islamic Society*. Edited by J.Y.N. Boll. Southern Illinois Univ. Press. Carbondale, Ill: 1982.

Burrows, M. "The Byzantine Tombs in the Garden of the Jerusalem School." *BASOR* 47: 28-35, 1932.

Butler, Howard Crosby, and Baldwin Smith. *Early Churches in Syria, fourth to seventh centuries*. University of Princeton: 1929.

Caetani, Leone. "Uthman and the Recension of the Koran." In, *The Origins of the Koran: Classic Essays on Islam's Holy Book*. Edited by Ibn Warraq. Prometheus Books. New York: 1998.

Cartalucci, Tony. CIA Coup-College. Activist Post: February, 2011. http://landdestroyer.blogspot.com/2011/02/cia-coup-college.html

Cartalucci, Tony. George Soros and Egypt's New Constitution: For Egyptians, the nightmare is just beginning. Activist Post: February 18, 2011. https://www.activistpost.com/2011/02/george-soros-egypts-new-constitution.html

Cartalucci, Tony. Google's Revolution Factory; Alliance of Youth Movements: Color Revolution 2.0. Activist Post: February 12, 2011. https://www.activistpost.com/2011/02/googles-revolution-factory-alliance-of.html

Cartalucci, Tony. Neo-Cons for Human Rights? Activist Post: February 16, 2011. https://www.activistpost.com/2011/02/neo-cons-for-human-rights.html

Cartalucci, Tony. US Department of Imperial Expansion: Deeper down the rabbit hole of US-backed color revolutions. Land Destroyer Report: March, 2011. http://landdestroyer.blogspot.com/2011/03/us-department-of-imperial-expansion.html

Cartalucci, Tony. Want to Understand the Egypt Issue? George Soros is Writing Egypt's Constitution. Truth is Treason: February 18, 2011. http://www.truthistreason.net/want-to-understand-the-egypt-issue-george-soros-is-writing-egypts-constitution

Chaulia, Sreeram. "Democratization, Color Revolutions, and the Role of the NGOs." *Global Research*: December 25, 2005. https://www.globalresearch.ca/democratisation-colour-revolutions-and-the-role-of-the-ngos-catalysts-or-saboteurs/1638

Clermont–Ganneau, C. "The Taking of Jerusalem by the Persians, A.D. 614". *PEFQst* 31: 36-54.

Committee to Protect Journalists (CPJ). At nonviolence rally in Cairo, attacks against the press. June 24, 2013. https://cpj.org/2013/06/at-nonviolence-rally-in-cairo-attacks-against-pres.php

Committee to Protect Journalists (CPJ). Journalists attacked while covering protests in Egypt. December 7, 2012. http://www.cpj.org/2012/12/journalists-attacked-while-covering-protests-in-eg.php

Conrad, Lawrence. "Kai elabon ten heram: Aspects of the Early Muslim Conquests in Southern Palestine." Paper presented at the 4th International Colloquium: From Jahiliyya to Islam. Hebrew University. Jerusalem: 1987.

Conrad, Lawrence. *The Byzantine and Early Islamic Near East: Elites Old and New*. Darwin Press. London: 2004.

Conybeare, F.C. "Antiochus Strategius' Account of the Sack of Jerusalem in A.D. 614". *English Historical Review* 25: 502-517.

Cook, David. *Contemporary Muslim Apocalyptic Literature*. Syracuse University Press. New York: 2008.

Cook, Michael. *Early Muslim Dogma: A Source Critical Study*. Cambridge University Press: 1981.

Corriente, F. "From Old Arabic to Classical Arabic." *Journal of Semitic Studies* 21, 1976: 62-98.

Counter Extremism Project. *Ayman al-Zawahiri.*
https://www.counterextremism.com/extremists/ayman-al-zawahiri/

Creswell, K.A.C. *A Short Account of Early Muslim Architecture.* Harmondsworth Publishing. UK: 1958.

Creswell, K.A.C. *Early Muslim Architecture.* Oxford: Clarendon Press, 1969.

Creswell, K.A.C. *The Origin of the Plan of the Dome of the Rock.* British School of Archaeology in Jerusalem. London: 1924.

Crone, Patricia. *God's Rule - Government and Islam: Six centuries of Medieval Islamic political thought.* Columbia Univ. Press: 2005.

Crone, Patricia. *Meccan Trade and the Rise of Islam.* Oxford University Press: 1987.

Crone, Patricia. *Slaves on Horses: The Evolution of the Islamic Polity.* Cambridge University Press: 2003.

Crone, Patricia. "The First Century Concept of Higra." *Arabica: Journal of Arabic and Islamic Studies* XLI, 1994: 386-387.

Crone, Patricia, and Michael Cook. *Hagarism: The Making of the Islamic World.* Cambridge: Cambridge Univ. Press: 1977, 1980.

Crone, Patricia, and Martin Hinds. *God's Caliph: Religious Authority in the First Centuries of Islam.* Cambridge University Press: 1986.

Crowfoot, J.W. and Fitzgerald, G.M. *Excavations in the Tyropoeon Valley, Jerusalem, 1927.* Annual of the Palestine Exploration Fund 5. London: Palestine Exploration Fund.

CSPI. Stats on texts devoted to the kafir. Center for the Study of Political Islam.
http://cspipublishing.com/statistical/TrilogyStats/AmtTxtDevotedKafir.html

Daily News Egypt. Egypt to aid Syrian rebels. DNE: June 15, 2013.
https://www.dailynewsegypt.com/2013/06/15/egypt-to-aid-syrian-rebels/

Das, Sujit. "Would the Earliest Quranic Manuscripts of Sana'a Spell the Downfall of Islam?" From, *Islam Watch: Telling the truth about Islam.* June 28, 2009. Retrieved on November 8, 2012.
http://www.islam-watch.org/authors/78-sujit/46-earliest-quranic-manuscripts-of- sanaa-downfall-of-islam.html

Dashti, Ali. Translated by F. R. C. Bagley. *Twenty-Three Years: A Study of the Prophetic Career of Mohammad.* Mazda Publications. Costa Mesa, CA: 1994.

Davies, J. Gordon. *The Origin and Development of Early Christian Church Architecture.* London: SCM Press, 1952.

Davies, J. Gordon. *The Architectural Setting of Baptism.* London: Barrie and Rockliff, 1962.

Defense and State Department Documents. https://www.judicialwatch.org/press-room/press-releases/judicial-watch-defense-state-department-documents-reveal-obama-administration-knew-that-al-qaeda-terrorists-had-planned-benghazi-attack-10-days-in-advance/
And: http://www.judicialwatch.org/wp-content/uploads/2015/05/JW-v-DOD-and-State-14-812-DOD-Release-2015-04-10-final-version.pdf And: https://www.judicialwatch.org/document-archive/jw-v-dod-and-state-14-812-state-release-2015-04-10-2/

Department of Defense. Information Report: August 12, 2014. http://www.judicialwatch.org/wp-content/uploads/2015/05/Pg.-291-Pgs.-287-293-JW-v-DOD-and-State-14-812-DOD-Release-2015-04-10-final-version11.pdf

Department of State. *Refugee Processing Center Affiliates.*
https://travel.state.gov/content/dam/visas/SIVs/Public%20Affiliate%20Directory.pdf

DePremare, Alfred-Louis. "Abd al-Malik B. Marwan and the Process of the Quran's Composition." In, *The Hidden Origins of Islam: New Research into Its Early History.* Edited by Karl-Heinz Ohlig and Gerd-R Puin. Prometheus Books. New York: 2009.

Dorstewitz, Michael. Syrian rebels accept help from US, pledge loyalty to al-Qaida. BIZPAC Review: June 14, 2013. http://www.bizpacreview.com/2013/06/14/syrian-rebels-accept-help-from-us-pledge-loyalty-to-al-qaida-77010

Egypt Brotherhood: The link was removed and replaced with this statement: The requested resource: /huff-wires/20121211/ml-egypt-brotherhood/is no longer available. Original link: http://www.huffingtonpost.com/huff-wires/20121211/ml-egypt-brotherhood/

Elam, Yohay. "Muslim Brotherhood Wants War with Israel." *FoxX*: January 31, 2011. https://www.forexcrunch.com/muslim-brotherhood-wants-war-with-israel/

Elaref, Aref. *A Brief Guide to the Dome of the Rock.* The Supreme Awqaf Council. Jerusalem: 1964.

El-Garhi, Mohamed. Al-Masry Al-Youm goes inside the Brotherhood's torture chambers. Egypt Independent: December 7, 2012.
http://www.egyptindependent.com/news/al-masry-al-youm-goes-inside-brotherhood-s-torture-chambers

El-Menawy, Abdel Latif. Egypt's countdown to June 30. Al-Arabiya: June 21, 2013. https://english.alarabiya.net/en/views/news/middle-east/2013/06/21/Egypt-s-countdown-to-June-30.html

El-Tabei, Haitham. Show of strength on Egypt streets: Brotherhood vs. rest of Egyptians. Middle East Online: November 25, 2012. http://www.middle-east-online.com/english/?id=55724

Emerson, Steve, John Rossomando, and Dave Yonkman. "Qatar's insidious influence on the Brookings Institution." *The Investigative Project on Terrorism*: October 28, 2014.
https://www.investigativeproject.org/4630/ipt-exclusive-qatar-insidious-influence-on#

Erizzo, F.M., editor. *Guillaume's note: Evangeliarum Hierosolymitanum.* Verona, Italy: 1861.

Eusebius Pamphilius. *Church History.* Edited by Philip Schaff. Christian Classics Ethereal Library: 1886.

Fick, Maggie. Ex-Qaeda allies ready to fight for Mursi in Luxor. Aswat Masriya: June 23, 2013. http://en.aswatmasriya.com/analysis/view.aspx?id=e9af075e-7dd8-4fe7-9e58-f30232889dcb

Foss, C. "The Persians in the Near East (602-630 AD)." *JRAS* 13: 149-170, 2003.

FoxNews. *Exclusive: Classified cable warned consulate couldn't withstand coordinated attack.* October 31, 2012. http://www.foxnews.com/politics/2012/10/31/exclusive-us-memo-warned-libya-consulate-couldnt-withstand-coordinated-attack.html

FoxNews. Hundreds of journalists attacked in Egypt since revolution, study finds. Fox News: May 30, 2013. http://www.foxnews.com/world/2013/05/30/hundreds-journalists-attacked-in-egypt-since-revolution-study-finds.html

FoxNews Business. "The Arming of Benghazi." June 27, 2015.
https://www.foxbusiness.com/politics/exclusive-the-arming-of-benghazi

Geva, H. "Jerusalem, the Byzantine Period." *New Encyclopedia of Archaeological Excavations in the Holy Land,* vol. 2: 768-85. Eds. E. Stern and A. Gilboa. Israel Exploration Society. Jerusalem: 1993.

Gibb, Hamilton A.R. "Arab-Byzantine Relations under the Umayyad Caliphate." *Dumbarton Oaks Papers* 12: 219-33, 1958.

Gibson, Dan. *Early Islamic Qiblas: A survey of mosques built between 1AH/622 CE and 263 AH/876 CE.* Independent Scholar's Press. Canada: 2017.

Gibson, Dan. *Quranic Geography.* Independent Scholars Press. Canada: 2011.

Gietmann, Gerhard, and Herbert Thurston. "Basilica." *The Catholic Encyclopedia.* New York: Robert Appleton Company, 1907.

Goldziher, Ignaz. *Muslim Studies.* Translated by C.R. Barber and S.M. Stern. Edited by S.M. Stern. Albany State University Press. New York: 1966.

Goldziher, Ignaz. "Read Anew: Islam and Parsism." In, *Early Islam: A critical reconstruction based on contemporary sources.* Edited by Karl-Heinz Ohlig. Prometheus Books. New York: 2013.

Griffith, Sidney. "Stephen of Ramlah and the Christian Kerygma in Arabic in Ninth Century Palestine. *Journal of Ecclesiastical History* 36: 23-45, 1985.

Gross, Markus. "New Ways of Qur'anic Research." In, *Early Islam: A critical reconstruction based on contemporary sources.* Edited by Karl-Heinz Ohlig. Prometheus Books. New York: 2013.

Guandolo, John. Why the MB is Still Not Designated as Terrorists in the US. The Counter Jihad Report: May 14, 2017. https://counterjihadreport.com/2017/05/14/why-the-mb-is-still-not-designated-as-terrorists-in-the-us/

Guandolo, John. The Primary Role of the Mosque is the Seat of the Islamic Government. UTT: January 15, 2019. https://www.understandingthethreat.com/primary-role-of-the-mosque/

Guillaume, A. *The Palestinian Syriac Lectionary of the Gospels.* Edited from two Sinai MSS and from P.de Lagarde`s edition of the *Evangeliarum Hierosolymitanum* by Agnes Smith Lewis and Magaret Dunlop Gibson, p. 187. London: 1899.

Guillaume, A. "The Version of the Gospels Used in Medina Circa 700 A.D." *Al-Andalus* 15: 289-296, 1950.

Hackensberger, Alfred. "From the Gospel to Islam: An interview with Christoph Luxenberg." *Chiesa Espresso Repubblica* 11: Italy, March 12-18, 2004.

Hagith, Sivan. *Palestine in Late Antiquity.* Oxford University Press. UK: 2008.

Haider, Kamran. "U.S. Supports Terrorists." *Swiss Info*: April 5, 2007. http://www.swissinfo.org.80/eng/international/ticker/detail/Iranian_speaker_says_US_supports_terrorists.html?siteSect=143&sid=7692846&cKey=1175790190000

Hall, Wynton. "7 Devastating Facts about Obama's Iran Nuclear Deal." *Breitbart*: July 17, 2015. https://www.breitbart.com/national-security/2015/07/17/7-devastating-facts-about-obamas-iran-nuclear-deal/

Hate and Violence in the Quran. https://thereligionofpeace.com/pages/articles/quran-hate.aspx; and: https://thereligionofpeace.com/pages/quran/violence.aspx

Hawting, G.R. "John Wansbrough, Islam, and Monotheism." In, *The Quest for the Historical Muhammad.* Edited with Translations by Ibn Warraq. Prometheus Books. New York: 2000.

Hawting, G.R. "The Disappearance and Rediscovery of Zamzam and the Well of the Kaba." *Bulletin of the School of Oriental and African Studies* 43: 44-54, 1980.

Healy, J.F. "The Early History of the Syriac Script: A Reassessment." *Journal of Semitic Studies* XLV/1: 55-67, Spring 2000.

Heger, C. "Koran XXV.1: Al-Furqan and the Warner." In, *What the Koran Really Says*. Ed. Ibn Warraq. Prometheus Books. New York: 2002.

Hill, D.R. *The Termination of Hostilities in the Early Arab Conquests*. Luzac. London: 1971.

Hosenball, Mark. Exclusive: Obama authorizes secret help for Libyan rebels. Reuters: March 30, 2011. https://www.reuters.com/article/us-libya-usa-order/exclusive-obama-authorizes-secret-help-for-libya-rebels-idUSTRE72T6H220110330

Hosko, Ron. "The truth about fatal shootings by police." *Fox News*: January 13, 2018. https://www.foxnews.com/opinion/ron-hosko-the-truth-about-fatal-shootings-by-police

Howley, Patrick. *Hillary Clinton-Linked Company: Our Alleged Payments to ISIS Are Under Review*. Breitbart: August 11, 2016. http://www.breitbart.com/2016-presidential-race/2016/08/11/hillary-clinton-linked-company-our-alleged-payments-to-isis-are-under-review/

Howley, Patrick. *Hillary Clinton Received Secret Memo Stating Obama Admin Support for ISIS*. Breitbart: June 14, 2016. http://www.breitbart.com/2016-presidential-race/2016/06/14/hillary-clinton-received-secret-memo-stating-obama-admin-support-for-isis/

Howley, Patrick. *Hillary Clinton Sponsored Secretive Arab Spring Program that Destabilized Middle East*. Breitbart: September 23, 2016. http://www.breitbart.com/2016-presidential-race/2016/09/23/hillary-clinton-sponsored-secretive-arab-spring-program-that-destabilized-middle-east/

Hubert, Jean. *L'Art pre-romain*. Paris: Les Edition d'Art et d'Histoire, 1938

Humphreys, Stephen. *Islamic History: A Framework for Inquiry*. Princeton University Press: 1991.

Husayn, Taha. *fi l-adab al-jahili*. Cairo, Egypt: 1927.

Ibn Hisham, abd al-Malik. *Al-Sira al-nabawiyya*. Eds. M. al-Saqqa et.al. Dar ihya al-turath al-arabi. Beirut, Lebanon: 1971.

Ibn Ishaq. *The Life of Muhammad*. Translated by A. Guillaume. Oxford University Press. London: 1955.

Ibn Kathir, Ismail. *Al-Jami we al-Sira al-Nabawiya*. Darussalam Publishing. Riyadh, Saudi Arabia: 2010.

Islamic Sharia Tribunal Begins Operating in Texas. https://jewtube.tv/islamic-sharia-law/america-is-going-muslim-islamic-shariah-tribunal-begins-operating-in-texas/?fbclid=IwAR3viMf0qZSvZJUZryDfY5MqkgYZQqoejZdJXxzMiIrB4-QlvJ6yOm4JuP4

Jeffery, Arthur. "Abu Ubaid on the Verses Missing from the Koran." In, *The Origins of the Koran: Classic Essays on Islam's Holy Book*. Edited by Ibn Warraq. Prometheus Books. New York: 1998.

Jeffery, Arthur. "A Variant Text of the Fatiha." In, *The Origins of the Koran: Classic Essays on Islam's Holy Book*. Edited by Ibn Warraq. Prometheus Books. New York: 1998.

Jeffrey, Arthur, Editor. *Materials for the History of the Text of Qur'an*. E.J. Brill. Leiden, Netherlands: 1937.

Jeffery, Arthur. "Progress in the Study of the Koran Text." In, *The Origins of the Koran: Classic Essays on Islam's Holy Book.* Edited by Ibn Warraq. Prometheus Books. New York: 1998.

Jeffery, Arthur. "The Quest of the Historical Muhammad." In, *The Quest for the Historical Muhammad.* Edited with Translations by Ibn Warraq. Prometheus Books. New York: 2000.

Jeffery, Arthur. "The Quran Readings of ibn Miqsam." In, *Which Koran? Variants, Manuscripts, Linguistics.* Edited by Ibn Warraq. Prometheus Books. New York: 2011.

Jensen, Robin Margaret. *Womb, Tomb, and Garden: The Symbolism of the North African Baptismal Fonts.* Newton, MA: Andover Newton Theological School. American Academy of Religion Annual Meeting, November , 1997.

Kaegi, Walter. *Heraclius: Emperor of Byzantium.* Cambridge University Press: 2003.

Kazhdan, Alexander P., Editor. *Oxford Dictionary of Byzantium.* New York: Oxford University Press, 1991.

Kennedy, Hugh. *The Prophet and the Age of the Caliphates: the Islamic Near East from the sixth to the eleventh century.* Routledge. New York: 2015.

Khoury, R.G. "Arafat." *Encyclopedia of the Quran,* vol. 1: 145-45, 2001.

King, Geoffrey. *Settlement in Western Arabia and the Gulf in the 6th-8th Centuries AD.* Paper presented at the 2nd Workshop on Late Antiquity and Early Islam: Land Use and Settlement Patters. London: April 1991.

King, Geoffrey, and Averil Cameron, eds. "The Byzantine and Early Islamic Near East". In, *Land Use and Settlement Patterns Vol. II.* Proceedings of the 2nd Workshop on Late Antiquity and Early Islam: Land Use and Settlement Patterns. Darwin Press. Princeton, NJ: 1994.

Kirkbridge, A.S. "Coins of the Byzantine-Arab Period." *Quarterly of the Department of Antiquities in Palestine* 62. Oxford University Press: 1947.

Kirkpatrick, David D. Egypt's Vote Puts Emphasis on Split Over Religious Rule. New York Times: December 3, 2011. http://www.nytimes.com/2011/12/04/world/middleeast/egypts-vote-propels-islamic-law-into-spotlight.html?pagewanted=all&_r=0

Kister, M.J. "Adam: A Study of Some Legends in tafsir and hadith Literature." *Israel Oriental Studies* 13: 113-174, 1993.

Kister, M.J. "Sanctity Joint and Divided: On Holy Places in the Islamic Tradition." *Jerusalem Studies in Arabic and Islam* 20: 1996.

Koren, Judith, and Yehuda D. Nevo. Methodological Approaches to Islamic Studies. In, *The Quest for the Historical Muhammad.* Edited with Translations by Ibn Warraq. Prometheus Books. New York: 2000.

Kritzeck, James. "Robert of Ketton's Translation of the Qur'an." *Islamic Quarterly* 2: 309-12, 1955.

Lammens, Henri. "Koran and Tradition: How the Life of Muhammad was Composed." In, *The Quest for the Historical Muhammad.* Edited with Translations by Ibn Warraq. Prometheus Books. New York: 2000.

Lammens, Henri. "The Age of Muhammad and the Chronology of the Sira." In, *The Quest for the Historical Muhammad.* Edited with Translations by Ibn Warraq. Prometheus Books. New York: 2000.

Lammens, Henri. "The Quest of the Historical Muhammad." In, *The Quest for the Historical Muhammad*. Edited with Translations by Ibn Warraq. Prometheus Books. New York: 2000.

Larcher, Pierre. "Pre-Islamic Arabic—Koranic Arabic—Classical Arabic: A Continuum?" In, *The Hidden Origins of Islam: New Research into Its Early History*. Edited by Karl-Heinz Ohlig and Gerd-R Puin. Prometheus Books. New York: 2009.

Lee, Ian, with Hamdi Alkhshali and Joe Sterling. Amid uneasy calm in Cairo, prime minister says some were paid to protest. CNN: September 16, 2012. http://www.cnn.com/2012/09/15/world/meast/egypt-us-embassy-protests/

Lester, Toby. "What Is the Koran?" In, *What the Koran Really Says*. Edited by Ibn Warraq. Prometheus Books. New York: 2002.

Lewis, Archibald R. *Naval Power and Trade in the Mediterranean, A.D. 500-1100*. Princeton University Press. NJ: 1951.

Lewis, Archibald, and Timothy Runyan. *European Naval and Maritime History*. Indiana University Press. IN: 1990.

Lippman, Thomas. "The Pioneers." *Saudi Aramco World*. Aramco Services Company: Houston, Texas. May/June 2004

Lucas, Fred. Obama Has Touted al-Qaeda's Demise 32 Times since Benghazi Attack. *CNS news*: November 1, 2012. http://www.netadvisor.org/wp-content/uploads/2017/01/2012-11-12-Obama-Has-Touted-Al-Qaeda's-Demise-32-Times-since-Benghazi-Attack.pdf

Luling, Gunter. "The Rediscovery and Reliable Reconstruction of a Comprehensive pre-Islamic Christian Hymnal hidden in the Koran under earliest Islamic Reinterpretations." In, *A Challenge to Islam for Reformation*. Motilal Banarsidass Publishers. Delhi, India: 2003.

Luxenberg, Christoph. "A New Interpretation of the Arabic Inscription in Jerusalem's Dome of the Rock." In, *The Hidden Origins of Islam: New Research into Its Early History*. Edited by Karl-Heinz Ohlig and Gerd-R Puin. Prometheus Books. New York: 2010.

Luxenberg, Christoph. "Relics of Syro-Aramaic Letters in Early Qur'an Codices in Higazi and Kufi Ductus". In, *Early Islam: A Critical Reconstruction Based on Contemporary Sources*. Edited by Karl-Heinz Ohlig. Prometheus Books. New York: 2013.

Luxenberg, Christoph. The Syro-Aramaic Reading of the Koran: A Contribution to the Decoding of the Language of the Koran. Schiler. Berlin: 2007.

Macler, Frederic, translator. Histoire d'Heraclius par l'Eveque Sebeos. Imprimerie Nationale. Paris: 1904.

Magister, Sandro. The Virgins and the Grapes: The Christian Origins of the Koran. Chiesa Espresso Online: 2004. http://chiesa.espresso.repubblica.it/articolo/7025bdc4.html?eng=y&refresh_ce

Magness, J. Reexamination of the Archaeological Evidence for the Sassanian Persian Destruction of the Tyropoeon Valley. Bulletin of the American School of Oriental Research 287: 67-74, 1992.

Margoliouth, David Samuel. "The Origins of Arabic Poetry." *Journal of the Royal Asiatic Society*. London: 1925, pp. 417-449.

Mauro, Ryan. *FBI Confirms Jihadi Training Camps in America*. Clarion Project: January 31, 2018. https://clarionproject.org/exclusive-fbi-confirms-jihadi-training-camps-america/

Mauro, Ryan. *Muslim Brotherhood: We're Spending $5 Million on PR in U.S*. The Counter Jihad Report: February 28, 2017. https://counterjihadreport.com/2017/02/28/muslim-brotherhood-were-spending-5-million-on-pr-in-u-s/

Mecca Climate: https://en.climate-data.org/location/3533/

MENA. Attacks on media reported at Islamist "no violence" rally. Egypt Independent: June 21, 2013. http://www.egyptindependent.com/attacks-media-reported-islamist-no-violence-rally/

MENA. Thousands converge on Tahrir; political leaders pledge to join sit-in. Egypt Independent: November 30, 2012. http://www.egyptindependent.com/news/update-thousands-converge-tahrir-political-leaders-pledge-join-sit

Meunier, Michael. *Will Obama and US stand with or against Egypt's people?* Fox News: July 01, 2013. http://www.foxnews.com/opinion/2013/07/01/will-obama-and-us-stand-with-or-against-egypt-people.html?intcmp=HPBucket

Meyendorff, John. *Byzantine Theology.* New York: Fordham University Press, 1999.

Mingana, Alphonse. *Odes and Psalms of Solomon,* ii. Damascus: 1920.

Mingana, Alphonse. *Sources Syriaques.* Leipzig, Germany: 1907.

Mingana, Alphonse. "Syriac Influence on the Style of the Kur'an." *Bulletin of John Rylands Library.* Manchester, UK: 1927.

Mingana, Alphonse. "Three Ancient Korans." In, *The Origins of the Koran: Classic Essays on Islam's Holy Book.* Edited by Ibn Warraq. Prometheus Books. New York: 1998.

Mohammad, Noor. "An Introduction to Islamic Law." In, *Modern Legal Systems Encyclopedia* 5A100.7: 1990.

More Muslim Stats: https://muslimstatistics.wordpress.com/2015/09/14/usa-muslim-refugees-91-4-on-food-stamps-68-3-on-cash-welfare/

Muslim Prayers. According to Tabari, Zamakhshari, the Tafsir al-Jalalayn, Tanwir al-Miqbas min Tafsir Ibn Abbas: https://www.altafsir.com/Tafasir.asp?tMadhNo=0&tTafsirNo=74&tSoraNo=1&tAyahNo=7&tDisplay=yes&UserProfile=0; and: https://www.altafsir.com/Tafasir.asp?tMadhNo=0&tTafsirNo=73&tSoraNo=1&tAyahNo=7&tDisplay=yes&UserProfile=0

Naggar, Y. Human Skeletal Remains from the Mamilla Cave, Jerusalem. *Atiqot* 43: 141-48, 2002.

Nashashibi, Sharif. Egypt's media is free... to praise Mursi. Al-Arabiya: January 7, 2013. http://www.alarabiya.net/views/2013/01/07/259076.html

Necipoglu, Gulru. "The Dome of the Rock as palimpsest: Abd al-Malik's grand narrative and Sultan Suleyman's glosses." In, *An Annual on the Visual Culture of the Islamic World, Vol. 25.* Eds. Gulru

Necipoglu and Julia Bailey. Brill. Leiden, Netherlands: 2008.

Negev, Avraham. *Nabatean Archaeology Today.* New York University Press. New York: 1986.

Negev, Avraham. "The Churches of the Central Negev: An Archeological Survey." *Revue Biblique* 81: 400-422, 1976.

Negev, Avraham. *The Greek Inscriptions from the Negev.* Franciscan Press. Jerusalem: 1981.

Nevo, Yehuda D. *Pagans and Herders: A Re-examination of the Negev Runoff Cultivations Systems in the Byzantine and Early Arab Periods.* IPS Press. Jerusalem: 1991.

Nevo, Yehuda D. *Sede Boqer and the Central Negev: 7th-8th century AD*. Paper presented at the 3rd International Colloquium "From Jahiliyyah to Islam." Hebrew University of Jerusalem: 1985.

Nevo, Yehuda D. "Towards a Prehistory of Islam." In, *What the Koran Really Says*. Edited by Ibn Warraq. Prometheus Books. New York: 2002.

Nevo, Yehuda D., Z. Cohen, and D. Heftman, eds. *Ancient Arabic Inscriptions from the Negev*. IPS Press. Jerusalem: 1993.

Nevo, Yehuda and Judith Koren. *Crossroads to Islam: The origins of the Arab religion and the Arab state*. Prometheus Books. New York: 1990; 2003.

North, James B. *A History of the Church*. Joplin, Missouri: College Press Publishing Company, 1991.

Obama: "decimated" (al-Qaeda is decimated).
https://www.youtube.com/watch?time_continue=7&v=GQjztrnJzCM

Obama: "al-Qaeda" (al-Qaeda is no longer a threat). https://www.businessinsider.com/obama-administration-al-qaeda-in-afghanistan-no-longer-a-threat-to-the-united-states-2011-6?op=1 And; https://www.alipac.us/f19/obama-admin-al-qaeda-no-longer-threat-intelligence-officials-revolt-303251/

Ohlig, Karl Heinz. *Early Islam: A critical reconstruction based on contemporary sources*. Prometheus Books. New York: 2013.

Ohlig, Karl-Heinz. "Evidence of a New Religion in Christian Literature "Under Islamic Rule"? In, *Early Islam: A critical reconstruction based on contemporary sources*. Edited by Karl-Heinz Ohlig. Prometheus Books. New York: 2013.

Ohlig, Karl Heinz. "From muhammad Jesus to Prophet of the Arabs". In, *Early Islam: A critical reconstruction based on contemporary sources*. Edited by Karl-Heinz Ohlig. Prometheus Books. New York: 2013.

Ohlig, Karl-Heinz. "Shedding Light on the Beginnings of Islam". In, *Early Islam: A critical reconstruction based on contemporary sources*. Edited by Karl-Heinz Ohlig. Prometheus Books. New York: 2013.

Ohlig, Karl-Heinz. "Syrian and Arabian Christianity and the Qur'an." In, *The Hidden Origins of Islam: New Research into Its Early History*, edited by Karl-Heinz Ohlig and Gerd-R Puin. Prometheus Books. New York: 2010.

Ohlig, Karl-Heinz, and Gerd-R Puin. *The Hidden Origins of Islam: New Research into Its Early History*. Prometheus Books. New York: 2010.

Parker, S. Thomas. *The Historical Development of the Limes Arabicus*. University of California Los Angeles, Ph.D. thesis: 1979.

Parker, S. Thomas. "The Roman Frontier in Central Jordan: Interim Report on the Limes Arabicus Project, 1980-1985." *BAR International Series* 340. Oxford: 1987.

Parry, James V. "Mapping Arabia." *Saudi Aramco World*. Aramco Services Company: Houston, Texas. January/February 2004.

Patrich, Joseph. "Issue Pessel u-Tmunah b'qerev ha-Nabbatim (prohibition of a graven image among the Nabateans)." *Cathedra* 26: 47-104. In Hebrew with English summary.

Peters, F.E. "The Quest of the Historical Muhammad." In, *The Quest for the Historical Muhammad*. Edited with Translations by Ibn Warraq. Prometheus Books. New York: 2000.

Pine, Shlomo. "Notes on Islam and on Arabic Christianity and Judaeo-Christianity." *Jerusalem Studies is Arabic and Islam* no. 4: 135-152, 1984.

Popp, Volker. "From Ugarit to Samarra: An Archeological Journey on the Trail of Ernst Herzfeld." In, *Early Islam*. Edited by Karl-Heinz Ohlig. Prometheus Books. New York: 2013.

Popp, Volker. "The Early History of Islam, Following Inscriptional and Numismatic Testimony." In, *The Hidden Origins of Islam: New Research into Its Early History*. Edited by Karl-Heinz Ohlig and Gerd-R Puin. Prometheus Books. New York: 2009, 2010.

Popp, Volker. "The Influence of Persian Religious Patterns on Notions in the Qur'an." In, *Early Islam*. Edited by Karl-Heinz Ohlig. Prometheus Books. New York: 2013.

Propaganda Organizations. http://www.cheriberens.net/white-helmetsnbspan-islamist-propagandist-group-and-funded-arm-of-us-government.html http://www.cheriberens.net/these-groups-are-propaganda-organizations-disguised-as-humanitarian-groups.html

Puin, Gerd-R. "Observation on Early Qur'an Manuscripts in San'a." In, *What the Koran Really Says*. Edited by Ibn Warraq. Prometheus Books. New York: 2002.

Quran Karim. Cairo, Egypt: 1972.

Rawandi, Ibn. "On Pre-Islamic Christian Strophic Poetical Texts in the Koran: A Critical Look at the Work of Gunter Luling." In, *What the Koran Really Says*. Edited by Ibn Warraq. Prometheus Books. New York: 2002.

Rawandi, Ibn. "Origins of Islam: A Critical Look at the Sources." In, *The Quest for the Historical Muhammad*. Edited with Translations by Ibn Warraq. Prometheus Books. New York: 2000.

Reich, R. "God Knows their Names: Mass Christian Grave Revealed in Jerusalem." *Biblical Archaeology Review* 22/2: 26-35, 1996.

Resist 2017: https://www.cnn.com/2017/05/15/politics/hillary-clinton-resistance-onward-together/index.html https://www.washingtonexaminer.com/washington-secrets/hillary-clinton-takes-lead-of-resist-jumps-into-midterm-elections https://townhall.com/tipsheet/mattvespa/2017/05/16/resist-clintons-antitrump-super-pac-is-now-active-n2327302

Richardson, Peter. *Building Jewish in the Roman East*. Baylor University Press: 2004.

Rippin, Andrew. "Literary Analysis of Koran, Tafsir, and Sira: The Methodologies of John Wansbrough." In, *The Origins of the Koran: Classic Essays on Islam's Holy Book*. Edited by Ibn Warraq. Prometheus Books. New York: 1998.

Rippin, Andrew. *Quranic Studies: Sources and Methods of Scriptural Interpretation*. Prometheus Books. New York: 2004.

Robinson, Chase F. *Islamic Historiography: Themes in Islamic History*. Cambridge University Press: 2002.

Rodinson, M. "A Critical Survey of Modern Studies on Muhammad." In, *Studies on Islam*. Edited by M. Swartz. New York: 1981.

Rodley, Lyn. *Byzantine Art and Architecture*. Cambridge: Cambridge University Press, 1994.

Roots of Violent Extremism: The Muslim Brotherhood. http://www.cheriberens.net/roots-of-violent-extremism-muslim-brotherhood.html

Rosenthal, Franz. *A Grammar of Biblical Aramaic*. Wiesbaden, Germany: 1963.

Rubin, Uri. *Between Bible and Quran: The Children of Israel and the Islamic Self-Image*. Darwin Press. UK: 1999.

Rubin, Uri. "Between Arabia and the Holy Land: A Mecca-Jerusalem Axis of Sanctity." *Jerusalem Studies in Arabic and Islam* 34: 345-62, 2008.

Rubin, Uri. *Between Bible and Qur`ān: The Children of Israel and the Islamic Self-Image*. Darwin Press. Princeton, NJ: 1999.

Rubin, Uri. "Islamic Retellings of Biblical History." In, *Adaptations and Innovations: Studies on the Interaction between Jewish and Islamic Thought and Literature from the Early Middle Ages to the Late Twentieth Century*. Eds. Y. Tzvi Langermann and Josef Stern. Peeters. Paris: 2007.

Rubin, Uri. "Moses and the Holy Valley Tuwan: On the biblical and midrashic background of a qur`anic scene." *Journal of Near Eastern Studies* 1: 73-81, 2014.

Rubin, Uri. "Muhammad's Night Journey to al-masjid al-Aqsa." In, *Aspects of the Earliest Origins of the Islamic Sanctity of Jerusalem*. Al-Qantara XXIX 1, enero-junio: 147-164, 2008.

Rubin, Uri. "Pre-Existence and Light—Aspects of the Concept of Nur Muhammad." *Israel Oriental Studies* 5: 97, 1975.

Rubin, Uri. "The Ark of the Covenant and the Golden Calf in Biblical and Islamic Historiography." *Oriens* 36: 196-214, 2001.

Salibi, K.S. "Islam and Syria in the Writing of Henri Lammens." In, *Historians of the Middle East*. Edited by B. Lewis and P.M. Holt. Oxford: 1962.

Sarwar, Shaikh Muhammad. *The Holy Quran: Arabic Text and English Translation*. Islamic Seminary. Elmhurst, NY: 1982.

Schacht, Joseph. "A Revaluation of Islamic Traditions." In, *The Quest for the Historical Muhammad*. Edited with Translations by Ibn Warraq. Prometheus Books. New York: 2000.

Schacht, Joseph. *An Introduction to Islamic Law*. Oxford University Press. Oxford: 1964.

Schacht, Joseph. *The Origins of Muhammadan Jurisprudence*. Oxford University Press. Oxford: 1967.

Schick, R. "The Christian Communities of Palestine from Byzantine to Islamic Rule: An Historical and Archaeological Study." In, *Studies in Late Antiquity and Early Islam 2*. The Darwin Press. Princeton: 1995.

Schock, C. "Adam and Eve." Encyclopedia of the Quran. Leiden: E.J. Brill. Leiden, Netherlands: 2001.

Seed, Tony. "Halifax International Security Forum." November 21, 2013. https://tonyseed.wordpress.com/2013/11/21/about-the-halifax-international-security-forum-the-haliax-candada-club/

Seed, Tony. "The Arab Spring: US black ops and subversion." May 26, 2016. https://www.investigation.net/en/the-arab-spring-us-black-ops-and-subversion/ And also, April 14, 2016: https://tonyseed.wordpress.com/2016/04/14/the-arab-spring-us-black-ops-and-subversion/

Serbia Revolution: https://washingtonmonthly.com/features/2001/0103.thompson.html
https://en.wikipedia.org/wiki/Overthrow_of_Slobodan_Milošević
https://www.washingtonpost.com/archive/politics/2000/12/11/us-advice-guided-milosevic-opposition/ba9e87e5-bdca-45dc-8aadda6571e89448/?noredirect=on&utm_term=.3fb53a7e6828
http://web.archive.org/web/20070109084028/http://www.washingtonmonthly.com/features/2001/0103.thompson.html

Shaban, M.A. *Islamic History A.D. 600-750: A New Interpretation.* Cambridge University Press: 1971.

Shah, Sirdar Ikbal Ali. *Selections from the Koran.* Octagon Press. London: 1980.

Shapira, Ian. *U.S. funding tech firms that help Mideast dissidents evade government censors.* Washington Post: March 10, 2011. http://www.washingtonpost.com/wp-dyn/content/article/2011/03/09/AR2011030905716.html

Shragai, Nadav. Second Temple-era mikveh discovered under al-Aqsa mosque. *Israel Hayom.* June 29, 2012. http://www.israelhayom.com/2012/06/29/second-temple-era-mikveh-discovered-under-al-aqsa-mosque/

Sivan, Hagith. *Palestine in Late Antiquity.* Oxford University Press: 2008.

Southern, R.W. *Western Views of Islam in the Middle Ages.* Harvard University Press. Cambridge, MA: 1962.

Stats about Muslims. http://www.cheriberens.net/stats-about-muslims-you-should-know.html

Stobart, James William. *Islam and Its Founder.* Society for Promoting Christian Knowledge. London: 1895.

Syrian Opposition Groups Defined. http://www.cheriberens.net/syrian-opposition-groups-defined.html

Tadros, Mariz. Politically motivated sexual assault: the Egypt story none want to hear. The Guardian: March 11, 2013. http://www.theguardian.com/global-development/poverty-matters/2013/mar/11/politically-motivated-sexual-assault-egypt

Taha, Rana Muhammed. Report: 359 torture cases during Morsi's first year in power. Daily News Egypt: June 26, 2013. http://www.dailynewsegypt.com/2013/06/26/report-359-torture-cases-during-morsis-first-year-in-power/

Taher, Abul. Querying the Koran. *The Guardian.* August 8, 2000. Retrieved November 8, 2011. http://www.theguardian.com/education/2000/aug/08/highereducation.theguardian

Teicher, Jacob L. "The Damascus fragments and the origin of the Jewish Christian sect." *Journal of Jewish Studies* 2: 115-43, 1951.

Teicher, Jacob L. "The Dead Sea Scrolls: Documents of the Jewish-Christian sect of Ebionites." *Journal of Jewish Studies* 2: 67-99, 1951.

The Arming of Benghazi. "Fox Affirms the Benghazi Brief." https://theconservativetreehouse.com/2015/06/28/fox-affirms-the-benghazi-brief-the-arming-of-benghazi/ And: FoxNews: "The Arming of Benghazi." FoxBusiness: June 27, 2015. https://www.foxbusiness.com/politics/exclusive-the-arming-of-benghazi

Theil, Stefan. "Challenging the Qur'an: A German scholar contends that the Islamic text has been mis-transcribed and promises raisins, not virgins." *Newsweek International:* July 28, 2003.

The Qur'an Dilemma: Former Muslims Analyze Islam's Holiest Book. Volume One. Pages 94-124. Canada: TheQuran.com, 2011.

Tisdall, William. *The Original Sources of the Qur'an*. Society for Promoting Christian Knowledge. London: 1905.

Torrey, C.C. *The Jewish Foundation of Islam*. Jewish Institute of Religion Press. New York: 1967.

Tschanz, David. "Journeys of Faith, Roads of Civilization." *Saudi Aramco World*. Aramco Services Company: Houston, Texas. January/February 2004.

Tsafrir, Yoram, and Gideon Foerster. *From Scythopolis to Baysan—Changing Concepts of Urbanism*. Paper presented at the 2nd Workshop on Late Antiquity and Early Islam: Land Use and Settlement Patterns. London: April 1991.

UTT. *Islamic Movement in U.S. Preparing for Battle*. Understanding the Threat: September 13, 2016. https://www.understandingthethreat.com/islamic-movement-in-u-s-preparing-for-battle/

UTT. *Ten years after the HLF Trial U.S. Jihadi Network still rolling*. Understanding the Threat: January 10, 2019. https://www.understandingthethreat.com/10-years-after-hlf/

Van Der Meulen, D. *The Wells of Ibn Saud*. Camelot Press. London: 1957.

Van Ess, Josef. Abd al-Malik and the Dome of the Rock: An Analysis of Some Texts. In, *Bayt al Maqdis: abd al Malik's Jerusalem*. Eds. Julian Raby and Jeremy Johns. Oxford University Press: 1992.

Walker, John. *A Catalogue of the Arab-Sassanian Coins*. Trustees of the British Museum. London: 1941.

Wansbrough, John. *Quranic Studies: Sources and Methods of Scriptual Interpretations*. Oxford Univ. Press: 1977.

Wansbrough, John. *The Sectarian Milieu: Content and composition of Islamic salvation history*. Prometheus Books. New York: 1978; 2006.

Warraq, Ibn. "A personal look at some aspects of the history of Koranic criticism in the nineteenth and twentieth centuries." In, *The Hidden Origins of Islam: New Research into Its Early History*. Edited by Karl-Heinz Ohlig and Gerd-R Puin. Prometheus Books. New York: 2009.

Warraq, Ibn. "Honest Intellectuals Must Shed Their Spiritual Turbans: Islam—The Final Taboo." In, *Virgins? What Virgins? and Other Essays*. Prometheus Books. New York: 2010.

Warraq Ibn. *Leaving Islam: Apostates Speak Out*. Prometheus Books. New York: 2003.

Warraq, Ibn. "Studies on Muhammad and the Rise of Islam: A Critical Survey." In, *The Quest for the Historical Muhammad*. Edited with Translations by Ibn Warraq. Prometheus Books. New York: 2000.

Warraq, Ibn. *The Origins of the Koran: Classic Essays on Islam's Holy Book*. Edited by Ibn Warraq. Prometheus Books. New York: 1998.

Warraq, Ibn. *The Quest for the Historical Muhammad*. Edited with Translations by Ibn Warraq. Prometheus Books. New York: 2000.

Warraq, Ibn. *Virgins? What Virgins? and Other Essays*. Prometheus Books. New York: 2010.

Warraq, Ibn. *What the Koran Really Says: Language, Text, and Commentary*. Prometheus Books. New York: 2002.

Warraq, Ibn. *Which Koran?* Prometheus Books. New York: 2011.

Whitby, Michael. *Rome at War: 293–696*. Osprey. London: 2002.

Wikileaks. "Egypt protests: secret US document discloses support for protesters." *The Telegraph*: Jan 28, 2011. https://www.telegraph.co.uk/news/worldnews/africaandindianocean/egypt/8289698/Egypt-protests-secret-US-document-discloses-support-for-protesters.html

Wikileaks. *Hillary Clinton Email Archive*. Situation Report No. 1 09/14/I. https://wikileaks.org/clinton-emails/emailid/16792

Wiktorowicz, Quintan. A Genealogy of Radical Islam. *Studies in Conflict and Terrorism*, vol. 28: 75-97, 2005.

Wilkinson, J. *Jerusalem Pilgrims before the Crusades*. Ariel. Jerusalem: 1977.

Winnett, Frederick, and J.L. Harding. *Inscriptions from Fifty Safaitic Cairns*. Toronto University Press: 1978.

WND. *35 terror training camps now operating inside U.S.* WND: January 2, 2012. https://www.wnd.com/2012/01/381953/

YouthMovements.com. *Alliance of Youth Movements: Attendee Biographies*. New York: December 3-5, 2008. https://allyoumov.3cdn.net/f734ac45131b2bbcdb_w6m6idptn.pdf

ABOUT THE AUTHOR

While living in Egypt, Cheri worked with the Egyptian Ministry of Culture researching and documenting the Egyptian culture through its traditions, festivals and celebrations. Cheri has researched, filmed and documented various regional traditions, Sufi sects, and the traditional music and dances unique to the various regions of Egypt.

First-hand experiences while living in Egypt, attending university in Egypt, and her eventual marriage to an Egyptian gave Cheri an in-depth, uncensored view of an Islamic society that she documents in her book, *An American Woman Living in Egypt*.

Cheri's dance experience in Egypt is extensive as well. She has studied with some of the most well-respected artists in Egypt: Mahmoud Reda, Ibrahim Akef, Mohammad Khalil, Farida Fahmi, Raqqia Hassan and many others. She has also trained with various folkloric troops throughout Egypt which specialize in regional folklore.

Previous to living in Egypt, Cheri was a legal researcher and trial brief writer. Prior to that, Cheri was head of the legal department for two daily newspapers. Cheri has a BA in Communications with a certification in Paralegal Studies.